Macmillan English Grammar In Context

Intermediate

with key

Macmillan Education
4 Crinan Street
London N1 9XW
A division of Macmillan Publishers Limited
Companies and representatives throughout the world

ISBN 978-1-4050-7140-6 (with key edition)
ISBN 978-1-4050-7141-3 (without key edition)

First published 2008

Design by Bigtop
Original design by Giles Davies
Illustrated by Andy Hammond, Joanna Kerr, Darren Lingard, Sarah Nayler, Andrew Selby
Cover concept by Giles Davies
Cover design by Katie Stephens
Cover photographs by Corbis, Digital Vision, Photodisc

The authors and publishers would like to thank the following for permission to reproduce
their material: Extracts from websites bbc.co.uk/schools/gcsebitsize/business & bbc.
co.uk/schools/gcsebitesize/physics copyright © bbc.co.uk reprinted by permission of the
publisher. Extract from www.equityschooltravel.co.uk copyright © Equity Educational
Tours, reprinted by permission of the publisher. Information 'Changing cities and urban
challenges' from Letts Revise KS3 Geography by A. Arnell & A. Browne; copyright © Letts
2004, reprinted by permission of the publisher, Huveaux Plc. Information 'Energy and
electricity' from Letts Revise KS3 Science by B. MacDuell & G. Booth, copyright © Letts
2002, reprinted by permission of the publisher, Huveaux Plc. Extracts from 'Weather and
Climate' (Usborne Science & Experiments) copyright © Usborne Publishing Limited 1992,
reprinted by permission of the publisher. Extract from 'Apple Computers – The Early Years'
taken from http://en.wikipedia.org/wiki/Apple-Computers, copyright © Wikipedia, the free
encyclopedia.

These materials may contain links for third party websites. We have no control over, and are
not responsible for, the contents of such third party websites. Please use care when accessing
them.

Although we have tried to trace and contact copyright holders before publication, in some
cases this has not been possible. If contacted we will be pleased to rectify any errors or
omissions at the earliest opportunity.

The author would like to thank Carl Robinson, Amanda Holmbrook and Sarah Curtis for
their support and help during this project. Special thanks are due to my editor Clare Shaw.
I would also like to thank the many teachers whose classes I have visited, and who have
commented on versions of this book.

The authors and publishers would like to thank the following for permission to reproduce
their photographic material: Alamy/ Pictorial Press p60, CoverSpot p116, The Print Collector
p124, FoodPix 128t, Elmtree Images p189l; Ardea/ M Watson p77; Bananastock/ pp 119,
189l, 191, 197, 198; Brand X/ pp 9bl, 97, 101, 117; Corbis/ Digital Stock pp 12, 21, 69, 136,
Smithsonian Institution p56, Bettmann pp64, 127, 162, 187, Cat Gwynne p84, Liu Liqun
p88, Peter M Fisher p89, Ed Kashi p113tl, James L Amos p113tm, Denis Scott p158, Atlantide
Phototravel p186, Kristy-Anne Glubish/Design Pics p189m, Andrew Brookes p189br; Dean
Ryan/ p113tr; Digital Vision/ p 25; Getty Images/ Hulton Archive p76, Sean Justice p96, The
Bridgeman Art Library p113b; John Foxx Images/ pp 8, 120, 129, 199; Mary Evans Picture
Library/ p92; Ordnance Survey/ p45; Photodisc/ pp 13, 15, 17, 27, 30, 31, 38, 95, 132, 150;
Photolibrary/ pp60, 125, Martyn Chillmaid p189r; Science Photo Library/ p142; Stockbyte/
pp 20, 43, 72, 80, 81, 151, 183, 189m; Superstock/ pp 19, 34, 46, 166, Age Fotostock p189r.

Printed in Thailand

2017 2016 2015 (with key edition)
18   17   16   15

2016 2015 2014 (without key edition)
16   15   14   13

Introduction

This book is designed to revise and consolidate grammar points at the level of Council of Europe Framework (CEF) B1 and B2. It assumes that some basic points have been covered. These can be practised in *Macmillan English Grammar In Context Essential*.

The practice material includes a wide range of topics to reflect both everyday language use and the kinds of subjects learners might be studying in schools or colleges. Many learners are likely to use English to learn another subject during their education and the choice of text tries to reflect this fact. Some texts contain information which learners should find interesting or challenging. The intention in general is that language should have a familiar context and that learners should have something to use language for.

Within each unit, exercises range in difficulty. This allows learners to build up their confidence with the simpler, more familiar tasks before moving onto the more challenging ones later in the unit. The longer, topic-based texts include highlighted words whose definitions can be found on the accompanying CD-ROM. This is a good opportunity for learners to widen their vocabulary and see grammar used in realistic contexts.

The Review section at the back of the book offers more activities for students who have finished the other exercises. It is also for students who feel that they haven't fully grasped the grammar point and need some further practice. In addition, it can be used as a means of testing or revising previous study, either in class or at home.

The CD-ROM
This includes two further exercises for each unit in this book, and a test section. Plus, where you see highlighted words like this, you will find the definitions in the glossary section. Just follow the link from the homepage.

To the student
Macmillan English Grammar In Context has been written to make grammar more interesting than other books on the market. We hope you find it enjoyable as well as useful. If you are studying at home, the units can be covered in any order but the exercises within each unit have been graded. If you find some exercises difficult, read the presentation page again. The extension activities and Review offer the opportunity of further practice.

To the teacher
Unlike many other grammar books, *Macmillan English Grammar In Context* puts grammar into context. The aim is to encourage students to see grammar used more realistically and in more interesting ways. The topics covered in the exercises can be used as a starting point for a lesson, as a subject for discussion, and as a means of helping to build students' vocabulary in useful areas. There is opportunity for individual study, group work and homework, plus testing, in the different sections of the book.

Contents

1 present simple

FORM

affirmative

I / You / We / They	want	go	take
She / He / It	wants	goes	takes

Most verbs add **-s** for third person she / he / it: want – wants   live – lives
Verbs ending **-ss, -sh, -ch, -x, -o**: add **-es**   pass**es**   wash**es**   relax**es**   go**es**

negative

I / You / We / They	**do not** (*don't*)	want	go
She / He / It	**does not** (*doesn't*)	relax	take

questions and short answers

Do	I / you / we / they	**work?**	Yes, I **do**. / No, I **do not** (*don't*).
Does	she / he / it	**work?**	Yes, he **does**. / No, he **does not** (*doesn't*).

USE

Use present simple for

- facts, or things that always happen.
  *Water **boils** at 100°C.*

- routines and habits.
  *The birds **return** to the island every spring.*

- timetable events.
  *The Drama Club **meets** every Thursday at 7.30.*

- plots of films, stories and plays.
  *At the party, Romeo **sees** Juliet and **falls** in love with her.*

yes / no questions and short answers

__Do__ male penguins __keep__ the eggs warm?   *Yes, they __do__.*
__Does__ water __boil__ at 80°C?   *No, it __does not__ / __doesn't__.*

question words

We put question words in front of present simple *yes / no* questions.

Why	*do people grow?*
Where	*does water come from?*
When	*do fish sleep?*
What	*does this word mean?*
Who	*do you sit next to?*
How	*does a camera work?*

what and who subject questions

With *what* and *who* it is possible to ask questions about the subject of a sentence.
In this case, we do not use a question form.

__Who knows__ the answer to this question?
__What makes__ it work?

1 Complete the sentence with the affirmative form of the verb in brackets.

a I (drive) ....drive.......... but my sister (cycle) ....

b The Sun (rise) .... in the east and (set) .... in the west.

c The Prime Minister (travel) .... abroad in his own private aeroplane.

d It (cost) .... $20 million to be a space tourist for one week in the International Space Station.

e The European Commission (meet) .... in Brussels.

f My dad (read) .... two books every week.

g I (understand) .... geography more than science.

h My favourite TV programme (start) .... at half past ten.

i The teachers at our school (give) .... us lots of homework.

j We (like) .... swimming because it's fun and good exercise.

2 Complete the sentence with the negative form of the verb in brackets. Use contractions.

a You (do) ....don't do.......... any of the cooking!

b My brother (play) .... tennis because he (like) .... it.

c I (think) .... that's a good idea.

d Teachers (work) .... at weekends.

e The government (agree) .... with the new EU laws.

f We (want) .... to see that film because it looks boring.

g His mum (drive) .... a fast car.

h Those new mp3 players (be) .... very expensive.

i These birds (stay) .... in the country during winter.

j He (sing) .... very well, does he?

3 Complete the sentence with the affirmative or negative form of the verb in brackets. Use contractions.

a The plane (leave) ....leaves.......... in half an hour but Nick (not / be) .... at the airport yet.

b My best friend (love) .... science fiction films but they (not / interest) .... me.

c I (not / study) .... chemistry because it (be) .... difficult.

d I (not / dance) .... because I (look) .... stupid.

e The Sun (not / go) .... round the Earth, the Earth (go) .... round the Sun!

f My new computer (do) .... lots more things than my old one, and it (not / crash) ....

g My dad (not / have) .... any qualifications but he (have) .... a really good job.

h Fire (need) .... oxygen to burn. It (not / burn) .... without oxygen.

i My teacher (not / own) .... a mobile phone because some people think they (be) .... bad for your health.

j According to scientists, animals (live) .... longer if they (not / eat) .... too much.

4 Complete the text with the affirmative form of the verbs in brackets.

Emperor penguins **a** (live) ....*live*............ in the Antarctic. The sea **b** (provide) .... all their food, so they are good swimmers. They **c** (dive) .... under the water and **d** (hold) .... their breath for up to 20 minutes. When the weather is very cold, the penguins **e** (stand) .... in a group. This **f** (keep) .... them warm. The Emperor is the only penguin that **g** (breed) .... in winter in Antarctica. Each female **h** (lay) .... one egg in May or June. They then **i** (return) .... to the sea to feed. Each male then **j** (stand) .... with an egg on his feet. His feet **k** (keep) .... the egg warm. He **l** (sleep) .... most of the time and **m** (eat) .... no food for about 65 days. When the egg **n** (hatch) ...., the female **o** (come) .... back and **p** (find) .... her mate. Now the females **q** (feed) .... the young penguins. The male **r** (spend) .... his time eating. After a few weeks, the male **s** (return) .... to the family, and then both parents **t** (look after) .... the chick.

GLOSSARY

5 Complete the text with the negative form of the verbs in brackets.

ROMEO AND JULIET

Two families, the Montagues and Capulets, live in Verona, Italy, but they **a** (get on) ...*don't get on*... with each other. Romeo, son of Montague, thinks he is in love with Rosaline, but unfortunately she **b** (love) .... him. He goes to see her at a party at the house of his enemy Capulet, but there he sees Juliet, Capulet's daughter. She **c** (know) .... his name because he has a mask. Tybalt, one of the Capulet family, tries to fight with Romeo, but Capulet **d** (allow) .... this. However, Tybalt **e** (agree) .... with him, and **f** (forgive) .... Romeo for coming to the house. Romeo manages to talk to Juliet, and he kisses her. They **g** (understand) .... that their families are enemies. When Romeo learns the truth, he **h** (care) .... that his love for Juliet could be very dangerous. Later he goes back to the house and stands in the garden. Juliet is standing on the balcony talking to herself about Romeo, but **i** (see) .... him below in the garden. After he talks to her, they soon show their love for each other, and agree to get married. However, they **j** (realize) .... that a terrible tragedy is about to happen.

GLOSSARY

6 Complete the question using the verb in brackets.
Check the factual answers on page 208.

a ....Do........ bones ......stop...... growing? (stop)

b How much water .... the brain .... ?
(contain)

c .... you .... hair on your tongue? (have)

d How many square metres .... an adult's skin
.... ? (cover)

e .... hair .... faster in hot weather? (grow)

f How long .... the heart .... to pump
blood around the body? (take)

g .... muscles .... or push? (pull)

h Which vitamin .... the liver .... ?
(produce)

i How many times a day .... you ....
in and out? (breathe)

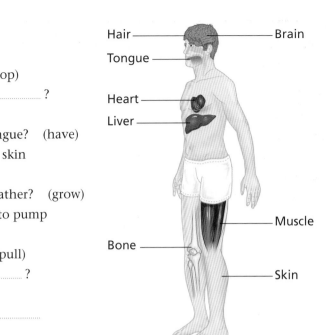

Hair — Brain
Tongue —
Heart —
Liver —
Muscle
Bone —
Skin

science

7 Complete the text with the affirmative, negative or question form of the verbs in brackets.

What **a** (do) ....does....... the body ....do....... to protect itself? Your body
b (prevent) .... harmful microorganisms entering and causing harm. The skin, for
example, **c** (allow) .... microorganisms to enter. Hairs and mucus in your nose
d (catch) .... invaders, and then you **e** (push) .... the mucus out when you
cough, sneeze or blow your nose. Enzymes and acids in the body, and white blood cells also
f (destroy) .... bacteria.
g (help) .... antibiotics .... ? Doctors **h** (use) ....
antibiotic drugs to fight bacterial infections, but antibiotics **i** (work) ....
against viruses. This is why doctors **j** (give) .... antibiotics to patients with a
common cold or flu.
How **k** (work) .... immunization .... ? Immunization
(or vaccination) is another way of protecting the body, by injecting the body with dead or
inactive microorganisms. After vaccination, the body **l** (start) .... to make
antibodies that destroy the microorganism. Because the microorganisms in the vaccination are
not dangerous, the person **m** (get) .... ill. When they
n (come) .... into contact with a live (dangerous) microorganism, then the
antibodies **o** (destroy) .... the infection before it makes them ill.

GLOSSARY

EXTENSION ACTIVITY

1 Make a list of five facts from this unit which
interest or surprise you.

2 Write ten sentences about your routines
and habits.

present simple

2 present continuous

FORM

affirmative

I	am ('m)	
You / We / They	are ('re)	moving.
She / He / It	is ('s)	

negative

I	am not ('m not)	
You / We / They	are not ('re not / aren't)	studying.
She / He / It	is not (isn't / 's not)	

questions and short answers

Am	I	going?	Yes, I am. / No, I am not ('m not).
Are	you / we / they	waiting?	Yes, they are. / No, they are not (aren't / 're not).
Is	she / he / it	singing?	Yes, he is. / No, he is not (isn't / 's not).

spelling rules

- One-syllable verbs ending in one vowel + one consonant, double the consonant and add *-ing*:
  sit – sitting   get – getting   put – putting
- Verbs ending in *e*, drop *e* before adding *-ing*:   *like – liking   write – writing*
- Verbs ending *-ie* change *-ie* to *-y*:   *lie – lying   die – dying*
- Two-syllable verbs ending in one vowel and one consonant usually double the final consonant and add *-ing*:   *travel – travelling   admit – admitting*
- All other verbs add *-ing*:   *play – playing   feel – feeling   try – trying*

USE

Use present continuous

- for actions happening at the moment of speaking, and not finished.
  *Sorry, I'm busy at the moment. **I'm doing** my homework.*
- for continuing, unfinished actions which are not actually happening at the moment of speaking, with verbs like *work, learn, read, study* etc.
  *What **are you doing** in science?   **We're learning** about the universe.*
- for changing situations, with verbs like *become, get, grow, change, increase*, or with expressions such as *more and more*.
  *The earth **is becoming** warmer.*
  *More and more people **are leaving** the countryside.*
- for a future arrangement, with a time reference (see **Unit 10**).
  ***We're leaving** tomorrow.*

Note: we do not repeat auxiliary *be* when we talk about two or more actions.
  *We **are doing** an experiment and **making** notes.*

present continuous or present simple?

*The Earth **moves** round the Sun.*	(present simple = a general fact)
*The floor **is moving**! It's an earthquake!*	(present continuous = at the moment)
*Most scientists **work** with computers.*	(present simple = a general fact)
*I'm **working** on my science project.*	(present continuous = at the moment)

verbs not usually in present continuous

Use present continuous with action verbs. For state verbs, which describe feelings, opinions etc, use present simple.

Thoughts and opinions	*think, understand, know, suppose, believe, want, remember, forget, depend, agree*
Feelings	*like, love, hate, feel, prefer, need*
Senses	*see, hear, smell*: basic sense meanings with *can. I can see* etc
	I see (= I understand) *I hear* (= people tell me)
	This meat smells (= has a smell)
Possession and existence	*belong, contain, have, include, mean, seem, weigh*

present simple and continuous with different meanings

Some verbs have a state meaning in present simple and an action meaning in present continuous.

I think it's a good idea.	Present simple for opinion
I'm thinking about it.	Present continuous for action (I haven't decided yet.)
It has four legs.	Present simple for description
I'm having a great time.	Present continuous for action (happening now)
The surface feels hard.	Present simple for description
I'm feeling sick.	Present continuous for action (happening now)
(*I feel sick* is also possible)	
I'm seeing Tom on Friday.	Present continuous for future action (I'm meeting)

1 Complete the sentence with the affirmative form of the verb in brackets.

a Look, all the people (leave) ....*are leaving.*....
b The Earth's temperature (rise) .... because people (use) .... too much energy.
c She (study) .... economics and he (study) .... philosophy.
d You (stand) .... too close to the road.
e We (stay) .... in a lovely hotel by the beach.
f I (go) .... to the supermarket now, do you need anything?
g The cat (chase) .... the dog.
h Technology (become) .... cheaper all the time.
i Pawel and Marek (train) .... for the football game next week.
j Manuela (listen) .... to music in her room.

2 Underline the correct form.

a Scientists *do not understand* / *are not understanding* everything about the universe.
b They disagree about some important facts. For example, *does it get* / *is it getting* larger or smaller?
c Although they *don't agree* / *are not agreeing* about everything, there are some facts about the universe which they are sure about.
d Take the planet Venus, for example. Here the temperature *reaches* / *is reaching* over 400°C.
e And another unusual fact about Venus is that a day there *lasts* / *is lasting* longer than a year.
f Many scientists *still search* / *are still searching* for life in other parts of the universe.
g *Do they look* / *Are they looking* for life on Venus?
h *It doesn't seem* / *isn't seeming* to be the kind of place where life might exist.
i The atmosphere of Venus *consists* / *is consisting* mainly of carbon dioxide (CO_2).
j And it *has* / *is having* an air pressure 90 times greater than that of Earth.

present continuous

11

3 Complete the text with the present continuous form of the verbs in brackets.

Good afternoon, everybody. I **a** (speak) ....._am speaking_..... to you from Mount Surprising, the giant volcano. A team of scientists **b** (visit) .... the volcano, and I'm here for Big TV, just in case anything exciting happens. I **c** (stand) .... here near the top of the crater, and **d** (look) .... down into the volcano. At the moment the four scientists **e** (climb) .... down into the crater. It doesn't look very dangerous, I must say, but they **f** (wear) .... special clothes and a rescue team **g** (stand by) .... just in case! A little bit of smoke **h** (rise) .... from the volcano, but that's normal. Now the scientists **i** (set) .... up their equipment. They **j** (try) .... to collect some gas, which will help them understand what exactly **k** (go on) .... under the volcano. Wait a minute! Something **l** (happen) .... ! The ground **m** (shake) .... ! The four scientists **n** (climb) .... out of the volcano as quickly as they can. They **o** (shout) .... something as well. I think it's time to leave!

Lava   Crater

4 Complete the sentence with the negative form of the verb in brackets. Use contractions.

a As you know, the Marina space mission (go) ....._isn't going_..... according to plan.

b As far as we can tell, the spacecraft (head for) .... the moon.

c We can't be sure because at the moment it (send) .... us any useful information.

d Some of the equipment on the spacecraft (work) .... properly.

e As a result, we (receive) .... radio signals.

f It seems that the solar power panels (point) .... at the Sun.

g So as a result, they (produce) .... enough power.

h And at the moment Marina's computer (respond) .... to our signals.

i We are trying to correct the problem but we (have) .... any luck.

j However, we (give up) .... hope.

5 Use the prompts to make a question.

a the weather in your country / change

....._Is the weather in your country changing_.... ?

b it grow / warmer or colder

.... ?

c storms / happen more often

.... ?

d less snow / fall in winter

.... ?

e summer / get hotter

.... ?

f the changes / become a problem

.... ?

g people / worry about this

.... ?

h they / do anything to help

.... ?

6 Complete the text with the present simple or present continuous forms of the verbs in brackets.

Population **a** (mean) ....*means*.......... the number of people who live in a particular area.
The population of the world **b** (not stay) .... the same. At the moment it **c** (grow)
.... at an increasing rate. In fact, scientists **d** (believe) .... that the world
population will increase until 2200, and then stop growing. However, things are not the same in all parts of the
world. At present in many Western industrial countries the population **e** (fall) ....
This **f** (happen) .... because families are small, and health conditions are good.
In developing countries, on the other hand, the population
g (rise) .... sharply. In Ghana, for
example, most families **h** (have) ....
several children. Many children in Ghana
i (die) .... from illness, so it is
important to have lots of children. They earn money
for the family and **j** (look after) ....
their parents in old age.

GLOSSARY

7 Complete the sentence with the present simple or present continuous form of the verb
in brackets.

a Everybody (know) ....*knows*.......... that the world's rainforests (disappear)
..*are disappearing*..

b Although rainforests (cover) .... only six per cent of the Earth's land
surface, they (contain) .... about 50% of all species of life on
the planet.

c They also (remove) .... carbon dioxide (CO_2) from the air and (produce)
.... oxygen (O_2).

d As they are important, why (they / vanish) .... ?

e Most scientists (agree) .... that there are two main reasons.

f First of all, the way of life in these forests (change) ....

g In some forests, big companies (cut) .... down more and more trees
(deforestation) and (cause) .... damage to the land.

h In other places, another kind of deforestation (happen) ....

i Here farmers (burn) .... more and more of the forest and (use)
.... the land to feed cattle.

j Now that governments (understand) .... the problem, they (begin)
.... to control these activities.

EXTENSION ACTIVITY

1 Write five true sentences about your continuing
activities, with *learn, read, write, study* and *try to*.

2 Write five true sentences about yourself, people you
know, your school etc describing changing situations.

*Need more practice? Go to the **Review** on page 192.*

3 past simple

affirmative

I / You / We / They / She / He / It **stopped.**

negative

I / You / We / They / She / He / It **did not** (*didn't*) **stop.**

questions

	Did	I / you / we / they / she / he / it	**wait?**
When	**did**	Leonardo da Vinci	**live?**
What	**did**	Leonardo da Vinci	**paint?**

short answers

Yes, I / you / we / they / she / he / it **did.**   No, I / you / we / they / she / he / it **didn't.**

spelling rules

- Verbs ending in *e*, add *-d*:   *decide – decided*
- For one-syllable verbs ending in one vowel + one consonant,
  double the consonant and add *-ed*:   *stop – stopped*
- Other one-syllable verbs, add *-ed*:   *wait – waited*
- Verbs ending in vowel + consonant + *y*, change *-y* to *-i* and add *-ed*:   *study – studied*
  Note: verbs ending in vowel + *y,* add *-ed*:   *play – played*
- Two-syllable verbs ending in one vowel + one consonant,
  double the consonant if the stress is on the last syllable and add *-ed*:   *prefer – preferred*
- If the stress is on the first syllable, add *-ed*:   *profit – profited*

irregular verbs   (see **List of irregular verbs** page 206)
Many verbs have irregular past simple forms eg   *drink – drank   see – saw*

Use past simple
- to talk about finished events in the past, when we think about a definite time.
  *Alexander's army **marched** beside the river and then **stopped** outside the city.*
- to describe the events in a story.
  *Oliver **heard** the sound of a bell. Soon afterwards, the door softly **opened**.*
- to describe habits and routines in the past. We usually use a time word or phrase.
  *Leonardo **painted** in his studio **every day**.*

Subject and object questions are both possible with past simple (see **Unit 1**).
   *What **did** Leonardo **paint**?*   object question: + auxiliary *did*
   *Who **painted** this portrait?*   subject question: no auxiliary *did*

Examples of time words and phrases we use with past simple:

yesterday	last night	last week	last year
on Tuesday	at 6.30	an hour ago	after that
in 1754	in January		

1 Complete the sentence with the past simple form of the verb in brackets.

a Aztec civilization (develop) _developed_ in the Valley of Mexico, 7,500 feet above sea level.

b The Aztecs (leave) _____ their own land of Aztlan at some time during the 12th or 13th century.

c They (believe) _____ that Huitzilopochtli their war god (want) _____ them to search for a new land.

d They (arrive) _____ in the Valley of Mexico during the 12th or 13th century AD.

e They (build) _____ their capital city, Tenochtitlan, on an island in Lake Texcoco.

f They (plant) _____ trees on the island to make the land better, (work) _____ hard and (improve) _____ the land.

g When the Spanish (arrive) _____ in 1519, Montezuma, the Aztec ruler, (think) _____ that Cortez was a returning god.

h When the Spanish (see) _____ the Aztecs' gold, they (decide) _____ to conquer the city.

i Later they (kill) _____ Montezuma, (defeat) _____ the Aztecs and (destroy) _____ Aztec religion and culture.

2 Complete the sentence with the past simple form of the verb in brackets. Then decide if each sentence is *True* or *False*. Check the factual answers on page 208.

a Greek actors (wear) _wore_ masks and special boots. *True*

b Spartan children (take) _____ baths only two or three times a year.

c The philosopher Socrates (drink) _____ poison and died.

d Alexander the Great's army (go) _____ as far as China.

e Heron of Alexandria (make) _____ a kind of jet engine.

f The Roman Emperor Caligula's name (mean) _____ 'Happy Soldier'.

g Roman mathematics (have) _____ no zero.

h Most Roman girls (get) _____ married at the age of 18.

i Roman soldiers (pay) _____ for their own equipment and food.

j The Romans (know) _____ how to make soap and cement.

3 Seven of the sentences (including the example) contain historical errors. Guess which ones are wrong and rewrite them with a negative past simple form. Check the factual answers on page 208.

a Alexander the Great married Cleopatra.
  Alexander the Great didn't marry Cleopatra.

b Nelson Mandela became President of South Africa in 1994.

c Leonardo da Vinci invented the Internet.

d Confucius the Chinese philosopher died in 1900.

e Marco Polo stayed in China for five years.

f The ancient Romans used steam engines in their battles.

g Genghis Khan invaded Italy and captured Rome.

h Christopher Columbus reached America by accident.

i William Shakespeare wrote *Don Quixote*.

4 Complete the question for each answer.

The Industrial Revolution in Britain

a When *did the Industrial Revolution happen in Britain* ?
The Industrial Revolution happened during the second half of the 18th century in Britain.

b How ?
Work changed with the building of large factories.

c What ?
The first factories produced iron, steel, and textiles.

d What ?
New technology encouraged the production of more ships, and railway equipment.

e What power ?
Factories used steam power.

f What ?
These factories required lots of coal for the steam engines.

g Where ?
Manufacturers constructed their factories close to coal mines.

h Why ?
They decided to do this because it was expensive to transport coal.

i What ?
Factories also needed limestone and iron ore, for the manufacture of steel.

j Where ?
Industry in the UK developed near the coal fields of South Wales, the Midlands, north-east England and central Scotland.

GLOSSARY

5 Rewrite each statement about the playwright William Shakespeare as a *yes* / *no* question.

a He came from a rich family.
Q *Did he come from a rich family* ?
A No, not really. His father was a glove maker.

b He grew up in London.
Q ?
A No, in Stratford upon Avon, a small town about 160 km from London.

c He went to school.
Q ?
A Yes, we think so.

d He knew Latin.
Q ?
A Yes, he learnt Latin at school, and some Greek as well.

e He got married.
Q ?
A Yes, he was only 18 when he married Anne Hathaway, aged 26.

f They had children.
Q ?
A Yes, a daughter Susanna, and twins, a boy Hamnet and a girl Judith.

g He began writing plays in Stratford.

Q ....?

A *We don't really know. We only know that after 1592 he was an actor and writer in London.*

h He wrote 37 plays all by himself.

Q ....?

A *Well, we know he wrote two plays together with John Fletcher. Some people think that all his plays were really written by somebody else.*

i He made up all the characters and plots of his plays.

Q ....?

A *Actually no. He borrowed lots of ideas from other writers. This was quite usual in his time.*

j He became rich and famous.

Q ....?

A *He certainly became quite rich, and his plays were popular. But he only became really famous in the 18th century and later.*

6 Complete the text with the past simple affirmative, negative or question forms of the verbs in brackets.

Louis Pasteur 1822–1895

As a young man, Pasteur **a** ....*studied*........ at the École Normale in Paris. Then at the age of just 32, he **b** (become) .... a professor at the University of Lille. In 1856, Pasteur **c** (receive) .... a visit from a man called Bigo who **d** (own) .... a factory that **e** (make) .... alcohol from sugar beet. He **f** (have) .... a question for Pasteur: why **g** (the alcohol / turn / to acid?) .... ? When this **h** (happen) ...., they **i** (not can) .... use it and **j** (throw) .... it away. Bigo **k** (ask) .... Pasteur to find out the reason for this.

At first, Pasteur **l** (not know) ...., but when he **m** (examine) .... the alcohol under a microscope, he **n** (find) .... thousands of tiny micro-organisms. He **o** (believe) .... that they **p** (cause) .... the problem. **q** (milk, wine and vinegar / behave / in the same way?) ....?

Other scientists **r** (disagree) .... with him, and newspapers **s** (make) .... fun of him. However, Pasteur **t** (continue) .... with his work, he **u** (invent) .... methods of testing his theory and **v** (prove) .... that he was right. Later he **w** (work) .... together with two doctors and **x** (develop) .... vaccines for diseases such as anthrax and rabies.

GLOSSARY

EXTENSION ACTIVITY

1 Write five sentences about a famous historical figure from your country.

2 Write ten true things that you did, using the time words and phrases on page 14.

Need more practice? Go to the Review on page 192.

science

3

past simple

17

4 past continuous, *used to do*

affirmative

| I / She / He / It | **was** | **reading.** |
| You / We / They | **were** | |

negative

| I / She / He / It | **was not** (*wasn't*) | **looking.** |
| You / We / They | **were not** (*weren't*) | |

questions and short answers

	Was	I / she / he / it	**waiting?**	Yes, I **was.**	No, I **wasn't.**
	Were	you / we / they	**watching?**	you **were.**	you **weren't.**
Where	**was**	he	**waiting?**		
What	**were**	they	**wearing?**		

USE

Use past continuous

- for a continuing unfinished action in the past.
  *When Sue arrived at 9.30 am, four people **were waiting** outside the office.*

	continuing past action	completed past event	
PAST	————————————————▶	▼	PRESENT
	were waiting	*arrived*	

- for a continuing unfinished action interrupted by a sudden past action.
  *While **we were doing** the maths test, the fire alarm went off.*

- for activities as background description.
  *The rainforest was full of sounds. Birds **were calling** from the trees and thousands of insects **were buzzing and humming**.*

- for two continuing events happening at the same time.
  *While Cortes **was talking** to the emperor, his army **was taking** over the palace.*

while, when

- Use *while* with past continuous for the time the event was happening.

- Use *when* with past simple for actions.

- We can use other more descriptive time phrases instead of *when*.
  ***At the moment** the earthquake struck, most people **were going about** their normal lives.*

habits in the past

For describing habits and states in the past, it is more natural to use *used to* + verb than past continuous, especially when we make contrasts with the present. We do not mention the exact date.

Used to is unchangeable, and has only a past tense form.
Negative: *didn't use to*   **Question:** *Did you use to?*

*Rainforests **used to cover** a third of the Earth, but now they are getting smaller.*
*Once people **didn't use to worry** about this problem.*
*What games **did you use to play** in the playground at school?*

Note: we also use **past simple** (+ frequency adverb) to describe habitual actions in the past.
*People **once thought** that the Sun travelled round the Earth.*

1 Underline the correct form.

a While *he took* / <u>*was taking*</u> a bath, Archimedes *discovered* / *was discovering* the principles of density and buoyancy.

b When Edouard Benedictus, a French scientist, *worked* / *was working* in his laboratory, he *dropped* / *was dropping* a glass bottle which had some plastic inside – and *invented* / *was inventing* safety glass.

c Columbus *arrived* / *was arriving* in America while he *tried* / *was trying* to reach the Far East.

d Alexander Fleming *discovered* / *was discovering* penicillin by accident while he *looked* / *was looking* at some old experiments.

e While Hiram Bingham *climbed* / *was climbing* in the mountains of Peru in 1911, he *discovered* / *was discovering* the lost city of Macchu Picchu.

f While Isaac Newton *sat* / *was sitting* under an apple tree, an apple *fell* / *was falling* on his head, and he *understood* / *was understanding* gravity.

g While Dr Harry Coover *tried* / *was trying* to invent a new kind of plastic, he *made* / *was making* a very soft substance which *stuck* / *was sticking* things together. It was Superglue.

h While he *observed* / *was observing* the Moon through his telescope, Galileo *realized* / *was realizing* that it had mountains and craters.

Macchu Picchu

2A Use the prompts to make a question. The answers are in Exercise 1.

a Where / Edouard Benedictus / work when he invented safety glass?
   Where was Edouard Benedictus working
   when he invented safety glass ?

b Where / Columbus / try to go when he reached America?
   _____
   _____ ?

c Where / Isaac Newton / sit according to the story about gravity?
   _____
   _____ ?

d What / Dr Harry Coover / hope to invent?
   _____
   _____ ?

e What Galileo / look at / through his telescope?
   _____
   _____ ?

2B Complete the sentence with the past continuous form of the verb in brackets. The sentences refer to Exercise 1.

f Edouard Benedictus (not try) _____
   _____
   to invent safety glass.

g Alexander Fleming (not hope) _____
   _____
   to discover penicillin.

h Hiram Bingham (not look for) _____
   _____
   the lost city of Macchu Picchu.

i Isaac Newton (not sit) _____
   _____
   in his study when he understood gravity.

j Dr Harry Coover (not conduct) _____
   _____
   an experiment to discover a kind of glue.

past continuous, used to do

3 Complete the sentence with the past simple or past continuous form of the verb in brackets.

Alexander the Great

a While he (grow up) ..*was growing up*.. , the philosopher Aristotle was his teacher. Alexander (become) .... interested in science, medicine, philosophy and literature.

b While his father Philip (attend) .... his daughter's wedding, a young nobleman (murder) .... him. Alexander was king of Macedonia at the age of 20.

c While he (fight) .... his enemies in the north, the Greeks in the south (start) .... a rebellion. He (destroy) .... all their cities.

d He (lead) .... his army against the Persian Empire through what is now Turkey. While he (stay) .... in the ancient city of Gordium, he (undo) .... the Gordian knot. A legend said that only a future king of Asia could do this.

e While his army (march) .... through Persia, it (defeat) .... Darius, the king of Persia.

f He (found) .... the city of Alexandria at the mouth of the Nile while he (visit) .... Egypt.

g While he (travel) .... with his army, he (give) .... his name to many other towns.

h He (kill) .... his friend Clitus in a quarrel, while they (have) .... dinner.

i While he (attack) .... the city of Mali in India, he (receive) .... a serious wound from an arrow.

j While he (attend) .... a banquet in Babylon in 323 BC, he (fall) .... ill and (die) ....

GLOSSARY

4 Complete the sentence with *used to* + a verb from the list.

~~write~~   spend   work   hold   help   act   teach   set   tell   do

a Charles Dickens, the novelist, ...*used to write*.. until early in the morning, and then go for long walks across London.

b William Shakespeare .... in some of his own plays.

c The German philosopher Immanuel Kant .... exactly the same things at the same time every day, so that people .... their watches by his actions.

d The author Agatha Christie .... her second husband with his archaeological excavations.

e The novelist James Joyce .... English in the Italian city of Trieste, and some people say that he .... his students the wrong meanings of words as a joke.

f The novelist Marcel Proust .... in a special soundproof room.

g The ancient Greek philosophers .... their classes outside in the open air.

h The Russian novelist Vladimir Nabokov .... his free time studying and catching moths and butterflies.

5 Complete the sentence with *used to* + the verb in brackets in positive, negative or question form.

a What things (be) ....*used to be*.... different in the past?

b For a start, all the continents (form) .... one large land mass.

c Obviously, there (be) .... cities and buildings, and forest covered a third of the Earth.

d The climate was different, and animals such as the hippopotamus and rhinoceros (exist) .... in northern Europe.

e Many mountains in Europe (be) .... active volcanoes.

f Early people (live) .... in complex societies, but in small groups in places where they could find food.

g What (eat) .... ? They (eat) .... whatever they could find.

h Early people (stay) .... in the same place, but (travel) .... long distances, following the animals they needed for food.

history

6 Complete the text with the past simple or past continuous form of the verbs in brackets.

The Vikings in America

According to Viking records, around the year 1000, while some Viking sailors **a** (look for) *were looking for* the coast of Greenland, they **b** (reach) .... the eastern coast of America. While they **c** (live) .... there, they **d** (try) .... to trade with the local Native Americans, known by the Vikings as Skraelings, but in the end the Native Americans **e** (fight) .... them and **f** (drive) .... them out. After several attempts to return, the Vikings **g** (give up) .... In 1968, while some archaeologists **h** (work) .... in Newfoundland, they **i** (discover) .... the remains of one of the Viking settlements, and **j** (prove) .... that this story was true.

Charles-Marie de la Condamine

In 1735 Charles-Marie de la Condamine **k** (sail) .... to South America. At that time, scientists **l** (argue) .... about the shape of the Earth. The French Academy **m** (want) .... him to take measurements on the Equator, along with two other scientists. The work **n** (take) .... them eight years and in the end, another scientific team **o** (find) .... the answer they **p** (look for) .... While de la Condamine **q** (travel) .... home along the River Amazon, he **r** (learn) .... many interesting things about the local people and their way of life. When he **s** (arrive) .... in Paris in 1745, he **t** (receive) .... a hero's welcome.

The River Amazon

GLOSSARY

past continuous, used to do

EXTENSION ACTIVITY

Make a list of ten things you used to do, but don't do any more, and say what you do now.

5 present perfect simple

affirmative

| I / You / We / They | **have ('ve)** | **decided.** | (past participle) |
| She / He / It | **has ('s)** | | |

negative

| I / You / We / They | **have not** (*haven't* / *'ve not*) | **decided.** |
| She / He / It | **has not** (*hasn't* / *'s not*) | |

questions

	Have	I / you / we / they	**decided?**
	Has	she / he / it	
Where	**have**	you	**put** it?
What	**has**	she	**done?**

short answers

| Yes, | I / you / we / they | **have.** | No, | I / you / we / they | **haven't.** |
| | she / he / it | **has.** | | she / he / it | **hasn't.** |

Regular verbs use *-ed* form as the past participle. Irregular verbs have irregular forms.

verb	past simple	past participle
wait (regular)	*waited*	*waited*
see (irregular)	*saw*	*seen*

See the **List of irregular verbs** on page 206.

USE

Use present perfect simple

- to describe an event in the past without a definite time.
  *Someone **has broken** a window in our classroom.*

- to describe what someone has completed or achieved in a period of time.
  ***I've finished** my homework, and I've cleaned my room.*

- to describe how many things someone has done.
  *Scientists **have found** more than 30 unknown insects.*

- to describe someone's experiences, what he or she has done in life.
  ***I've travelled** by plane, but I **haven't flown** in a helicopter.*

- to describe changes, comparing past and present.
  *Our climate **has become** much warmer.*

> **action verb happening in a period of time up to the present,
> exact time not known**
> ?   ?   ?   ?   ?   ?   ?   PRESENT
> *Someone **has broken** a window.*

We often use time words and phrases with present perfect simple to make the meaning clear.

just, recently	Someone has **just** broken a window.
	Scientists have **recently** found more than 30 unknown insects.
ever?, never	Have you **ever** flown in a helicopter? I've **never** travelled by plane.
already (sooner than expected)	I've **already** finished my homework. It was easy!
yet? (we expect something to happen soon)	Have you finished **yet**?
not ... yet (for things which have not happened so far)	Peter has**n't** phoned **yet**. I'm still waiting.

for and *since*

We use *for* with a length of time.

   She's worked here **for ten years**.

We use *since* with a point of time to describe when the period of time began.

   They've lived here **since 2001**.

been and *gone*

A number of astronauts **have been** to the Moon.	(and have returned)
The space probe Voyager **has gone** past the planet Neptune.	(it hasn't returned)

1 Complete the sentence using a verb from the list in present perfect simple form.

collect	install	organize	paint	plant
put up	recycle	replace	~~send~~	show

What we have done to make our school a greener place

a We ......*have sent*...... information leaflets to all parents.

b We .... information posters in every classroom.

c We .... over five tonnes of litter for recycling.

d We .... fifteen trees in front of the school.

e We .... 50 light bulbs with energy-saving bulbs.

f We .... 25 ink cartridges from computer printers.

g We .... three films about how to save energy.

h We .... signs on all the doors reminding people to turn off the lights.

i We .... five new energy-saving heaters.

j We .... teams of students to turn off unused lights.

2 Read these sentences about fish. Then put the verb in brackets into present perfect simple form.

a About 15% of protein eaten by humans (always come) ...*has always come*... from fish.

b Recently, however, the number of fish (fall) ....

c Several things (cause) .... this problem.

d Most scientists agree that governments (not do) .... enough to stop overfishing.

e This means that fish populations (grow) .... smaller.

f Many fish (not reproduce) .... fast enough to replace their numbers.

g The population of North Sea cod, for example, (reach) .... a dangerous level.

h EU laws (reduce) .... the numbers of fishing boats.

i As a result, many fishermen in traditional fishing ports (lose) .... their jobs.

j In recent years, fish in the UK (become) .... expensive, and many people (stop) .... eating it.

present perfect simple

3 Use the prompts to make a question.

  a you / ever / see a humming bird?   *Have you ever seen a humming bird?*   ?
     It's the world smallest bird.

  b you / ever / read *War and Peace*?   _____   ?
     It's one of the longest 19th-century novels.

  c you / ever / visit San Marino?   _____   ?
     It's Europe's second smallest country.

  d you / ever / swim in the Pacific Ocean?   _____   ?
     It's the largest ocean in the world.

  e you / ever / take a trip to the Sahara Desert?   _____   ?
     It's one of the hottest places in the world.

4 Complete each sentence with one of the time words in the list. You will need to use some words more than once.

> yet   for   already   since

In the laboratory ....

  a 'Haven't you left ......*yet*...... ?'
  b 'No. I've been here .... 8.00 this morning.'
  c 'Have you checked the results of the experiment .... ?'
  d 'Yes, I've .... done that.'
  e 'We've worked on this project .... three weeks. Unfortunately we haven't
     discovered anything interesting .... '
  f 'No, nothing has happened .... last Tuesday.'
  g 'Yes, I know. I've .... seen your report.'
  h 'So I'm going to do the experiment again. But I haven't started it .... '
  i 'Don't bother. I've .... started it. I haven't checked ...., but I think we're
     going to get the same results.'

5 Complete the sentence with *have been* or *have gone*.

  a Two scientists from a laboratory in Oxford a ..*have gone*.. to Antarctica, and will stay there
     for three months. They b .... there to investigate the effects of global warming on
     the polar ice. Colleagues in Oxford, who c .... to Antarctica on earlier expeditions,
     will keep in touch with them by radio.

  b A team from London has arrived in China. They d .... there to join a project
     which is searching for the fossil remains of dinosaur eggs. 'We e (not) .... to China
     before,' said team leader Mark Jones, 'though two of us f .... to the USA where
     there is a similar project.'

  c A dangerous spider is missing from a private zoo in Manchester. 'Herbie is a Brazilian
     wandering spider, and we're not sure where he g .... ' said spokesperson Anne
     Graham. 'He only arrived in the zoo last month, so he h (not) .... here long.
     A lot of children i .... to the zoo in the past few days, and we are worried that
     someone has taken Herbie, or that he j .... out in somebody's pocket, and they
     don't know about it.'

6 Use the prompts to make a present perfect simple question about scientific advances. Then answer *yes* or *no*. Check the factual answers on page 208.

a scientists / discover a cure for the common cold?
Have scientists discovered a cure for the common cold?

b people / live for long periods in space?

....

c human beings / land on Mars yet?

....

d scientists / invent time travel yet?

....

e doctors / manage to transplant human hearts?

....

f archaeologists / find the lost city of Atlantis?

....

g scientists / ever teach an animal to talk?

....

geography

7 Read the text about climate change. Choose the correct form, A or B, to complete the sentence.

At the moment, scientists agree that the world's climate **a** _B_ warmer over the past 50 years, but they disagree about the causes. Some believe that human activities **b** .... climate change. They argue that for 1,000 or 2,000 years before 1850, when records **c** .... , the temperature was more or less stable. Short warm or cold periods **d** .... during that time, but the climate always **e** .... to the same level. However, since the Industrial Revolution, human beings **f** .... more and more fossil fuels, such as coal and oil. In 1800 the atmosphere **g** .... around 280 parts per million of carbon dioxide (CO_2). Since then there **h** .... an increase of about 31%. This extra carbon dioxide **i** .... the world's temperature because of the greenhouse effect.

Other scientists disagree that human activities over the past 50 years **j** .... global warming. They point out that volcanoes and other natural processes **k** .... CO_2 into the atmosphere, and that human activity **l** .... a rise in CO_2 of only three per cent.

In 1999, 156 countries **m** .... the Kyoto protocol, part of a United Nations agreement on climate change, which **n** .... into force in 2005. They **o** .... to reduce their emissions of CO_2 and other greenhouse gases, although so far, some countries, such as the USA and Australia, **p** .... any action.

a A *became*	B *has become*
b A *caused*	B *have caused*
c A *began*	B *have begun*
d A *occurred*	B *have occurred*
e A *returned*	B *has returned*
f A *burned*	B *have burned*
g A *contained*	B *has contained*
h A *was*	B *has been*
i A *raised*	B *has raised*
j A *caused*	B *have caused*
k A *always released*	B *have always released*
l A *contributed*	B *has contributed*
m A *signed*	B *have signed*
n A *came*	B *has come*
o A *agreed*	B *have agreed*
p A *did not take*	B *have not taken*

present perfect simple

EXTENSION ACTIVITY

Make a list of ten things you have done, or have never done in your life so far.
Need more practice? Go to the **Review** *on page 192.*

6 present perfect continuous

FORM

affirmative

I / You / We / They	**have** (*'ve*)	**been**	**reading**.
She / He / It	**has** (*'s*)		

negative

I / You / We / They	**have not** (*haven't / 've not*)	**been**	**working**.
She / He / It	**has not** (*hasn't / 's not*)		

questions

	Have	I / you / we / they	**been waiting**?
	Has	she / he / it	
What	**have**	you	**been doing**?
Where	**has**	she	**been staying**?

short answers

Yes,	I / you / we / they	**have.**	No,	I / you / we / they	**haven't.**
	she / he / it	**has.**		she / he / it	**hasn't.**

USE

Use present perfect continuous

● to talk about recent continuing activities.
*What **have** you **been doing** lately?*
***I've been revising** for my exams.*

● to explain how recent continuing activities have caused the present situation.
*My eyes ache. **I've been reading** all day.*

● to talk about recent continuing activities which will probably continue in the future.
*This diagram shows how the climate **has been changing**.*

● with *how long* questions.
*How long **have you been studying** French?*
(this is a continuing process, and isn't finished)

● with time words *lately, recently, all (day), every (morning), for, since.*

covering a period of time up to the present
PAST ⟶ PRESENT
***I've been studying** all morning.*
(It's still morning now and I haven't finished my work yet)

present perfect simple or present perfect continuous?

Present perfect simple	*I've **written** my project.* (finished, but we don't know when)
Present perfect continuous	*I've **been writing** my project.* (continuing up to the present, and not finished)

With verbs that describe continuing states eg *work, live,* there is little difference in meaning.
*I've **worked** here for three years. / I've **been working** here for three years.*
Note that we **do not** say ~~I am working here for three years~~.

1 Complete the sentence using the verb in brackets in the present perfect continuous form.

a I'm sorry to keep you waiting. I hope you (not wait) ....*haven't been waiting*.... long.

b There you are! We (look for) .... you all morning!

c I feel really tired. I (study) .... hard lately.

d Anna has got a really good suntan. She (go) .... to the beach a lot.

e Tom needs cheering up. He (have) .... a lot of problems lately.

f I haven't seen you for ages. What (you / do) .... ?

g I (work) .... here for the past three years, and I really like it.

h Sam and Chris (paint) .... their room, and their clothes are covered in paint!

geography

2 Underline the correct form.

A Scientists a *have recently identified* / *have been identifying* a new species of animal in the rainforest of Borneo. They b *have been searching* / *searched* for this creature for several years, after reports from local villagers, and say it is a type of lemur.

A lemur

B Archaeologists in Guatemala c *have found* / *have been finding* a Mayan wall painting which they think is more than 2,000 years old. Archaeologist William Saturno d *explored* / *has been exploring* the site since 2002.

C Scientists using the Hubble Space Telescope think they e *found* / *have found* two new moons circling the planet Pluto. Astronomers f *have been looking* / *looked* closely at Pluto since 1978 when they g *spotted* / *have spotted* its first moon. The telescope h *worked* / *has been working* for fifteen years, and i *has been producing* / *has produced* more than 700,000 images of the universe.

D Australian scientists j *have been discovering* / *have discovered* a new coral reef over 60 km long in the Gulf of Carpentaria by using satellites to spot the reefs in deep water. Recently divers k *have managed* / *have been managing* to reach the reefs and take photographs.

GLOSSARY

3 Use the prompts and *how long* to make a question.

a astronomers / look for Pluto's moons?
  How long have astronomers been looking for Pluto's moons ?

b archaeologists / hope to find Atlantis?
  .... ?

c scientists / use satellites to discover new reefs?
  .... ?

d physicists / investigate the origin of the universe?
  .... ?

e scientists / observe Vesuvius?
  .... ?

f biologists / try to find new species of mammal?
  .... ?

g archaeologists / excavate the palace in Guatemala?
  .... ?

h doctors / search for a cure for HIV?
  .... ?

*Need more practice? Go to the **Review** on page 192.*

present perfect continuous

7 past perfect

past perfect simple

affirmative

I / You / We / They / She / He / It **had ('d)** **left**. (past participle)

negative

I / You / We / They / She / He / It **had not** (*hadn't*) **left**.

questions

	Had	I / you / we / they / she / he / it	**left?**
What	**had**	they	**found?**

short answers

Yes,	I / you / we / they / she / he / it	**had.**
No,		**hadn't.**

Use past perfect simple to describe a past event which happens before another event in the past. Only use it when it is important to make clear that one event in the past happened before another.

> On 12 July 1771, Cook's ship The Endeavour *arrived* back in Britain. Cook **had not discovered** a new continent, but he **had visited** places never seen before.

In this example, '*not discovered*' happened before '*arrived*'.

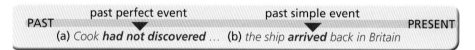

PAST	past perfect event	past simple event	PRESENT
	▼	▼	
	(a) Cook **had not discovered** …	(b) the ship **arrived** back in Britain	

We do not use past perfect simple simply to show that an event happened a very long time ago. We can sometimes use *before* or *after* with past simple to make the order of events clear.

> By the time the ship reached the island, more then twenty sailors **had died**.
> More than twenty sailors **died before** the ship reached the island.

forgot, remembered, realized

With *forgot, remembered, realized, knew*, we use past perfect simple to describe the past events that happened before the moment we forgot, remembered or realised something.

> When Franklin checked the ship's position, he **realized** he **had made** a mistake.

past perfect continuous

affirmative

I / You / We / They / She / He / It **had been waiting.**

negative

I / You / We / They / She / He / It **had not** (*hadn't*) **been waiting.**

questions				
	Had	I / you / we / they / she / he / it	**been**	**waiting?**
What	**had**	they	**been**	**doing?**

short answers			
Yes,	I / you / we / they / she / he / it	**had.**
No,		**hadn't.**

(USE)

Use past perfect continuous

● in a past tense narrative, to describe a continuing action in a period of time before something
else happened.
*Anna **returned** from France, where she **had been studying** French.*

● to explain a past situation, by describing the events happening before.
*Both boys **were** wet and muddy. They **had been playing football** in the rain.*

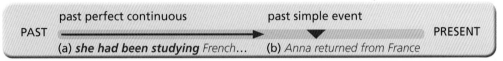

See also **Unit 16, Indirect (Reported) Statements**.

....

1 Read the following information about famous moments in history. Then <u>underline</u> the correct
form. Only one verb in each paragraph is past perfect.

A Columbus left Spain in August 1492 with three
ships, to try and find a way to India by sailing
west instead of east. When his ships **a** *finally
reached / had finally reached* land on 12 October,
he thought he was there, but the ships **b** *actually
arrived / had actually arrived* in America instead.

B Captain Robert Scott wanted to reach the South
Pole first. He and his companions finally arrived
there on 1 January 1912 after a terrible journey
across the ice, but **c** *found / had found* a Norwegian
flag. Unfortunately for Scott, Roald Amundsen **d**
got / had got there on 14 December, 18 days earlier.

C Leonardo painted his famous The Last Supper
between 1495 and 1498, but the painting started
to deteriorate within 50 years. The most common
explanation for this used to be that Leonardo
e *used / had used* the wrong kind of paint, but
experts have always disagreed about this, and
many believe that the damp in the wall is the
cause of the damage. Between 1978 and 1999,
experts **f** *restored / had restored* the painting, and
the public can now see it again.

2 Complete the sentence with the past simple or past perfect simple form of the verb in brackets.

a When I (try) .....*tried*........... to use my laptop, I realized the battery (run) .... down.

b I (turn) .... the computer off, but forgot that I (not save) .... my work.

c I only remembered I (not pay) .... the bill when my Internet connection (stop)
.... working.

d When I (receive) .... the e-mail, I couldn't understand who (send) .... it.

e When I (check) .... the instructions, I understood what I (do) ....

f I knew I (receive) .... a virus when I (run) .... the anti-virus program.

g As soon as I (download) .... the document, I knew I (make) .... a mistake.

h I could see what (go) .... wrong as soon as I (look) .... inside the printer.

i I knew I (press) .... the wrong key when nothing (happen) ....

j When the screen (go) .... blank, I couldn't understand how it (happen) ....

3 Read these sentences about Julius Caesar. Then complete the sentence with the past simple or past perfect form of the verb in brackets.

a Julius Caesar (come) _____came_____ from an aristocratic Roman family, though his family was not rich by Roman standards.

b When he was 15 his father (die) _____, and to avoid political problems in Rome, Caesar (serve) _____ as a soldier in the east.

c By the time he (return) _____ to Rome, he (win) _____ awards for bravery.

d He (become) _____ a member of the Senate, and governor of what is now Spain.

e By the age of 40 he (rise) _____ to the top of the political world, and (form) _____ a political alliance with a powerful general, Pompey, and a rich man, Crassus.

f Between 58 BC and 49 BC he (fight) _____ a war against the people of what are now France, Belgium, Switzerland and parts of Germany.

g By the end of this war, according to the historian Plutarch, three million men (die) _____

h In 50 BC the Senate (order) _____ Caesar to return to Rome. By that time, Crassus was dead and Pompey (become) _____ Caesar's enemy.

i In the civil war that followed, Caesar (defeat) _____ all his enemies.

j By the time a group of Roman senators (murder) _____ him in 44 BC, he (be) _____ the most powerful man in Rome for only a year.

geography

4 Choose the correct form, A, B or C, to complete the sentence.

On 26 December 2004, Tilly Smith, a 10-year-old British schoolgirl, **a** __C__ on the beach with her family. They **b** _____ Christmas in Thailand. Suddenly Tilly **c** _____ that something was wrong. She could see that the water **d** _____ and waves **e** _____ up the beach. The beach **f** _____ smaller and smaller. She **g** _____ that there had been an earthquake in Sumatra that morning, but she **h** _____ a geography lesson she **i** _____ at school just two weeks before. So she **j** _____ her mother what she **k** _____ about earthquakes and giant waves. Luckily for the Smith family, Tilly's teacher Andrew Kearney **l** _____ the class about earthquakes and **m** _____ them a video of a tsunami in Hawaii. Tilly **n** _____ screaming at her parents to get off the beach. They **o** _____ Tilly back to their hotel, which was not too close to the shore, and **p** _____ the alarm. One of the staff, who was Japanese, **q** _____ the word *tsunami*, and **r** _____ everyone to leave the beach. From their room on the third floor, the Smiths **s** _____ the terrible effects of the tsunami on the area. Thanks to Tilly, everybody from that beach **t** _____ that terrible day.

	A	B	C
a	A walked	B had walked	C was walking
b	A spent	B had spent	C were spending
c	A felt	B had felt	C was feeling
d	A rose	B had risen	C was rising
e	A came	B had come	C were coming
f	A got	B had got	C was getting
g	A did not know	B had not known	C was not knowing
h	A suddenly remembered	B had remembered suddenly	C was suddenly remembering
i	A had	B had had	C was having
j	A told	B had told	C was telling
k	A learnt	B had learnt	C was learning
l	A taught	B had taught	C was teaching
m	A showed	B had shown	C was showing
n	A started	B had started	C was starting
o	A took	B had taken	C were taking
p	A raised	B had raised	C were raising

	A	B	C
q	A understood	B had understood	C was understanding
r	A ordered	B had ordered	C was ordering
s	A watched	B had watched	C were watching
t	A survived	B had survived	C was surviving

GLOSSARY

5 Read the story of Archimedes and his bath. Then complete the text with the correct form of the verb in brackets.

Archimedes, the Greek mathematician, is probably most famous for the story of King Hieron II of Syracuse and the gold crown. The king **a** (want) ...*wanted*... to give a gold crown as a gift to the gods, and **b** (give) .... a carefully weighed amount of gold to a goldsmith. The man **c** (produce) .... a beautiful crown, but the king was worried that the craftsman **d** (not use) .... all the gold to make the crown. Dishonest craftsmen often **e** (mix) .... gold with silver, which was cheaper, but the king could not find a way of proving that the man **f** (do) .... this. He **g** (ask) .... Archimedes to solve the problem. Archimedes **h** (know) .... that gold and silver have different densities. The problem was that nobody could calculate the mass of an object like a crown. While Archimedes **i** (think) .... about this problem, he decided to go to the public baths to relax. While he **j** (climb) .... into the bath, he **k** (notice) .... some water on the floor. It **l** (spill) .... over the side of the bath, and he **m** (realize) .... that he **n** (solve) .... the problem by accident. The total amount of water that **o** (spill) .... out of the bath must be the same as the volume of his body. He could use a piece of pure gold and calculate its volume, and then test the crown and see if it was the same. According to the story, he **p** (jump) .... straight out of the bath and **q** (run) .... down the street calling 'Eureka – I've found it.' The goldsmith soon **r** (admit) .... that he **s** (cheat) .... the king, and was punished. Archimedes **t** (discover) .... a principle of buoyancy.

GLOSSARY

6 Read the sentences about two mountain climbers. Then complete the sentence with the past perfect simple or past perfect continuous form of the verb in brackets.

a The two climbers stopped to rest. They (climb) ....*had been climbing*.... for hours and were exhausted. Things were not looking good.

b They were very cold, because it (snow) .... heavily since mid-morning, and one of them (hurt) .... his ankle.

c They (look) .... for shelter for the past two hours, because they realized that the weather was going to get worse.

d They (already phone) .... the rescue centre for help.

e They (also leave) .... details of their planned route at the village where they stayed the night.

f They were experienced climbers and they (prepare) .... carefully for their trip. They knew there was a cave halfway up the mountain.

g They spent a long time searching for the cave before they realized that they (head) .... in the wrong direction. Then the snow stopped, and they could see the dark entrance of the cave nearby.

h Luckily they (bring) .... warm clothes and plenty of food with them, and they waited safely in the cave.

EXTENSION ACTIVITY

Read the sentences from Exercise 6 again. Make sure you have checked the answers to this exercise. Translate the story into your language.

Need more practice? Go to the ***Review*** *on page 192.*

8 tense contrasts

past simple: decided   **past continuous:** was looking
past perfect simple: had happened   **past perfect continuous:** had been working

Use past simple, past continuous and past perfect for events in a narrative (story).

- Past simple to describe actions or states in the past.
  *That afternoon **he decided** to check the old experiments.*

- Past continuous to describe continuing actions, or to set the scene.
  *While **he was looking** at them …*

- Use past perfect when we need to make clear that one past action happened before another past action.
  *… he noticed that something unusual **had happened**…*
  *… while he **had been working** on the new experiments.*

past simple: What did you do?   **past continuous:** What were you doing?
  *We **were** in a maths lesson. Water **started** dripping from the ceiling. We **changed** rooms.*
  *What **were** you **doing**? (when something happened)*   *We **were writing** a test.*
  *What **did** you **do**? (an action)*   *We **changed** rooms.*

present perfect simple and continuous: has won, has been winning
past perfect simple and continuous: had won, had been playing

- Present perfect events are connected to the present in some way. Past perfect events are past events that take place before other past events.
  *She **has just won** the Grand Slam. She **has been playing** tennis for only six years.*
  (She plays now – she started six years ago.)
  *When Anna **won** the Grand Slam in 2001, she **had been playing** tennis for only six years.*
  (All the events are in the past: she won in 2001, she started playing six years before that.)

past simple: discovered   **present perfect:** have discovered

- Use past simple for finished events in the past. We can use a definite date or time.
  *Clyde Tombaugh **discovered** the planet Pluto **in 1930**.*

- Use present perfect for recent events without a definite time.
  *Astronomers **have discovered** a new planet recently. They **have named** it Sedna.*

- We can use *since* + **point in time** with present perfect but not with past simple.
  I've been here since 8.30! (I'm still here.)

- We can use *for* + **period of time** with present perfect for unfinished time, or past simple for finished time.
  I've been in the team for two years. (I'm still in the team.)
  I was in the team for two years. (Finished – I'm not in the team now.)

present perfect simple: have taken   **present perfect continuous:** have been taking

- Use present perfect simple when an action has recently finished. Use present perfect continuous to describe a continuing action up to the present moment.
  ***Have** you **taken** your medicine? (just now or very recently)*
  ***Have** you **been taking** your medicine? (over a long period up to now)*

- Present perfect continuous can suggest that the action might continue into the future.
  ***I've done** a lot of work lately. (but now I've finished)*
  ***I've been doing** a lot of work lately. (and it is still going on)*

present perfect simple and continuous: have lived, have been living
present simple and continuous: live, am living

- Use present perfect to describe a period of time that continues up to the present, and includes the present.
  *How long **have you been living** here? (We don't say ~~How long are you living here?~~)*
  ***I've been** here since 2002. (We don't say ~~I am here since 2002~~.)*

present simple, present continuous: have, am having

● Use present simple for facts, things that always happen, habits and state meanings.

*Rabbits **live** in holes in the ground.*   *I **travel** to work by bus.*
*I **enjoy** Italian food.*   *I **have** three sisters.*

● Use present continuous for events that are happening at the moment, or are changing, and for action meanings.

*It's **raining**.*   *Things **are getting** better.*
*I'm really **enjoying** this party.*   *I'm **having** a great time.*

1 <u>Underline</u> the correct form.

a When the police *stopped / were stopping* Smith's car for a routine check, they realized that he was the man who *robbed / had robbed* the bank.

b I woke up in the middle of the night and *turned on / was turning on* the light. Someone or something *climbed / was climbing* in my window!

c Unfortunately Jan *arrived / was arriving* at the station at 3.25, and found that she *missed / had missed* the train.

d The doctors *tried / had been trying* their best, but while they were performing the operation, the patient *died / was dying*.

e We'd been watching the film for half an hour before we realized that we *were making / had made* a terrible mistake. We *went / had gone* into the wrong cinema!

f On the morning of the accident, Mr Davis *just finished / had just finished* a night shift at a local factory, and *didn't have / hadn't had* any sleep for 24 hours.

g I'm sorry I *didn't answer / wasn't answering* the phone earlier, but I *was painting / had been painting* the ceiling in my bedroom.

h The office Marlowe was visiting was on the 15th floor, and unfortunately the lift *wasn't working / hadn't been working*, so by the time he arrived at the top of the stairs, he *was / had been* out of breath.

i On Christmas morning when they *woke up / were waking up*, the children looked eagerly out of the window. It *snowed / had been snowing*, and the garden was covered in a thick white carpet.

j After the two film stars *landed / were landing* at the small airport, they left quickly in a van that *was waiting / had been waiting* for them since the early morning.

2 Complete the sentence with the past simple or present perfect form of the verb in brackets.

a I (leave) ......*left*...... my bag on the train this morning.

b Helen (complete) .... the test half an hour before the end.

c The match can't begin yet because the other team (not arrive) ....

d We (not play) .... chess for ages. Do you feel like a game?

e I (like) .... their last album, but I'm not keen on the new one.

f When (you go) .... to the cinema last?

g Sam (not take) .... a day off since last April.

h (you see) .... my wallet? I'm sure I left it here on the desk.

i When (you realize) .... that you wanted to be a musician?

j I (have) .... an idea! Why don't we go skating tomorrow?

tense contrasts

3 Complete the text with the past simple, past continuous or past perfect simple form of the verbs in brackets.

Mozart was born in 1756, the son of a professional musician. His father soon **a** (give up) _gave up_ composing when he recognized his son's musical talent. By the age of three, the young Mozart **b** (learn) .... to play several pieces of music. While he and his father **c** (travel) .... round Europe, Mozart met many famous musicians and composers. Before he was 17, he **d** (compose) .... several operas. While he **e** (visit) .... the Vatican in Rome, he **f** (listen) .... to a piece of music which, up to this point, the Vatican authorities **g** (keep) .... secret. No one **h** (publish) .... a copy of the piece before, but Mozart **i** (manage) .... to write it down from memory after he **j** (listen) .... to it once. By the age of 30 he **k** (become) .... one of the most famous composers in Europe, and **l** (have) .... a large apartment in Vienna, which is now a tourist attraction. It was here that he **m** (write) .... his famous opera *The Marriage of Figaro*. In 1791, while he **n** (work) .... on his *Requiem*, he **o** (fall) .... ill and died at the age of 35.

GLOSSARY

4 Choose the correct form, A, B, C or D, to complete the sentence.

a I ......_A_...... this computer for more than ten years, so I'm thinking of getting a new one.

b You're half an hour late! I .... here for ages!

c I .... these black trousers better than those blue ones.

d Can I borrow a pen? I .... mine.

e I'd like to dance with you, but I .... for my friend.

f Kate .... in Poland since last October. She's really enjoying it.

g Carol's great, isn't she? .... her long?

h Paul .... in all day today, so now he feels like going out.

i You'd better borrow this umbrella. .... really hard.

j I .... on my project all morning, and I need a break.

a **A** *have had*	**B** *have been having*	**C** *have*	**D** *am having*
b **A** *have waited*	**B** *have been waiting*	**C** *wait*	**D** *am waiting*
c **A** *have liked*	**B** *have been liking*	**C** *like*	**D** *am liking*
d **A** *have lost*	**B** *have been losing*	**C** *lose*	**D** *am losing*
e **A** *have waited*	**B** *have been waiting*	**C** *wait*	**D** *am waiting*
f **A** *has taught*	**B** *has been teaching*	**C** *teaches*	**D** *is teaching*
g **A** *Have you known*	**B** *Have you been knowing*	**C** *Do you know*	**D** *Are you knowing*
h **A** *has stayed*	**B** *has been staying*	**C** *stays*	**D** *is staying*
i **A** *It has rained*	**B** *It has been raining*	**C** *It rains*	**D** *It is raining*
j **A** *have worked*	**B** *have been working*	**C** *work*	**D** *am working*

5 <u>Underline</u> the correct form.

a   How **a** *do you get on* / *<u>are you getting on</u>* in Paris? Sorry **b** *I haven't written* / *I'm not writing* before but **c** *I train* / *I've been training* hard for my basketball team. We **d** *played* / *have played* in a tournament last week – we **e** *come* / *came* third! I really **f** *enjoy* / *enjoyed* taking part, but **g** *I haven't done* / *I wasn't doing* anything else for the past month.

b   Unfortunately, when Sarah's big day **h** *arrived* / *was arriving*, things **i** *have gone* / *went* disastrously wrong at first. For a start, it **j** *was raining* / *has been raining* and as the traffic was so heavy, she **k** *arrived* / *was arriving* nearly ten minutes late for her interview. Then while she **l** *was crossing* / *has crossed* the road, a passing bus **m** *splashed* / *was splashing* her with water. But inside the building her luck **n** *changed* / *has changed*. 'Mr Fortescue **o** *is expecting* / *has expected* me,' she **p** *was telling* / *told* the receptionist.

'He **q** *hasn't arrived* / *doesn't arrive* yet,' she was told. 'Just take a seat.' Perhaps everything would be all right after all!

c   An art historian **r** *has discovered* / *is discovering* two missing paintings by Fra Angelico (c 1395– 1455) in the home of a pensioner from Oxford who **s** *has died* / *died* earlier this year. Jean Preston **t** *bought* / *has bought* the paintings when she **u** *was working* / *has been working* in America in the 1960s. Shortly before her death, a friend **v** *recognized* / *has recognized* them as part of a group of six small paintings which Angelico **w** *painted* / *has painted* in 1439. Miss Preston **x** *paid* / *was paying* about £200 for the pair, but experts **y** *say* / *said* they are now worth around £1 million.

EXTENSION ACTIVITY

1   Look through the unit again and find two examples for each of these tenses: present simple, present continuous, past simple, past continuous, present perfect simple, present perfect continuous, past perfect simple, past perfect continuous.

2   Look at the explanation page again. Choose an example sentence from each section. Translate it into your language.

*Need more practice? Go to the **Review** on page 192.*

tense contrasts

9 will, shall, be going to

(FORM)

affirmative

I / You / We / They / She / He / It	**will** (*'ll*)	**go.**
	shall	

negative

I / You / We / They / She / He / It	**will not** (*won't*)	**go.**
I / We	**shall not** (*shan't*)	

questions

	Will	I / you / we / they / she / he / it	**go?**
	Shall	I / we	
What	**will**	you	**do?**
How long	**will**	it	**take?**

short answers

Yes,	I / you / we / they / she / he / it	**will / shall.**
No,		**won't / shan't.**

(USE)

Use *will*

- to say what we expect to happen in the future.
  *It **will take** 50 years for temperatures to return to normal.*

- with *definitely, probably, possibly* to show how certain or uncertain we are.

certain *definitely, certainly*	**less certain** *probably*	**uncertain** *possibly*

  *It will **probably** take 50 years for the climate to stabilize.*
  *The climate **will** definitely change before then.*

- to make a social arrangement.
  *I'll **see** you tomorrow.*

- to make a promise, warning or threat.
  *I'll **give** you my homework on Monday.* (promise)
  *Careful! **You'll fall**.* (warning)
  *I'll **deal** with you later!* (threat)

- to make an offer.
  *I'll **carry** the projector for you. / **Shall** I carry it for you?*

- in a formal rule.
  *Students **will wear** protective clothing at all times.*

- to make a decision in a situation.
  Which pullover do you want? **I'll have** this one, I think.*

Use *won't*
- to mean 'refuse'.
  *Jack **won't give** me back my ruler!*

See **Unit 24** for other uses of *will*.

Use *shall*
- in formal speech or writing with *I / we*.
- to make offers – see **Unit 26**.

FORM

> *going to* is formed with **be + *going to* + verb**
>
> | I | am ('m) | | |
> |---|---|---|---|
> | You / We / They | are ('re) | **going to** | try. |
> | She / He / It | is ('s) | | |

USE

Use *going to*

- to talk about a personal plan or intention.
  We're going to try *and recycle more of our household rubbish.*

- to make a prediction about the future, especially when this has already started to happen.
  *Most people can see that the Internet **is going to be** just as much a part of the future for us all as the telephone or electricity is today.*
  *Something strange is happening to the computer screen. The program **is going to crash**!*

- to make a decision with a result in the distant future, not 'instant', as with *will*.
  *I've decided about my future. I'm **going to study** law at university.*

....

1 Read these famous failed predictions. Then complete the sentence using *will* + the verb in brackets.

  a We are in September 1914: according to most newspapers in Britain and Germany, the war (be) ....*will be*........ over by Christmas. They cannot imagine that the war (continue) .... until 1918, and (claim) .... the lives of about 9 million in the military and a further 7 million civilians.

  b We are in 1919: according to geologist Albert Porta, the conjunction of six planets (cause) .... the Sun to explode. In fact, the Sun (probably destroy) .... the Earth one day, when it becomes a red giant in about 4.5 billion years.

  c We are in 1977: according to Ken Olson, head of a computer company, people (never want) .... a computer in the home. Latest predictions (2005) suggest that computer ownership (reach) .... 1.3 billion machines worldwide by 2010.

  d We are in 1999: according to many scientists, computers (crash) .... and (cause) .... chaos on the first day of the new millennium.

  e And one to look forward to: according to the Aztec calendar, the world (come) .... to an end on 22 December 2012. We (have to) .... wait and see.

2 Complete the sentence with *will* + a verb from the list.

> carry   cost   take place   provide   sell   use   ~~hold~~

  a Most people know that London ....*will hold*........ the 2012 summer Olympic Games.
  b Most of the Games .... in three areas of London: in the Olympic Park in East London; along the River Thames; and in Central London.
  c The Olympic Village, in the same area, ... accommodation for over 17,000 athletes.
  d A new railway link .... spectators to the Olympic Park.
  e The organizers .... 8 million tickets for the Olympic Games, and a further 1.6 million for the Paralympics.
  f 75% of the tickets .... less than €70.
  g For some events the Games .... well-known places in Central London such as Hyde Park and Horse Guards Parade.

will, shall, be going to

3 Match sentences a to j with their responses 1 to 10.

a Why can't I play with the Bunsen burner?
b We're really tired.
c Put away these books, please.
d I can't write on this blackboard.
e Why is Maria annoying you?
f I don't understand this problem.
g Please stop throwing things, George.
h Shall I move this desk?
i I still haven't got your project!
j Is that the end of the lesson?

1 Sorry, I won't do it again.
2 She won't stop taking my things.
3 Yes, there's the bell. I'll see you tomorrow.
4 No, you'll hurt yourself. I'll do it.
5 I'll hand it in on Monday, I promise.
6 It's dangerous. You'll burn yourself.
7 Ok, I'll explain how to do it.
8 We'll have a short break in a few minutes.
9 Shall I put them in the cupboard?
10 I'll clean it for you.

geography

4 Read the information about environmental problems and their solutions. Then make five statements about what you're going to do and five about what you're not going to do to solve these problems.

There are a number of things we can do if we want to help save our planet. For example, if we stop wasting paper, and recycle paper and cardboard, we'll save some of the millions of trees which are cut down every year. As far as the problem of rubbish is concerned, if we recycle bottles and cans and organic waste, and stop taking plastic bags from the supermarket, this will all make a big difference. We also have to stop making unnecessary car journeys so as to cut down air pollution. Try walking or using a bike instead, and if you buy local fruit and vegetables, this reduces lorry traffic to supermarkets. Water is another problem, and we should all take showers, not baths, to save water. Finally, we need to stop using so much energy, so try changing to low-energy light bulbs, and turning off unnecessary lights.

a I'm not going to ..... *waste paper*
b I'm going to .....
c .....
d .....
e .....
f .....
g .....
h .....
i .....
j .....

GLOSSARY

5 Say what you think will happen in each picture. Use a verb from the list.

| blow down | hit | flood | disappear | snow | erupt |

a   *The volcano is going to erupt.*   d ....

b   ....   e ....

c   ....   f ....

a   b   c

d   e   f

6 Use *will*, *shall* or *going to* + the verb in brackets

a   Next year you have to choose between two lessons, either biology or a second foreign language. Make your decision.
I've made up my mind. (do)   *I'm going to do biology.*

b   You have to miss school to see the dentist, but you promise your teacher to be back at two o'clock. What do you say? (be) ....

c   You are doing an experiment in science, and you can see that it isn't going well. (work) ....

d   You are near the light switch and it's getting dark. Offer to turn the lights on. (turn)

e   Your teacher asks you who you want to sit with. You decide to sit with Helen. (sit)

f   Your teacher asks you about your career plans, and you say you are planning to study engineering. (to)

EXTENSION ACTIVITY

1   Make ten predictions for the future about yourself, your friends, your country, the world etc.

2   What are your plans for the rest of the day, and the rest of the week? Write five sentences.

will, shall, be going to

10 future time

present continuous future

- Use for a fixed arrangement in the future eg an event already written in a diary.
  I'm coming back next Thursday.
  We're having a party next Friday. Would you like to come?

Note that there is usually a time reference.
*What are you doing **next week**?*

present simple

- Use for an event that always happens at a certain time, or is part of a timetable.
  *The conference **begins** on Tuesday at 10.00.*

will, going to or present continuous?

When we make predictions *will* and *going to* are both possible.
*I think Helen **is going to win**.   I think Helen **will win**.*

We use *going to* when we talk about plans.
*We're **going to go** to France next year. (a plan)*

We use present continuous when we talk about an arrangement that is definitely fixed.
*We're **leaving** for France on Monday. (we've bought the tickets)*

When we see that an event has already started to happen, we use *going to*.
*Look at that ship! **It's going to hit** the rocks!*

future continuous

will + **be** + *-ing*

Use future continuous

- to describe an activity in progress in the future, with a time reference.
  *This time next week **I'll be starting** at my new school.*
  *What **will** you **be doing** in ten years' time?*

future perfect

will + **have** + *past participle*

Use future perfect

- to look back from the future to an earlier event, often with *by* or *by the time*.
  *By the time we get home, the match **will have begun**.*

future time clauses following time words

A future time clause follows a time word or phrase.
after   as   as soon as   before   by the time   until   when

In sentences referring to the future, the verb following the time word or phrase is present simple, and the main verb is a *will*-future.
*By the time we reach the station, it **will be** too late.*

When we emphasize completion or achievement, we can use a present perfect simple verb instead of a present simple verb.
*We'll let you know when **we have reached** a decision.*

1 Complete each sentence using a verb from the list in the present simple form. Then match each sentence **a** to **j** with a description **1** to **10** of where you might read or hear it.

close	continue	expire	leave	open
~~retire~~	rise	start	take off	take place

a Mrs Douglas ....*retires*........ at the end of this term, and we wish her all happiness for the future.   7

b There has been a change to the schedule and your flight now .... at 18.40.

c The exhibition .... until 31 December. Don't miss it!

d The match .... at three o'clock, so please be here by two.

e The opening ceremony .... on 27 July.

f Saturday 18 March. The sun .... at 6.08.

g The licence for this software .... one year from the agreement date.

h This offer .... on 30 September so buy now to avoid disappointment!

i The 4.30 to York .... from Platform 1. Cross the footbridge at the end of this platform.

j Doors .... at 18.00.

---

1 Cinema door   **5** Travel information desk   **8** Newspaper review

2 Advertisement   **6** CD-Rom leaflet   **9** Notice on a sports club notice board

3 Airport check-in desk   **7** ~~School newsletter~~   **10** Diary

4 News announcement

2 Complete each sentence using a verb from the list in the present continuous form.

arrive	come	give	~~hold~~	leave
meet	pick up	serve	show	take

a We ....*are holding*........... a science fair next weekend. There will be displays of students' work, and a guest speaker.

b Professor Tamsin Anderson .... from Cambridge to talk to us.

c She .... a talk on the Genome Project on Saturday morning.

d In the afternoon she .... us a film.

e Then at 5.30 we .... tea and cakes.

f 'Have you heard from Dr Anderson?' 'Yes. She .... at 6.00 on Friday evening.'

g '............................ anyone .... her at the station?'

h 'David and his parents .... her .... and .... her to the hotel.'

i 'And after the conference?' 'She .... on Sunday at 12.30.'

SCIENCE Fair

17th December

Come and see some great projects!

Everyone gets a prize!

Come and hear our mystery Guest Speaker!

Refreshments included!

future time

41

3 Underline the correct form.

a 'Be careful with that test tube. It _will break_ / _breaks_.'

b 'The egg is cracking. The baby bird _will come out_ / _is going to come out_ / _comes out_.'

c 'Can you hurry up please. The film _will start_ / _is going to start_ / _starts_.'

d 'Carry this very carefully.' 'Don't worry, _I'm not dropping it_ / _I won't drop it_.'

e '_We're playing_ / _We'll play_ football this afternoon. Do you want to play too?'

f 'This dictionary costs €50, but the red one is cheaper.'

'Ok, _I'll take_ / _I'm taking_ / _I'm going to take_ the red one.'

g 'Have you decided about next year yet?'

'Yes, _I'm studying_ / _I'm going to study_ / _I'll study_ journalism. Well, that's the plan anyway.'

h 'Ok, bye for now.'

'Bye, _I'll see you_ / _I'm going to see you_ / _I'm seeing you_ at the same time on Friday.'

4 Complete each sentence with a phrase from the list.

| I'll be waiting | I'll be watching | I'll be starting | I'll be catching |
| I'll be lying | I'll be living | I'll be going | I'll be working |

a Next Tuesday at this time _I'll be lying_ on the beach!

b _____ outside the cinema at 7.30. See you then!

c All tomorrow afternoon _____ on my history project.

d This time next week _____ my holiday!

e In three years' time _____ into the army.

f Don't phone at 9.00, because _____ the match then.

g In ten years' time, I expect _____ in my own flat.

h This time tomorrow _____ the plane to Brazil!

5 Complete each sentence using _will have (done)_ or _won't have (done)_ + the verb in brackets, according to your opinion.

In my opinion, by the end of the 21st century:

a People (start) _will have started_ living on other planets.

b Scientists (invent) _____ artificial food.

c We (find) _____ a solution to the problem of poverty.

d Doctors (discover) _____ a cure for cancer.

e Most people (move) _____ to very large cities.

f We (use) _____ all the fossil fuel on Earth.

g The world (become) _____ a peaceful place.

h People (make) _____ the environment cleaner.

6 Complete the text with the present simple
or *will* form of the verb in brackets.

The future of our solar system

The Sun (continue) _will continue_ much as it is today until it b (enter) ....
its red giant phase in 4 to 5 billion years. Then, the core c (grow) .... smaller and
hotter until it finally d (finish) .... burning the fuel in its nuclear core. When this
e (occur) .... the core f (become) .... so dense that helium fusion will
begin. When the helium atoms g (collide) ...., they h (form) ....
carbon (from 3 helium atoms) and oxygen (from 4 helium atoms). When this process i (begin) ....,
the Sun j (produce) .... enormous amounts of energy. The Sun k (grow) ....
larger as this energy l (increase) .... It m (be) .... over a hundred
times its present size by the time it n (stop) .... growing. This is why we use the term red
giant. As the Sun o (expand) ...., it is probable that it p (absorb) ....
the Earth. When the Sun q (use) .... up all its energy, it r (become) ....
a small white dwarf, and s (not make) .... any more energy. After a few billion years, when
it is completely cool, it t (be) .... just a cold dark object.

GLOSSARY

7 Choose the correct form, A, B or C, to complete the sentence.

a We seem to be completely lost. What _____A_____ now?

b Just think, this time next week we .... a taxi to the airport.

c As soon as we hear any news, we .... you know.

d The new film of *Hamlet* starring Johnny Depp .... next week.

e Some scientists believe that they .... a cure for most types of cancer by 2050.

f .... a press conference about our new discovery on Tuesday.

g Look at that helicopter! It .... on the sports field!

h In a year's time I .... in the music industry.

i Hold on to the camera. .... drop it.

j We .... a new area in the Zoo where visitors will be able
to get closer to the animals.

a A *are we going to do*   B *are we doing*   C *will we do*
b A *are going to take*   B *take*   C *will be taking*
c A *are letting*   B *will have let* C *will let*
d A *will have come out*   B *comes out*   C *will come out*
e A *discover*   B *are discovering* C *will have discovered*
f A *We'll have held*   B *We hold*   C *We're holding*
g A *will land*   B *is going to land* C *lands*
h A *am going to work*   B *am working*   C *will be working*
i A *You drop*   B *You're going to drop* C *You'll be dropping it*
j A *open*   B *will have opened* C *are going to open*

EXTENSION ACTIVITY

1 Look at the explanation
page and read the section
*future time clauses
following time words.*
Write seven sentences
about yourself, using the
time words in the list on
the explanation page.

2 Make a diary for next week,
to remind you what you are
doing on each day.
Then write a sentence for
each day.
*Need more practice? Go to
the Review on page 192.*

future time

11 there, it

there

Use *there + be*

- to say that something exists or doesn't exist.
  There's a diagram on page 36.   **There weren't any lessons** yesterday.
- to say that something happens, using a time reference.
  There's a disco **tonight**.
- to describe numbers or amounts.
  There are two ways of doing this.
  There was a lot of rain last night.
- in some expressions.
  There's no point in waiting.

Use *there*

- with *appear* and *seem*.
  There appears / seems to be a problem.
- with modals.
  There can't / could / might / must / should be an answer.
- to refer to place.
  Who lives **there**?

there, they're, their

These all have the same pronunciation.

they're = they are   *their = possessive form of they*
  This is Tom, and this is Peter. **They're** brothers.
  And this is **their** sister, Helen.

it

Use *it + be*

- with adjectives.
  It's important / difficult / easy / interesting / best to use a computer.
- with some nouns.
  It's a pity / a shame to be indoors on a day like this.
- for dates, days and times.
  It's June 4th. It's Friday. It's half past three.
- with verbs of weather.
  It's raining / snowing.

Use *it*

- with *seem / appear*.
  It seems / appears that somebody found the money in the street.
- with *looks as if*.
  It looks as if it's going to rain.
- with some expressions.
  It doesn't matter.   **It's time** to go.   **It takes** an hour to get there.
- to refer to something we have already mentioned.
  This is my new bike. **It's** really fast!

it's, its

it's = it is   **It's** a lovely day today!
its = possessive of it   The company gave all **its** employees a holiday.

1 Underline the correct form.

The surface of the Earth is not flat. **a** <u>There</u> / They are mountains and high land and **b** there / they are also low areas. **c** There / They are steep slopes in some places, but in others
d there / they are gentle ones. **e** There / They are special symbols on maps which show the height and shape of the land.
f There / They include colour and contour lines, and
g there / they are also height numbers for some high places.

On detailed maps, **h** there / they are contour lines.
i There / They show how steep the slope is. **j** There / They usually appear every ten metres and **k** there / they are numbers on them to show the height.

l There / They are also numbers at the bottom and on the side of the map. **m** There / They are used to identify each square on the map. **n** There / This is called a grid reference.
o There / They is a grid reference for every place on the map.

2 Rewrite the sentence so it begins as shown. Make any necessary changes.

a A match takes place on Tuesday.
There _is a match on Tuesday._

b You can do this in three ways.
There _____

c A lot of snow fell yesterday.
There _____

d We haven't got any milk.
There _____

e A strange man seems to be outside.
There _____

f A lot of people were at the rock concert.
There _____

g Crowds of people were on the train.
There _____

h An interesting television programme is on at 8.00.
There _____

3 Complete the sentence with *there*, *they're* or *their*.

a Whales have been hunted for centuries for _their_ oil and meat.

b _____ now in danger of disappearing completely.

c _____ are now less than 12,000 of these beautiful creatures left.

d _____ have been laws to protect whales since 1967.

e _____ numbers have increased slightly in recent years.

f _____ still a source of food and oil in some parts of the world.

g _____ meat is sold in several countries.

h _____ also in danger from sonar equipment on ships.

i _____ confused by the sound signals.

j As a result, they lose _____ way and swim into shallow water, and die.

there, it

4 Complete the sentence with *it's* or *its*.

a Come on, let's go home. _It's_ getting late.

b I'm taking my umbrella because _____ going to rain.

c The horse had a white star on _____ forehead.

d The school at the end of my road has given _____ pupils a holiday on Friday.

e _____ time to go now.

f I think _____ a pity you couldn't stay longer.

g My cat has broken one of _____ back legs.

h _____ easy to get things wrong if you're not careful.

5 Complete the sentence with *it* or *there*.

a _There_ is a problem with the computer. Can you help?

b Will _____ be a party at the end of term?

c _____ is a pity she wasn't here to get her prize.

d 'Who's at the door?' '_____ is me.'

e _____ is a very good restaurant not far from my house.

f _____ is a long time since I went to the dentist's.

g _____ is easy to book a ticket on-line.

h If you want to look up a word, _____ is a list in the back of the book.

i Hello, Sue. _____ is really good to see you.

j _____ is no point in phoning him again. He must be out.

6 Complete the text with *it* or *there* in each space.

Tropical forests grow near the Equator where a _it_ is warm and wet. b _____ are only two seasons, rainy and dry. c _____ is normally 20–25°C in a tropical forest and d _____ is only a drop of about 5°C in the coldest months. e _____ is a lot of rain, on average more than 200 cm per year. f _____ is poor soil, and g _____ is difficult for plants on the forest floor to develop, as tall trees (25–35 metres) block the light. h _____ are many plants, birds, animals and insects. i _____ are different kinds of tropical forests with different kinds of trees. j _____ depends on the temperature and the amount of rainfall.

In temperate forests, k _____ are four seasons with a cold winter. l _____ is impossible for the trees to grow all the year round in a temperate forest, and m _____ is a growing season of only 140–200 days. n _____ is also a greater range of temperatures, from –30 to 30°C, and o _____ rains throughout the year (75–150cm). As p _____ is cooler and drier here, trees are smaller, q _____ is more light, and the soil is richer. r _____ are many deciduous trees in these forests, and s _____ is common to find many animals and birds. Again, t _____ is a range of forest types depending on the annual rainfall.

GLOSSARY

7 Choose the correct form, A, B, or C, to complete the text.

When **a** ......C...... winter, frogs stay in a dormant state at the bottom of ponds or in holes where
b .... wet. In spring **c** .... important for the frogs to reproduce, and **d** .... usually
return to a place they know to lay their eggs. **e** .... may be necessary for them to travel a long distance,
and **f** .... not unusual for frogs to take risks. **g** .... cross from one side of a busy road to the
other, for example. When **h** .... , they call to each other. Each species of frog has a particular set of
sounds, because **i** .... important that frogs of the same species find each other. The frogs mate in the
water and the fertilized eggs live in a layer of jelly in the water. **j** .... large numbers of eggs, because
k .... likely that predators will eat most of them. **l** .... about ten days before the tadpoles
leave the eggs. **m** .... like small fish, with a large body and a tail, and live in the water until
n .... to change into frogs. **o** .... an amazing story.

a	A *there is*	B *they are*	C *it is*	**i**	A *it is*	B *they are*	C *there is*
b	A *it is*	B *there is*	C *there are*	**j**	A *It is*	B *They are*	C *There are*
c	A *there is*	B *they are*	C *it is*	**k**	A *they are*	B *it is*	C *there is*
d	A *it*	B *they*	C *there*	**l**	A *It takes*	B *There is*	C *They take*
e	A *They*	B *It*	C *There*	**m**	A *It looks*	B *Looks*	C *They look*
f	A *they are*	B *there is*	C *it is*	**n**	A *they begin*	B *it begins*	C *begin*
g	A *They might*	B *It might*	C *There might*	**o**	A *There is*	B *They are*	C *It is*
h	A *it arrives*	B *they arrive*	C *arrive there*				

GLOSSARY

EXTENSION ACTIVITY

1 Write a short description of your room or your neighbourhood using *there is / there are*.

2 Write some opinions beginning *It's important / difficult / easy / interesting to…*

12 question formation

inversion

We make questions with *be* by putting the verb in front of the noun or pronoun. This movement of the verb is called *inversion*. When *be* is part of the verb tense we also put it in front of the noun or pronoun.

Statement (noun + verb)	**Question** (verb + noun)
*Everest **is*** the highest mountain.	***Is Everest*** the highest mountain?
The Romans were expecting an attack.	***Were the Romans expecting*** an attack?

Do the same when *will*, *have* and *had* are part of the verb tense.

Will we arrive on time?

Have you read War and Peace?   ***Had Napoleon intended*** to fight the battle?

Present simple tenses form questions with *do / does*, and past simple with *did*, using the verb stem.

Do ants show any kind of intelligence?   ***Does a cat know*** how to swim?

Did Columbus discover America?

modal auxiliaries, *have to* (see Units 22–25)

Modals form questions by moving the auxiliary in front of the pronoun.

Can bats hear well?   ***Should we stop*** eating white sugar?

Have to forms questions with *do / does* and *did*. *Have to* is generally used as a question form of *must*.

Do I have to turn on the computer first?   ***Did Roman slaves have to work*** hard?

yes / no questions, short answers

Questions without a question word have the answer *yes* or *no*. When we answer this kind of question, we often give a short answer which repeats part of the question.

Is Everest the highest mountain?	Yes, it **is**. / No, it **isn't**.
Was Columbus the first European to reach America?	No, he **wasn't**. / Yes, he **was**.
Do ants show any kind of intelligence?	Yes, they **do**. / No, they **don't**.
Had Napoleon intended to fight the battle?	No, he **hadn't**. / Yes, he **had**.
Can bats hear well?	Yes, they **can**. / No, they **can't**.
Did Roman slaves have to work hard?	Yes, they **did**. / No, they **didn't**.

wh- questions

We put a question word in front of question forms.

Which is the highest mountain?

How do ants show intelligence?

Who was the first European to reach America?

Why is the climate changing everywhere?

When will the ice at the Poles melt completely?

How well can bats hear?

embedded questions

Statements or questions with verbs like *know* and *wonder*, or polite requests like *Can you tell me ...* can introduce a second question. The second question is in statement form.

direct question	**embedded question**
How hot is it on Mars?	*I wonder **how hot it is** on Mars.*
Where does the blue wire go?	*Can you tell me **where the blue wire goes**?*
Who is Romeo?	*Do you know **who Romeo** is?*
What is the answer?	*I know **what the answer is**.*
What was the time?	*I didn't know **what the time was**.*

question phrases

Many questions are formed from a question word and other words.

What is the difference between X and Y?   ***What kind of*** plant is this?

How strong / large is this?   ***What effect*** does heat have on water?

What is the relationship between X and Y?   ***How does*** this **work**?

1 Rewrite the sentence as a *yes / no* question.

a The Nile is the longest river.
  Is the Nile the longest river ?

b Earthquakes have occurred in this country.
  ?

c The volcano had erupted before.
  ?

d 200 million years ago there was only one continent.
  ?

e People were expecting a tsunami in 2004.
  ?

f Our climate will be different in 50 years' time.
  ?

g The capital city has continued to grow.
  ?

h The Arabian Desert and the Gobi Desert are similar in size.
  ?

i The ice at the Poles has started to melt.
  ?

j Many people were injured in the earthquake.
  ?

2 Complete a short answer for each question.

a Do all birds spend winter in a different part of the world?   No, they don't

b Is the peregrine falcon the fastest bird?   Yes,

c Can a racehorse run faster than a lion?   No,

d Does the giant scolpender centipede really eat mice?   Yes,

e Have termites really built nests seven metres tall?   Yes,

f Do millipedes really have a thousand legs?   No,

g Are we really discovering more species of insect all the time?   Yes,

h Is it true that wasps make paper to build their nests?   Yes,

i Can some fish really climb trees?   Yes,

j Did unicorns really exist once?   No,

3 Match questions **a** to **j** with their answers **1** to **10**. Then complete the questions.

Questions

a Where does the name volcano come from? 5
b How many ____ on Earth?
c Where ____ come from?
d Why ____ of the volcano?
e What ____ mean?
f How long ____ remain active?
g How ____ that a volcano will erupt?
h What ____ with?
i What ____ volcanoes are going to erupt?
j What ____ caused volcanic eruptions?

Answers

1 Scientists predict when a volcano will erupt by measuring movements in the Earth.
2 The hot lava comes from deep in the Earth's crust.
3 They often release sulphur dioxide gas (SO_2) as a sign that they are going to erupt.
4 *Dormant* means that the volcano is not active at the moment – but it could erupt again.
5 The name volcano comes from the Roman god of fire, Vulcan.
6 Most volcanoes remain active for thousands or even millions of years.
7 People once thought that coal and sulphur (S) burning below ground caused volcanic eruptions.
8 It's hard to give an exact number, but there are more than 30 well-known ones.
9 They measure the movements with an instrument called a seismometer.
10 The lava comes out because of pressure from below.

49

4 Use the prompts to make a question. Then choose answer A, B or C. Check the factual answers on page 208.

a you know / what / be / the capital of Argentina? *Do you know what the capital of Argentina is* ?
b you know / how long / be / the River Nile? _____ ?
c you know / where / be Lake Titicaca? _____ ?
d you know / what colour / be / the flag of Mali? _____ ?
e you know / how many states / there be / in Australia? _____ ?
f you know / how high / be / Mount Everest? _____ ?
g you know / what / be / the capital of the Republic of Gambia? _____ ?
h you know how many / has got / official languages / Switzerland? _____ ?
i you know / what / be / the Finnish name for Finland? _____ ?
j you know / what / be / the population of the Republic of San Marino? _____ ?

a A *Montevideo*   B *Buenos Aires*   C *Valparaiso*
b A *6,695 km*   B *8,695 km*   C *10,695 km*
c A *between Bolivia and Peru*   B *in central Asia*   C *on an island near Hawaii*
d A *red, white and blue stripes*   B *green, yellow and red stripes*   C *blue and white stripes*
e A *12*   B *9*   C *8*
f A *6,848 metres*   B *7,848 metres*   C *8,848 metres*
g A *Conakry*   B *Thimphu*   C *Banjul*
h A *4*   B *3*   C *2*
i A *Republika e Shqipërisë*   B *Suomen tasavalta*   C *Eesti Vabariik*
j A *about 270,000*   B *about 27,000*   C *about 2.7 million*

5 Rewrite each question beginning as shown. Check the factual answers on page 208.

a Where is Llanfairpwllgwyngyllgogerychwyrndrobwllllantysiliogogogoch?
   Do you know _____ *where Llanfairp (etc) is* _____ ?
b Is it the name of a real place?
   Do you have any idea _____ ?
c Was it an invented name?
   Can you tell me _____ ?
d Why did they decide to make up a name?
   I wonder _____ ?
e What do the local people say?
   Could you tell me _____ ?
f Where does the name Taumatawhakatangihangakoauauotamateaturipukakapiki-
   maungahoronukupokaiwhenuakitanatahu come from?
   Do you have any idea _____ ?
g How do you pronounce it?
   Do you know _____ ?
h What does it mean?
   Do you understand _____ ?
i Which language is this word from?
   Can you tell me _____ ?
j What's the longest place name in your country?
   Could you tell me _____ ?

6 Read the text about earthquakes. Then complete the question for each answer.

Earthquakes

When an earthquake occurs, part of the Earth's surface moves. In fact, the surface of the Earth moves all the time. The tectonic plates which make up the surface press against each other very slowly. Over thousands of years, this movement creates great stress. In some places where the layers of rock are weak, this eventually causes a sudden movement – an earthquake. Thousands of earthquakes happen every day, but most are very small and cause no damage. A large earthquake shakes buildings to the ground, or causes a tsunami wave. The effects are usually very serious.

Severe earthquakes are common in southern Europe, and on 1 November 1755 a powerful earthquake hit the city of Lisbon in Portugal. Between 60,000 and 100,000 people died. After the earthquake a tsunami struck the city, and there was also a fire, which caused nearly total destruction. People as far away as Finland felt the shock, and the tsunami reached Barbados in the West Indies. Geologists now believe that the strength of the earthquake was as high as 9 on the Richter scale. This is the same strength as the Indian Ocean earthquake of 26 December 2004.

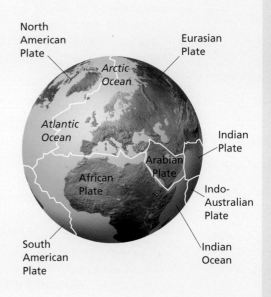

North American Plate • Eurasian Plate • Arctic Ocean • Atlantic Ocean • Indian Plate • Arabian Plate • African Plate • Indo-Australian Plate • South American Plate • Indian Ocean

a What *moves when an earthquake occurs* ?

Part of the Earth's crust moves when an earthquake occurs.

b What .... ?

The movement of tectonic plates creates this stress.

c How many .... ?

Thousands happen every day.

d What .... ?

It shakes buildings or causes a tsunami wave.

e When .... ?

On 1 November 1755.

f How many .... ?

Between 60,000 and 100,000.

g In which distant country .... ?

In Finland.

h What .... ?

That the strength of the earthquake was as high as 9 on the Richter scale.

GLOSSARY

EXTENSION ACTIVITY

1 Make a list of ten questions which you would like to ask a famous person.

2 Make a list of ten quiz questions and ask another person in the class. You must know the answer!

13 tag questions

tag question forms

We can put a tag at the end of a statement to make a question. We use the verb in the statement to make the tag, using an auxiliary if necessary. The noun in the statement becomes a pronoun in the tag. In the most common types of tag question, a positive verb has a negative tag.

*You **like** pizza, **don't you**?* (I'm not sure)

A negative verb has a positive tag.

***Andrew** won't be angry, **will he**?* (I want you to tell me that he won't)

types of tag questions

- positive verb, negative tag

  When we use a positive verb and a negative tag, we generally expect a *yes* answer.

  *Russia produces a lot of natural gas, **doesn't it**?*   *Yes, **it does**.*

  *A lot of diamonds come from South Africa, **don't they**?*   *Yes, **they do**.*

- negative verb, positive tag

  When we use a negative verb and a positive tag, we generally expect a *no* answer.

  *There aren't any active volcanoes in Scotland, **are there**?*   *No, **there aren't**.*

  *Switzerland doesn't belong to the EU, **does it**?*   *No, **it doesn't**.*

- positive verb, positive tag

  When we use a positive verb and a positive tag, we are showing surprise.

  *You liked the film, **did you**?* (I didn't expect that you would like it)

intonation and meaning

The meaning of the question depends on the intonation we use.

*Budapest is the capital of Hungary, **isn't it**? Yes, it is.*

When the intonation falls or is level, we are checking information we already know.

*There are mountains in New Zealand, **aren't there**? Yes, that's right.*

When the intonation rises, we are asking a question.

*That's not the Greek flag, **is it**?*   *No, you're right. The Greek flag is blue and white.*

so and *neither* answers

In speech, we use *so* or *neither* to add similar information without repeating the main verb. We use only an auxiliary (*be*, *have*, *can* etc) after *so* and *neither*.

We use *so* to add information following a **positive** statement.

Stromboli is an active volcano.   ***So** is Etna.*

Volcanoes cause great damage.   ***So** do hurricanes.*

We use *neither* to add information following a **negative** statement.

Japan doesn't produce its own oil.   ***Neither** does Korea.*

A computer can't work without electricity.   ***Neither** can a car.*

13

1 Add a positive tag to each sentence.

a Madagascar isn't in the Atlantic Ocean, _is it_ ?

b Astronauts haven't landed on Mars, _____ ?

c The climate won't get any worse, _____ ?

d The Romans didn't sail to America, _____ ?

e Chickens can't fly, _____ ?

f The world's population isn't growing in all

countries, _____ ?

2 Add a negative tag to each sentence.

a You were at the same school as Maria,

weren't you _____ ?

b This is the way to the station, _____ ?

c You've forgotten to buy the tickets, _____ ?

d They understand this problem, _____ ?

e Helen is coming to the party, _____ ?

f The bus took a long time, _____ ?

3 Choose the correct sentence, A or B, for each situation.

a ___A___ You always know the answer, in fact!

A You know the answer, don't you?   B You don't know the answer, do you?

b _____ I'm sure I left it here, but now I can't find it.

A You have seen my bag, haven't you?   B You haven't seen my bag, have you?

c _____ I knew that he would pass.

A Jack passed the exam, didn't he?   B Jack didn't pass the exam, did he?

d _____ Oh no! That means I'm going to get wet!

A It's raining, isn't it?   B It's not raining, is it?

e _____ You ought to get one. It's a much better way to travel in the city.

A You've got a bike, haven't you?   B You haven't got a bike, have you?

f _____ So we can talk about the final plans then.

A You'll be here next week, won't you?   B You won't be here next week, will you?

g _____ You're really good at it, so I'm sure it isn't the first time.

A You've played this game before, haven't you?   B You haven't played this game before, have you?

h _____ Why didn't you tell me, I thought he'd already left.

A Mr Jones is still waiting for me, isn't he?   B Mr Jones isn't still waiting for me, is he?

4 Use the information to write two sentences. Begin the second sentence with the word in capitals.

a Most portable radios and most CD players need batteries for power.   SO

Most portable radios need batteries for power. So do most CD players.

b Airships and helicopters don't need a runway to land.   NEITHER

_____

c Diesel engines and petrol engines produce exhaust fumes.   SO

_____

d Wind power and wave power don't cause air pollution.   NEITHER

_____

e Computers and calculators use electronic microchips.   SO

_____

f A wireless keyboard and wireless mouse don't require a connecting cable.   NEITHER

_____

g Some cookers and lighting systems can use solar power.   SO

_____

EXTENSION ACTIVITY

1 Make a list of ten personal check questions with tags and ask another member of the class.

2 Make a list of ten quiz check questions with tags and ask another member of the class.

*Need more practice? Go to the **Review** on page 192.*

tag questions

14 infinitive after verbs and adjectives

Many verbs and adjectives are followed by infinitive constructions, either with bare infinitive (*go*) or *to*-infinitive (*to go*). A good dictionary gives examples of the patterns used.

verbs followed by bare infinitive

make and *let*   (*make / let* + object + bare infinitive)
> Factory owners **made young children work** twelve hours a day.
> My parents **don't let me hold** noisy parties.

would rather ('d rather)
> Do you want to watch a DVD?   No, **I'd rather** play cards.

verbs followed by bare infinitive, or *to*-infinitive

help, dare
   (*help / dare* + object + bare infinitive / *to*-infinitive)
> Computers can **help us analyse** / **to analyse** large amounts of information.
> Nobody **dared to make** / **make** a noise.

verbs followed by *to*-infinitive

aim, fail, intend, learn how, long, manage, need, offer, plan, prefer, refuse, try, want
> We **aim to complete** the work by next week.
> Please **try to arrive** punctually at 8.30.

verbs followed by *to*-infinitive, or *that*-clause

decide, expect, hope, promise, threaten, warn
> We **decided to leave** early.
> We **decided that we would** leave early.

As these verbs often refer to the future, the *that*-clause often contains *would*.
With the verb *pretend*, the *that*-clause often contains a past tense verb.
> Jack **pretended to be** ill.   Jack **pretended that he was** ill.

verbs followed by an object and *to*-infinitive

advise, allow, dare, encourage, forbid, force, instruct, order, permit, persuade, remind, teach, tell
> They **advised me to try** again later.
> Tom's mother **taught him to cook**.

verbs followed by *to*-infinitive, or *-ing* (see also **Unit 15**)

begin, start, hate, like, love
> After an hour, the spectators **began to leave** the stadium.
> After an hour, the spectators **began leaving** the stadium.

adjectives followed by *to*-infinitive

- These can describe how someone feels about something, for example: *afraid, anxious, ashamed, careful, determined, free, frightened, happy, keen, quick, ready, sorry, willing.*
  Peter was **determined to pass** the exam.
  Some adjectives can also be followed by a preposition. See **Unit 42**.

- We can give an opinion about something, using adjectives such as *agreeable, amusing, boring, difficult, easy, hard, impossible, nice, good, important, necessary.*
  It's **easy to fall** over on the ice.

- Adjectives can be used in phrases with *be*, for example: *be supposed to, be expected to, be allowed to, be prepared to.*
  Sorry, but **you're not allowed to wait** here.

1 Underline six other examples of verb or adjective followed by the *to*-infinitive, and one example of verb or adjective followed by the bare infinitive.

In India all children <u>are supposed to go</u> to school between the ages of six and 14. In fact in the countryside it is very difficult for young children to get an education because the government has failed to build enough schools, and also because transport is difficult, and children need to take the bus to get to school. There are few buses, so most children go on foot. On top of all these problems, many parents never went to school themselves, so they don't expect their children to go. Many parents are also so poor that they don't let their children go to school, but prefer to send them to work instead, because they need the money. Children from richer families, on the other hand, often live near good schools, and their parents encourage them to pass their exams so that they can get good jobs.

2 Complete each sentence using a verb from the list.

> decide to   ~~hope to~~   learn how to   manage to   prefer to

a In developed countries, most students ......*hope to*...... continue into higher education.
b They know that if they .... get a university degree, they will stand more chance of getting a good job.
c Those who .... leave school at the age of 16 usually have opportunities to continue in education in a college of further education.
d This is the kind of college where you can .... become a chef or a tourist guide, and concentrates on the practical side of a job.
e And for those who .... go straight into employment at this age, there is always the chance of training on the job, or going back to full-time education at a later date.

> aim to   fail to   long to   need to   try to

f Do you ever .... get away from school and try something different?
g Then perhaps you .... go for work experience.
h Many schools .... give their pupils the chance to find out what work is like, by sending them to work for a few hours a week.
i Employers say that very few pupils .... learn useful skills.
j 'We .... make sure that all the children who work here understand themselves a bit better when they leave,' commented one employer.

3 Complete each sentence so that it means the same as the first sentence, using either *make* or *let* in a suitable form.

a In ancient Sparta, girls had to practise running, wrestling and throwing javelins.
The ancient Spartans ...*made girls practise running, wrestling and throwing javelins.*...
b A baby was not allowed to live if it was not fit and strong.
The ancient Spartans did not ....
c They encouraged young children to fight each other to make them tough.
The ancient Spartans ....
d People were not allowed to take a lot of baths.
The ancient Spartans didn't ....
e The children had to sleep on rushes, a kind of grass.
The ancient Spartans ....

14

infinitive after verbs and adjectives

55

f Eating a lot of food was not allowed.

The ancient Spartans ....

g All the boys had to join the army.

The ancient Spartans ....

h Boys were not allowed to cry when they fought.

The ancient Spartans ....

4 Rewrite each sentence so that it contains the word in capitals.

The conquest of the Incas

a Francisco Pizarro decided that he would return to South America in 1532.   TO

  Francisco Pizarro decided to return to South America in 1532.

b He hoped that he would conquer the Incas.   TO

c He also expected that he would become rich.   TO

d When he reached the Inca city of Cajamarca, he pretended that he was a friend.   TO

e He threatened that he would kill his prisoner, the Emperor Atahualpa, unless
  the people brought him their gold and silver.   TO

f But he had no intention of letting the Emperor go free.   INTEND

g His aim was to make sure that the Incas had no leader.   AIMED

h He made a promise that he would set the Emperor free, but killed him.   PROMISED

i Pizarro also killed his friend Almagro, who wouldn't obey his orders.   REFUSED

j Almagro's friends succeeded in killing Pizarro three years later.   MANAGED

GLOSSARY

5 Complete each sentence so that it means the same as the first sentence.

a Learning how to live in space is difficult.

  It's ..... *difficult to learn* .... how to live in space.

b Eating in weightless conditions isn't easy.

  It isn't .... in weightless conditions.

c Taking enough exercise is difficult.

  It's .... enough exercise.

d Being in good health is very important for astronauts.

  It's very important for astronauts .... in good health.

e Imagining what astronauts have to do is difficult.

  It's .... what astronauts have to do.

f Living a completely normal life in space is impossible.
It's .... a completely normal life in space.

g Going into space is never boring.
It's never .... into space.

h Returning to Earth makes most astronauts feel happy.
Most astronauts feel .... to Earth.

6 Complete the text with one word from the list in each space.

allow	careful	decided	encouraged	failed
forced	learned	let	managed	prepared
refused	~~sorry~~	supposed	threatened	trying

I'm a .....*sorry*..... to say that we have b ....
to close the science laboratory until further notice.
Although we have always c .... pupils to
conduct safe experiments, and have always believed it was
important to d .... students discover
science for themselves, recent events have made it difficult
for us to e .... such work to continue.
I am referring of course to the robot that Class 5
f .... to construct recently while they were
g .... to be constructing a simple computer.
Although at first the builders of this machine were
h .... to hide their machine from members of
staff, unfortunately they i .... to control the
robot. It not only j .... how to leave the
laboratory, but walked into the town centre and broke
into the National Bank in Green Street. It is impossible to
imagine what it was k .... to do. The pupils who
built it have l .... to say whether they were
controlling its actions. In any case, the police were not
m .... to permit this situation to continue,
especially when the robot n .... to attack
members of the bank staff, and o ....
them to fill a large bag with money. Please remember, this
is not what science is for!

GLOSSARY

EXTENSION ACTIVITY

1 Choose eight verbs from page 54 and write true sentences about yourself.

2 Choose eight adjectives from page 54 and write true sentences about yourself.

infinitive after verbs and adjectives

15 -ing form

This is the name for the form of the verb ending -ing. When we use it as a noun, we can also call it a *gerund*, and when we use it as an adjective or verb, we also call it the *present participle*, though it is often difficult to decide which is which.

- **verbs of feeling and opinion etc followed by -ing**
admit, avoid, consider, deny, dislike, enjoy, fancy, feel like, finish, can't help, involve, keep, mean, mind, miss, practise, risk, can't stand, suggest
> *Having a healthy lifestyle **involves following** a balanced diet, which **means eating** a variety of fruit and vegetables and **avoiding** too many sweet or fatty foods, and also **taking** regular exercise.*

- **expressions with *it's***
it's no good, it's no use, it's not worth
> ***It's not worth taking** an umbrella. It's not going to rain.*

- **expressions with *spend***
spend (one's) time, spend (quality) time
> *I **spent my time swimming** and **sunbathing**.*
> *Anna **spent a lot of time researching** her project.*

- **expressions with *like***
We can use -ing and *to*-infinitive after *like*.
> *I don't **like getting** up early.*   *I **like to watch** TV late at night.*

- **verbs followed by -ing or *to*-infinitive with different meanings**

stop	*It's a good idea to **stop eating** sweets between meals.* (stop an activity)
	*They **stopped to buy** food, and then continued their journey.* (stop in order to)
try	***Try going** for a swim – it's a good way to get fit.* (see if it works)
	*They **tried to reach** the island, but it was too far away.* (make an effort)
remember	***Remember to warm up** before you start exercising.* (don't forget)
	*I **remember going** to school for the first time.* (past memory)

- **prepositions followed by -ing**   (See **Unit 42**)
We use the -ing form after a preposition. A preposition can follow a verb or an adjective.
be interested in, apologize for, be used to, accuse (someone) of, specialize in, succeed in, insist on
> *Are you **interested in joining** a tennis club?*
> *I must **apologize for arriving** late.*
> *I am not **used to staying up** so late.*
> *They **accused Rick of stealing** the money.*

- ***come* and *go* followed by -ing**
There are many expressions of this kind, mainly connected with sport, but not team games. We also use *shopping* in this way.
> *Do you want **to come swimming** / **sailing** / **running** with us?*
> Not ~~*She's gone playing tennis.*~~
> *They've **gone shopping**.*

- **-ing form as subject**
We can use -ing form as a noun subject.
> ***Adding** and **subtracting** decimals is similar to adding and subtracting whole numbers.*

1 Underline the correct word or phrase.

a New research shows some young people *can't help* / *consider* / *risk* eating food which contains large amounts of sugar, salt, and animal fat.

b Many young people also *avoid* / *enjoy* / *keep* taking any exercise.

c They don't even *avoid* / *enjoy* / *suggest* walking to school or playing active games with their friends.

d For too many young people, enjoyment *feels like* / *involves* / *keeps* sitting in front of the television, or in front of a computer playing games.

e Of course if they *involve* / *keep* / *suggest* doing this, they are very likely to have health problems at an early age.

f Health experts *consider* / *mean* / *suggest* taking hard exercise at least three times a week.

g This *can't help* / *keeps* / *means* running, cycling or swimming.

h So even if you don't *avoid* / *feel like* / *risk* taking exercise, it's important to organize regular exercise activities.

i You could *go* / *involve* / *practise* swimming or jogging, for example.

j You may also *consider* / *involve* / *keep* changing your diet, and eating more fruit and fresh vegetables.

2 Complete each sentence **a** to **h** with an ending from **1** to **8**.

a For a Roman soldier, joining the Roman army meant ____6____

b He received wages, but had to spend money too, since being in the army involved _____

c In the early days of Rome, everyone became a soldier and young men couldn't avoid _____

d However, as time went on, fewer Romans served as soldiers. The army stopped _____

e When the army was at the height of its power, an enemy who considered _____

f Unless the enemy had very large numbers of soldiers or attacked by surprise, they risked _____

g Foreign armies were often disorganized and ran away, but the Romans always kept _____

h The Romans were more successful because their soldiers spent more time _____

1 ... being completely destroyed by the ancient world's best fighting force.

2 ... buying his own food, uniform and weapons.

3 ... attacking it faced very serious problems.

4 ... taking all the young Roman men, and service became voluntary.

5 ... fighting, until the end if necessary, and rarely surrendered.

6 ~~... remaining in service from 20 to 30 years.~~

7 ... training to use their weapons, and fighting in organized groups.

8 ... serving in the army if there was a war, as it was compulsory.

3 Complete the text with the *-ing* or *to*-infinitive form of the verbs in brackets.

People who remember **a** (do) ___to do___ everything they have planned are usually people who organize their tasks in some way, and avoid **b** (get) _____ into a muddle. A shopping list is a good example of this technique, provided you remember **c** (take) _____ the list with you when you go **d** (shop) _____

It's sometimes possible to remember a fact, for example, if first of all you stop **e** (think) _____ for a few moments. When you try **f** (remember) _____ something, this will be easier if you have learnt it in an organized way. If you are not sure how to do this, try **g** (write) _____ brief notes about the text you are reading. Many people find this an effective way of learning. After all, it's easy to read something and not understand or remember it, usually because you have stopped **h** (pay) _____ attention.

-ing form

4 Complete the text with a word from the list. You will have to use some words more than once.

| at | between | by | for | in | on | of |

Galileo

As well as being a scientist, Galileo was interested **a** ......*in*...... painting and music. He started his studies **b** .... attending medical school in Padua. Unlike most scientists at that time, who usually relied **c** .... discussing the facts, not trying to prove them, he recognized the importance **d** .... doing experiments to prove the facts. He is famous **e** .... dropping different weights from the Tower of Pisa to prove that all bodies fall at the same rate, though this is probably not a true story. Through practice, he also became good **f** .... observing the stars, and identified craters on the Moon, sunspots, and the moons of Jupiter. As a result **g** .... studying the planet Venus, he succeeded **h** .... proving that Copernicus was correct, and that the Earth moved around the Sun. Unfortunately, the Church authorities accused him **i** .... publishing unacceptable ideas. In the end he was forced to choose **j** .... being punished by the Church, or denying his own ideas. He spent most of the last nine years of his life imprisoned in his own house.

GLOSSARY

5 Rewrite each sentence so that it contains the word in capitals.

> *Fossils are the remains of animals, plants, and other organisms preserved in rocks. The word fossil comes from the Latin word* fossus, *meaning 'having been dug up'.*

    a Does fossil-collecting interest you?   INTERESTED
       Are you interested in fossil-collecting?

    b Do you have to walk long distances?   INVOLVE

    c I often find rocks that aren't really fossils.   KEEP

    d When you look for fossils on a cliff, you could fall.   RISK

    e I really think this is the wrong place to look for fossils.   HELP

    f You have to get up early to go on the club trip.   MEANS

    g I left my hammer at home.   REMEMBER

    h I want to sit down and have a rest!   FEEL

    i I know how to find fossils.   GOOD

    j Don't take up a hobby unless you're serious about it.   WORTH

6 Rewrite each sentence so that it begins with an –*ing* form as subject.

a It can be very relaxing to collect fossils.
Collecting fossils can be very relaxing.

b It can be very difficult to give up smoking.
_____

c It isn't a good idea to do an exam without revising.
_____

d It is fun to learn a new sport.
_____

e It takes lots of hard work to learn a foreign language.
_____

f It was very exciting to see my favourite band play live.
_____

g It will never be possible to live on Mars.
_____

h It took a long time to write the report.
_____

i It is so tiring walking up this mountain!
_____

j It is illegal to drive without a licence.
_____

history

7 Complete the text with the –*ing* form or *to*-infinitive of the verbs in brackets.

The first explorers to cross Australia

John Stuart decided **a** (cross) ____*to cross*____ Australia from south to
north in 1859. He wanted **b** (win) _____ a prize offered by the
South Australian government. This meant **c** (travel) _____
across mountains and desert for 3,000 kilometres. He and his three companions
kept **d** (ride) _____ for eight months before reaching the centre
of the continent. What had they expected **e** (find) _____? So far
they had only succeeded in **f** (discover) _____ a huge desert. On this
expedition Stuart failed **g** (reach) _____ the coast, and turned back ill and
short of food. He tried **h** (complete) _____ the journey the next year, but failed again.
Finally in 1861 he managed **i** (arrive) _____ at the northern coast, near the modern city of
Darwin. Ever since he has been famous for **j** (cross) _____ the continent, though sadly he
died soon after his return to Adelaide.

Darwin

NORTHERN
TERRITORY

QUEENSLAND

WESTERN
AUSTRALIA

SOUTH
AUSTRALIA

NEW
SOUTH
WALES

Adelaide

GLOSSARY

EXTENSION ACTIVITY

1 Choose eight verbs from page 58 and write true
sentences about yourself.

2 Make a list of ten things you are interested in.

Need more practice? Go to the Review on page 192.

–*ing* form

16 reported statements

Direct speech is the actual words people say. We use speech marks.

Napoleon said: 'I have fought sixty battles and I have learned nothing.'

Reported or indirect speech tells us what people have said. We do not use speech marks.

*Napoleon **said that he had fought** sixty battles and had learned nothing.*

tense changes

In reported speech we usually begin with a past tense reporting verb (eg *said*) so we change all the verbs that follow, and put them back further in the past.

*'I **know** the answer,' she said.*	*She said (that) she **knew** the answer.*
*'**I've done** it,' she said.*	*She said (that) she **had done** it.*
*'**I'll** see you later,' he said.*	*He said **he would** see us later.*

people: personal pronouns

We also change the word we use to refer to the person who spoke.

*Jack said: '**I** have finished.'*   *Jack said that **he** had finished.*

words referring to time and place

In direct speech time words like *now*, *today*, *tomorrow*, change because there is no longer a 'here and now' reference. The point of view has changed.

*'I'll see you **tomorrow**.'*   *He said he would see me **the following day**.*

Reference words like *here* and *this* also change.

*'I like **this** painting.'*	*She said that she liked **the** painting.*
*'I don't understand **this**.'*	*He said that he didn't understand **it**.*

tomorrow →	*the following day, the next day*
yesterday →	*the day before*
here →	*there*
this (pronoun) →	*it*
this (determiner) →	*the*

say and tell

We always put an object after *tell*.

*He **said** that he felt ill.*   *He **told them** that he felt ill.*

We use *tell* in the phrases *tell a lie* and *tell the truth*.

*She **told her teacher a lie**.*   *He **told me the truth**, I'm sure.*

We don't say *He said the truth* or *He said a lie*.

no changes

- When we report immediately what someone says, or talk as if it was very recent, we use a present tense reporting verb and we do not make tense changes.

  *Helen **says she'll be back** later.*

- When we report a state meaning (eg *like, live, believe* etc) it is possible to make no changes if we want to show that the state continues.

  *'I still don't believe you.' He said that he still **doesn't** believe me.*

  We can also make the tense change, but it can suggest that the state belongs to the past.

  *He said that he **didn't** believe me at that time.*

- When we report a narrative we need not change past simple to past perfect.

  'I was standing at the bus-stop, and I saw everything that happened,' he said.

  ***He said he was standing** at the bus stop and **saw** everything that **happened**.*

- We do not make tense changes when we report quotations.

  *Napoleon said that **you must** never interrupt your enemy when **he is making** a mistake.*

1 Rewrite each sentence as reported speech with tense changes.

a 'I get up every day at 6.30,' she said.
She .said..(that)..she..got..up..every..day..at..6.30.

b 'I forgot to phone the doctor,' he said.
He ....

c 'Everybody likes comedy films,' he said.
He ....

d 'I'm thinking about it,' he said.
He ....

e 'I was reading the paper,' she said.
She ....

f 'Scientists don't understand everything,' she said.
She ....

g 'I've decided to look for a new job,' he said.
He ....

h 'I can swim 5,000 metres,' he said.
He said ....

i 'I'm going to have a baby,' she said.
She ....

j 'I'll phone on Friday,' he said.
He ....

2 Read the information about the Trojan War. Then put one pronoun or reference word in each space.

A 'I love you, Helen, and I want you to come with me to Troy,' Paris told Helen.
Paris told Helen that he loved **a** ....her....... and he wanted **b** .... to go to Troy with **c** ....

B 'I'm going to attack Troy and get my wife back because she loves me best!' Menelaus told his brother.
Menelaus told his brother that he was going to attack Troy and get **d** .... wife back because **e** .... loved **f** .... best.

C 'We'll come with you to Troy and get your wife back,' the Greek heroes told Menelaus.
The Greek heroes told Menelaus that **g** .... would go with **h** .... to attack Troy and get **i** .... wife back.

D 'We've been fighting here for nine years and we want to get back to our families,' the Greeks said.
The Greeks said that they had been fighting **j** .... for nine years and they wanted to get back to **k** .... families.

E 'I'm going to take some soldiers with me inside this wooden horse,' Odysseus told them.
Odysseus told them that he was going to take some soldiers with **l** .... inside **m** .... wooden horse.

F 'My plan has worked, and the city is ours,' Odysseus told the Greeks.
Odysseus told the Greeks that **n** .... plan had worked and the city was **o** ....

3 Read the information about Heinrich Schliemann.
Then complete the text by writing *said* or *told* in each space.

Heinrich Schliemann –
an interview in the 1860s

Heinrich Schliemann was a German archaeologist who excavated a city in
Turkey in 1871 and decided that it was ancient Troy. He found evidence
of destruction by war, and also discovered some gold objects. Nowadays
archaeologists believe that his methods of excavation were unscientific, and
they also believe that some of his discoveries were false.

Recently many experts have **a** ....*said*........ that Schliemann had a habit of not telling the truth, and this
has raised doubts about his work. For example, he **b** .... everyone he was a US citizen, but in
fact this wasn't true. He also **c** .... he had a degree from the University of Rostock, but in fact
the university rejected his thesis. He **d** .... he had found gold jewellery at Hissarlik, but some
people believe these were modern pieces. In fact, his servant later **e** .... people that no jewellery
had been found in the places that Schliemann claimed to have found it. He also **f** .... the
authorities in Turkey that he was an archaeologist, but he didn't have any qualifications. When he talked about
his work, he always **g** .... people that he had dreamed of finding Troy when he was a small
boy, but many people feel that he invented this story later. However, although many archaeologists at the time
h .... that his work was inaccurate, we have to remember that archaeology was not a science in
Schliemann's time. He may not have always **i** .... the truth, but he brought a lot of energy to the
discovery of the ancient world, and devoted his life and his wealth to his excavations.

GLOSSARY

4 Rewrite each sentence about Schliemann as reported speech.

a 'I have always been interested in the story of Troy,' he told journalists.
   He told journalists (that) he had always been interested in the story of Troy.

b 'My father read the stories to me when I was a child,' he said.

c 'I have always believed that Troy was a real place,' he said.

d 'At an early age I decided to discover the site of the city,' he said.

e 'For many years I worked as a merchant in the USA and Russia,' he said.

f 'I am a wealthy man and I have retired from business,' he said.

g 'I first went to the site at Hissarlik in 1868,' he said.

h 'Since then I have spent a lot of my own money on the excavation,' he said.

i 'I am working with a British archaeologist,' he said.

j 'We are hoping to prove that Hissarlik is the site of ancient Troy,' he said.

5 Read the statement from a news conference held at an archaeological site. Then answer the questions.

'Good morning everyone, my name is Julia Richmond, and I'm the director of this dig. Thank you for coming to this news conference. First I want to explain how we found this site, and what we've been doing here. I'm sure you have read the publicity handout, so you know something about this. It's important to give you the latest information. Then I'm going to give a description of some of the interesting discoveries we have made here. I'll give you a general account of the project, and I'll show some slides of the site. Then there will be a chance for all of you to look at some fascinating objects. We've brought some of the more spectacular finds. They are waiting for you in the room next door, and you will be able to take photographs. You've been very patient. So now let's begin …'

What did the archaeologist say about …

a … her job?

She told the journalists ___(that) she was the director of the dig.___

b … finding the site?

She said _____

c … the publicity handout?

She told _____

d … the latest information?

She said _____

e … interesting discoveries?

She told _____

f … a general account of the project?

She said _____

g … slides?

She told _____

h … fascinating objects?

She said _____

i … spectacular finds?

She told _____

j … the room next door?

She said _____

k … photographs?

She told _____

l … being patient?

She said _____

EXTENSION ACTIVITY

1 Choose five sentences and their answers from Exercise 1 and translate them into your language. Are the tense changes and punctuation rules the same?

2 Read Exercise 3 again. Write four things that Schliemann told people, using direct speech.

reported statements

17 reported questions, commands, and reporting verbs

reported questions

- *yes / no* questions

We report these questions using *if* or *whether*. We follow the tense-change rules (see **Unit 16**). We change the question form of the verb to the statement form. We do not use a question mark.

> *'Do you understand the question?' she asked us.*
> *She asked us **if / whether we understood** the question.*

- reported questions with a question word

We report these questions using the question word and the following tense-change rules. We change the question form of the verb to the statement form.

> *'**What temperature is** the water?' she asked.*
> *She asked **what temperature the water was**.*

reported requests and commands

Use *ask* to report requests: *ask* + object + *to*-infinitive.

> *'Please turn on your computers.'* He **asked us to turn on** our computers.

Use *tell* to report commands: *tell* + object + *to*-infinitive.

> *'**Turn on** your computers!'* He **told us to turn on** our computers.
> *'**Don't turn it on**!'* He **told us not to turn it on**.

report verbs

Some verbs explain what people say, or summarize their words. Using a report verb often means you can summarize the actual words people say, without repeating them.

> *'I'll bring my homework tomorrow, honestly, I will, really!'*
> *He **promised to** bring his homework the next day.*

- verb + *that*-clause

suggest	*'Why don't you use a calculator?'*	He **suggested (that) I used** a calculator.
promise	*'I'll do it.'*	He **promised (him) (that) he would** do it.

- verb + *-ing*

suggest	*'Why don't you use a calculator?'*	He **suggested using** a calculator.
deny	*'I didn't break the jar.'*	He **denied breaking** the jar.

- verb + *to*-infinitive

offer	*'I'll help you.'*	He **offered to help** her.
promise	*'I'll bring it tomorrow.'*	She **promised to bring** it the next day.
refuse	*'I won't sit down!'*	He **refused to sit** down.
agree to	*'Ok, I'll pay (you) €300.'*	He **agreed to pay (him)** €300.

- verb + object + *to*-infinitive

advise	*'I would (wouldn't) stop, if I were you.'*	She **advised me (not) to** stop.
remind	*'Don't forget to lock the door.'*	She **reminded him to** lock the door.
warn	*'Don't touch that wire!'*	She **warned me not to** touch the wire.

- verb + object

invite	*'Would you like to come to dinner?'*	He **invited me to** dinner.
offer	*'Would you like some ice cream?'*	He **offered her** some ice cream.

- other patterns

explain	*'This is how you do it.'*	She **explained how to** do it.
agree with	*'Yes, I think the same.'*	She **agreed with** him.
congratulate	*'Well done, you've won.'*	He **congratulated her on** winning.

1A Complete the reported *yes* / *no* questions.

a 'Have you done your homework?'
The teacher asked me ____if I had done my____
____homework.____

b 'Are we starting a new lesson?'
I asked the teacher ____

c 'Are you paying attention?'
The teacher asked me ____

d 'Do I have to write it down?'
I asked the teacher ____

e 'Are you feeling all right?'
The teacher asked me ____

1B Rewrite the sentence as direct speech. Include necessary punctuation.

f I asked the teacher if she had a spare pen.

g The teacher asked me if I was going to start.

h I asked the teacher if it was all right to use a pencil.

i The teacher asked me if I knew the answer.

j I asked the teacher if it was the end of the lesson.

Are you guys paying attention?

2A Complete the reported questions without past tense shift.

a How many colours are there in a rainbow?
The teacher asked us ____how many colours____
____there are in a rainbow.____

b What does a tadpole turn into?
The teacher asked us ____

c How do fish take oxygen from the water?
The teacher asked us ____

d How many stomachs does a cow have?
The teacher asked us ____

e What do scientists mean by gravity?
The teacher asked us ____

2B Complete the reported questions with past tense shift.

f When did the Second World War begin?
The teacher asked us ____

g Why did Romeo drink the poison?
The teacher asked us ____

h What did Edison do in 1877?
The teacher asked us ____

i What was Gregor Mendel famous for?
The teacher asked us ____

j What did Marie Curie discover?
The teacher asked us ____

reported questions, commands, and reporting verbs

3A Complete the reported questions.

a 'Do you live here?' I asked.
I asked him _____if/whether he lived there._____

b 'What's your name?'
He asked me _____

c 'What time is it?'
I asked her _____

d 'Are you sitting here?'
She asked me _____

e 'Do you want some coffee?'
I asked her _____

3B Rewrite the sentence as direct speech. Include necessary punctuation.

f He asked me when the next train left.
_____

g I asked him where the bus station was.
_____

h She asked me whether I had any change.
_____

i I asked her what she was staring at.
_____

j They asked me if I was waiting for them.
_____

4 Complete the reported requests or commands.

a 'Fill the jar with water, John.'
The teacher _____told John to fill the jar with water._____

b 'Please help him, Angela.'
The teacher _____

c 'Michael, don't spill the water!'
The teacher _____

d 'Please pour a little water into here, Alison.'
The teacher _____

e 'Light the gas, Steve.'
The teacher _____

f 'Don't touch it with your finger, Alan.'
The teacher _____

g 'Sarah, heat the water gently until it boils.'
The teacher _____

h 'All of you, please watch the water carefully.'
The teacher _____

5 Match the sentences **a** to **h** with the same words reported in **1** to **8**.

a This is how you turn on the computer. 1 He explained how to turn on the computer.

b I wouldn't turn on the computer if I were you. 2 He warned me not to turn on the computer.

c I'll turn on the computer. 3 He invited me to turn on the computer.

d It's not true – I didn't turn on the computer. 4 He suggested I turned on the computer.

e Careful – don't turn on the computer. 5 He refused to turn on the computer.

f Why don't you turn on the computer? 6 He denied turning on the computer.

g Would you like to turn on the computer? 7 He offered to turn on the computer.

h No, I won't turn on the computer! 8 He advised me not to turn on the computer.

6 Read the advice from a sports expert. Then complete each sentence using one word from the box and any other necessary information.

'Hello, my name's Vernon Marchewski and I'm going to tell you about the best ways to improve your fitness. If you're interested in being an athlete, or just doing sport for fun, this advice is for you.

I think the most important thing is to choose a workout that you enjoy. Don't cycle if you don't like cycling. You need to do something that will motivate you, so avoid activities that are too hard for you, or boring.

To make your workout more fun and challenging, do it a bit differently each time. Try a new activity, or vary how long you spend doing something, and how difficult you make it.

Another great way to motivate yourself is to make sure you have goals. For example, if you run 5 km a day, try to increase it to 6. But be careful, don't overtrain. This can lead to injury, and your body needs to rest as well as work hard.

Look after yourself, remember to eat good food and drink lots of water. A healthy diet is the best way to a healthy body.

Finally, only use proper equipment. If you cycle, have your bicycle checked and repaired regularly. Only wear good running shoes, and invest in comfortable clothing.'

| explained | warned | reminded | told | ~~said~~ | advised | shouldn't | suggested |

a Vernon _said his advice was_ _____ for people interested in being athletes.

b He _____ the audience _____ they enjoyed.

c He _____ too hard, or boring.

d To make your workout fun, Vernon _____

e He _____ goals is a good way to motivate yourself.

f He _____ lead to injury.

g He _____ good food.

h He _____ bad equipment.

EXTENSION ACTIVITY

1 Make sure you have the correct answers for Exercise 3. Translate the answers into your own language.

2 Write sentences in direct speech giving examples of these actions:
suggesting, denying, refusing, advising, inviting

social studies

reported questions, commands, and reporting verbs

GLOSSARY

18 conditionals: true, real and unreal

always true (zero conditional)
if X happens, Y happens
These sentences describe what always happens in certain circumstances eg scientific facts.

present simple	present simple
When / If you **press** *the switch, the light* **comes** *on.*	

real conditions (conditional 1)
if X happens, Y will happen
These sentences describe what the speaker thinks will possibly happen as a consequence of a real situation.

present simple	*will* future
If we **do not deal** *with the global warming problem, temperatures* **will rise.**	

If we **leave** *now,* **we'll catch** *the bus. If we* **don't leave** *now, we* **won't catch** *it.*

In informal speech, we often use *going to* instead of *will*.
> *If you* **don't take** *an umbrella, you're* **going to get** *wet.*
> We also use *might* or *can / could* in place of *will*. See **Unit 25**

We can also use imperatives in real conditions.
> *If you don't know a word,* **look it up** *in the dictionary.*

Sentences beginning *If you will...* are only used when *will* means *insist*, or is used as a polite form.
> **If you will stay up** *so late, then of course you'll feel tired.*   (insist)
> **If you'll wait** *here, I'll see if the manager is ready.*   (polite)

unless
Unless means *only if not*. We use it when we say that if something does not happen, something else will happen.
> **Unless we deal with** *the global warming problem, average temperatures* **will rise.**

provided, as long as + present simple
Provided and *as long as* mean *only if*.
> **Provided / as long as** *we* **reduce** *energy consumption, we can slow down global warming.*

in case + present simple
This describes a possible situation we want to be prepared for.
> *Take an umbrella* **in case it rains.**

unreal conditions (conditional 2)
if X happened, Y would happen
These sentences describe what the speaker thinks would happen in an imaginary situation.

past simple	*would* + verb
If you **were** *on Venus, you* **would see** *the Sun rise in the west.*	

> *What* **would happen** *if the Earth* **stopped** *turning?*
> *If the Earth* **didn't have** *a Moon, there* **wouldn't be** *any tides.*

The past simple tense we use in an *if*-sentence does not describe past time, but unreal time. We also use *might* or *could* in place of *would*. See **Unit 25**.

if I were you
We give advice with *If I were you*.
> *I* **wouldn't** *do that,* **if I were you**. or **If I were you, I wouldn't** *do that.*

real or unreal?

This depends on the situation of the speaker, or what the speaker is thinking.

For example, we're in the classroom. There are some heavy tables. I think a friend is going to lift them. I give a warning.

*'If you **try** to lift those tables on your own, you**'ll hurt** yourself.'*

Same situation. Nobody is thinking of lifting the tables. I make a comment.

*'Those tables look heavy! If you **tried** to lift them, you**'d hurt** yourself.'*

1 Complete the answers using the word or words in capitals.

a What happens when you heat water to 100°C?   BOIL
   If you   *heat water to 100°C, it boils*

b What does water turn into when you boil it?   STEAM
   If you

c What happens when you cool the steam?   TURNS BACK
   If you

d What happens when you heat a piece of metal?   EXPANDS
   If you

e What happens when you freeze a piece of metal?   CONTRACTS
   If you

f What happens when you freeze water?   EXPANDS
   If you

2 Use the words to complete an *if*-sentence about solutions to environmental problems.

Solution A – recycle paper, metal and glass

a everyone / recycle paper / companies / not cut down so many trees
   If everyone recycles paper, companies won't cut down so many trees.

b everyone / recycle metal and glass / we not waste valuable resources

c everyone / recycle paper, metal and glass / we not produce so much rubbish

Solution B – turn off lights, don't drive so much, insulate your house

d everyone / turn off unwanted lights / save a lot of electricity

e everyone / walk or cycle / not waste so much oil and petrol

f everyone / insulate their houses / not waste so much energy for heating

Solution C – use renewable energy

g countries use more wind and water power, not depend so much on power stations

h countries use power stations less, cause less air pollution

3 Use the prompts to complete the question.
Then choose the most likely answer.
Check the factual answers on page 208.

a what / happen if you / travel through the Earth to the other side?

What would happen if you travelled through the Earth to the other side?

b what / happen if the Earth suddenly stop / going round?

c what / happen if we not / have a Moon?

d what / happen if all the ice at the poles / melt?

e what / happen if there be / no more electricity?

f what / happen if aliens receive / messages from Earth and decide / to visit us?

a A *You would fly out the other side into space.*	B *This would be impossible because the Earth's core is hot.*	C *You would fall to the centre and then stop.*
b A *We would enjoy longer and warmer days*	B *It would start moving in the opposite direction*	C *Even if the Earth stopped, we would keep moving!*
c A *There would not be any ocean tides.*	B *The Earth would spin more slowly*	C *The Sun would grow stronger.*
d A *Sea levels would fall.*	B *Sea levels would stay the same.*	C *Sea levels would rise.*
e A *The universe would no longer exist.*	B *People would use candles for light and fires for heat.*	C *The world would be a safer place.*
f A *They wouldn't know exactly where we were.*	B *They wouldn't arrive for millions of years, as they would be so far away.*	C *They wouldn't understand our messages anyway.*

GLOSSARY

4A Rewrite each sentence so that it contains *unless* or *as long as* and begins as shown.

a If you don't train hard, you won't succeed in sport.
You *won't succeed in sport unless you train hard.*

b If you train regularly, you can improve your performance.
You can improve

c If you enjoy your sport, it doesn't really matter whether you succeed or not.
It doesn't really matter

d If you don't eat and sleep properly you won't develop as an athlete.
You won't

4B Rewrite each sentence so that it contains *in case*.

    e Take a spare pair of running shoes, because it's possible that you will need them.
      Take a spare pair of running shoes ....

    f Take a waterproof coat with you because it's possible that it will rain.
      Take a waterproof coat with you ....

    g take a warm jumper because it's possible that you will get cold when you stop.
      Take a warm jumper ....

    h Take a first-aid kit because it's possible that someone will get injured.
      Take a first-aid kit ....

5 Use the words to complete the conditional *if*-sentence. Use an always true, real or unreal conditional to suit the meaning.

    a Scientists are planning a way of writing extremely small letters, using xenon (Xe) atoms. If you (use) ......*used*...... this system, you (be able) .... to write ten copies of the Bible on the area of a postage stamp.

    b Humans are among the few animals to have colour vision. If you (be) .... a horse, for example, you (see) .... everything in black and white.

    c The brain works in two parts, the left side and the right side. Scientists can put one side of the brain to sleep, and see what happens. For example, if they (turn off) .... the right side of the patient's brain, the patient (not be able) .... to sing, because musical ability comes from the right side of the brain.

    d Beetles are one of the most numerous species on the planet. In fact, if other insects and animals (not eat) .... beetles, in about a year and a half the beetle population (weigh) .... as much as the whole Earth!

    e Parts of the body send messages to other parts of the body when they have to do things. For example, if you (not have) .... enough water in your body the brain (let) .... you know that you need more, by making you feel thirsty.

    f If you (look) .... inside your own eye at the images there, they (be) .... upside down, and they (be) .... moving.

    g If you (smoke) ...., chemical changes (take place) .... in your cells, which do not receive enough oxygen and die.

    h The world's oceans contain huge amounts of salt. In fact, if you (remove) .... all the salt from the oceans, you (be able) .... to use it to build a wall about 300 km wide and a kilometre tall all around the Earth!

EXTENSION ACTIVITY

  1 Write five sentences about your life which begin *Unless I …*

  2 Write a list of eight interesting scientific facts you found in this unit, which begin *If …*

  *Need more practice? Go to the **Review** on page 192.*

conditionals: true, real and unreal

19 conditionals: impossible past, wishes

impossible or past conditions   (conditional 3)

if X had happened, Y would have happened

These sentences describe what the speaker thinks would have happened as a consequence of a situation which is in the past, so is impossible to change.

> On 18 June 1815 the Coalition Army under Wellington and Blucher defeated Napoleon
> **would have + verb**   **past perfect**
> and the French army. But what would have happened if Napoleon had won the battle?
> **would have + verb**
> The history of Europe would certainly have been different.

> I'm sorry I didn't talk to you yesterday, but I simply didn't see you!
> **If I'd seen** you, I **would have** said hello.

We also use *might have* or *could have* in place of *would have*. See **Unit 25**.

past condition with a result in the present

if X had happened, Y would be different

We often think about past events, and their effects on the present.

> **If** Chris **hadn't gone** to the hospital, he **wouldn't be** alive today.

wishes

● about the present

When we use *wish* to make a wish about the present, we use the *unreal past simple*, as in an unreal conditional sentence. We can also use *could / was able to*.

> **I wish I knew** more about European history.
> (= If I knew more about it now, I would be happier.)
> **I wish I could** swim really fast.

● wishes about the past

When we use *wish* to make a wish about the past, we use the past perfect, as in an impossible past conditional sentence.

> **I wish I had been** present at the battle of Waterloo.
> (= If I had been present at the battle of Waterloo, I would have been happy!)

● wishes with *would*

We also use *wish* with *would* when we want someone to do something or not to do something. This is often because we think it is a bad habit.

> **I wish you wouldn't** keep staring at me!
> **I wish Pete would** phone.

● *if only*

We can use *if only* to make a stronger kind of wish about the present or the past.

> **If only I knew** more about European history!
> **If only I had studied** harder!

1 Complete the sentence using the verbs in brackets.

a If Alexander the Great (march) ....had marched.... west instead of east, he (conquer) .... the whole of Europe.

b If more Vikings (go) .... to North America, the Viking settlements (succeed) ....

c If the ancient Egyptians (build) .... bigger boats, they (cross) .... the Atlantic and (land) .... in America.

d If a storm (not hit) .... Bartolomeu Dias's ship off the coast of Africa in 1487, they (not arrived) .... in the Indian Ocean by accident.

e If Cheng Ho and other Chinese explorers (continue) .... further on their voyages, they (sail) .... up the west coast of Africa and reached Europe in the early 15th century.

f If Columbus (not read) .... about Marco Polo's trip to China, he (not try) .... to sail there by crossing the Atlantic.

g If Columbus (sail) .... east in 1492, he (reach) .... China or Japan.

h If the Aztecs (not think) .... that Cortes and his men were gods, the Spaniards (not conquer) .... Mexico so easily.

i If Lewis and Clark (not find) .... a way across America from St Louis to the Pacific in 1806, thousands of settlers (not make) .... the journey in later years to settle in the central and western parts of North America.

j If Charles Darwin (not take) .... a voyage to South America between 1831 and 1836, he (not write) .... his famous book *The Origin of Species*, which argued that living creatures evolved over millions of years.

2 Use the information to make an impossible past conditional sentence which has a result in the present.

a Columbus 1492: 'Don't worry men, I've brought a map with me, so I know exactly where we are. If I ....hadn't brought a map...., we .... lost!'

b Galileo 1640: 'I've explained my new ideas to the Church, but now I'm in trouble! If I ...., I .... !'

c Marco Polo 1300: 'It's true, I have exaggerated and made up some of the descriptions in the book about my travels. I suppose that's why people don't believe the true things. If I ...., perhaps more people .... ,'

d Mrs Abraham Lincoln, April 1865: 'We went to the theatre last night, and now my poor husband the President is dead, shot by a political opponent. If we .... he .... alive today!'

e Leonardo da Vinci, 1518: 'I've done a lot of things in my life, but perhaps I haven't spent enough time on my paintings. I didn't always manage to finish them, I'm afraid. If I ...., more of them .... ,'

f Napoleon, 1820, in exile on the island of St Helena: 'Looking back, I can see that invading Russia was a mistake. Without that, perhaps I wouldn't have lost the war. If I .... Russia, perhaps I .... Emperor of France!'

Isabella of Castile

3 Use the information to make an impossible past conditional sentence, beginning as shown. It is not necessary to use all the information.

a The Trojans saw the wooden horse, and decided to take it into Troy. Once it was inside the walls, the Greeks hidden inside the horse came out, opened the gates, and the Greek army captured Troy.
If the Trojans *hadn't taken the wooden horse into Troy*, the Greeks *would not have captured the city.*

b In September 490 BC, an army from Athens and Plataea met the Persian army of Darius I on the Greek coast at Marathon, about 35 km from Athens. It seemed that nothing could stop Darius conquering Greece. However, the Greek army won a total victory, and the Persian army went home.
If the Greeks .... ,
Darius and his army ....

c On 10 January 49 BC, Julius Caesar crossed the River Rubicon on the border of Italy with his army. This led to civil war which Caesar won, and so became leader of the Roman state.
If Julius Caesar .... ,
he ....

d In 1469, Isabella of Castile married Ferdinand of Aragon. Their marriage combined the two kingdoms and created the kingdom of Spain, which soon became one of the most powerful countries in Europe.
If Isabella .... ,
Spain ....

e In September 1066, Duke William of Normandy sailed with an army to England. He believed that he, and not Harold, was the rightful king. Harold marched to meet William but his army was tired after fighting a battle in the north against the Vikings. William won the battle that followed, and became king of England.
If Harold's army .... ,
William ....

GLOSSARY

4 Complete the *wish*-sentence with the verb in brackets.

a What on earth is the answer to this problem! (know) I *wish I knew the answer to this problem.*
b Unfortunately, I haven't got a calculator. (have) I ....
c The trouble is, I don't really understand the problem. (understand) I ....
d And my teacher never explains things to me. (explain) ....
e I think I'd prefer to be in a different class. (be) ....
f In fact, I'd rather do French instead. (do) ....
g I love France – it would be great to live there! (live) ....
h But at the moment I have to my homework! (have to do) ....

5 Complete the *wish*-sentence with the information provided.

a Juliet: 'Considering what happened later, meeting Romeo was a mistake.'
I *wish I hadn't met* him!
b Christopher Columbus: 'Sailing to America was a mistake, perhaps, and it would have been better to stay at home!'
I .... at home!
c Harry Potter: 'Learning to be a wizard has turned out to be rather dangerous. Deciding to go to a wizard school was a mistake!'
I .... school !
d Marco Polo: 'It was great being in China. Perhaps it would have been better to stay there, and not come home to Italy.'
I wish .... China.

e Newton: 'Actually the story of the apple falling on my head is true, and I can tell you it really hurt! Sitting under the apple tree was a big mistake!'

I .... tree !

f Helen of Troy: 'I didn't really like Paris very much. Running away with him was a mistake.'

I .... with him !

g Dr Frankenstein: 'This monster is causing a lot of trouble. Making him was a mistake.'

I .... him !

h Archimedes: 'Jumping out of my bath and running down the street shouting 'I've found it!' was a great idea. But it was a mistake not to put some clothes on first!'

I .... clothes on !

6 Rewrite the sentence as a complaint, using *wish* with *would* or *wouldn't*. Use contractions.

a You never hand your work in on time!   I *wish you'd hand your work in on time* .... !

b You always make so many mistakes!   I .... !

c You always drop litter on the floor!   I .... !

d You never pay attention!   I .... !

e You always talk during the test!   I .... !

f You never listen to what I'm saying!   I .... !

g You always interrupt people!   I .... !

h You always throw things across the room!   I .... !

i You never behave!   I .... !

j You always make so much noise!   I .... !

science

7 Complete the text with the verbs in brackets.

Sloths live in trees and eat mainly leaves, twigs and fruit. In fact, if you **a** (be) .... *were* .... a sloth, you **b** (spend) .... most of your life hanging upside down from a tree. This is the safest place for sloths. If a sloth **c** (stay) .... completely still, predators **d** (not realize) .... it is there, because it has green algae living on its skin, and it is difficult to see. Sloths move very slowly on the ground, but if they **e** (go) .... in water, they **f** (swim) .... extremely well. However, they have a low body temperature, and if they **g** (remain) .... too long in hot sunlight, they **h** (die) .... Sloths are not large animals, growing to about a metre in length. On the other hand, if you **i** (be) .... in North America 20,000 years ago, you **j** (see) .... a giant ground sloth, as large as an elephant! These giant sloths died out thousands of years ago. Modern sloths live in the rainforest of South America, and they are in danger, like many rainforest animals. If human beings **k** (continue) .... to destroy the rain forest, sloths **l** (become) .... extinct.

A sloth

GLOSSARY

EXTENSION ACTIVITY

1 What would your life have been like, if you had lived a hundred years ago? Write five sentences.

2 Write a list of wishes about things you want to change about yourself.

conditionals: impossible past, wishes

20 the passive and its uses

FORM

Use be + past participle to form the passive.

present simple active	We **find** oil and gas beneath the ground or sea.
present simple passive	*Oil and gas **are found** beneath the ground or sea.*
present continuous active	The police **are questioning** two men.
present continuous passive	*Two men **are being questioned** by the police.*
past simple active	Teachers **trained** Aztec boys to fight.
past simple passive	*Aztec boys **were trained** to fight.*
present perfect active	Tourism **has harmed** some countries.
present perfect passive	*Some countries **have been harmed** by tourism.*
will active	We **will choose** a new class representative on Monday.
will passive	*A new class representative **will be chosen** on Monday.*

USE

Use the passive

- to move important information (the object of the active sentence) to the beginning.
  *Two men **are being questioned** by the police.*

- when we want to be impersonal and not mention the name of the person who performs the action.
  We often use the passive in scientific or technical processes.
  *Oil and gas **are found** beneath the ground or sea.*

- when it is obvious who performed the action, eg teachers, or we do not want to use a general
  subject eg *people, they.*
  *Aztec boys **were trained** to fight.*
  *Two missing children **have been found** safe and well.*

- more often in formal speech and writing than in everyday speech.

transitive and intransitive

Verbs which have an object are called transitive verbs; verbs without an object are intransitive.
Only transitive verbs can be made passive.

transitive	**subject**	**verb**	**object**	
	I	*lost*	*my wallet*	*on the way to school.*
intransitive	*I*	*swim*	*–*	*every day.*

Use *by*

- when it is important to know the 'agent' or person who performed the action
  *Some countries have been harmed **by tourism**.*

- only when it is really necessary.
  The two men were arrested. (by the police – this is obvious)

Use *with*

- for objects which perform actions.
  *The game was played **with a ball of solid rubber**.*

1 Complete the sentence with the past simple passive form of the verb in brackets.

a In ancient times, fires (light) ....*were lit*........ to use smoke as a signal over long distances.

b Morse code (invent) .... by an American called Samuel Morse.

c The world's first television images (show) .... to scientists in Scotland in 1926.

d Radios (use) .... to broadcast coded messages during the Second World War.

e The World Wide Web (design) .... originally to make it easier for nuclear physics researchers to communicate.

f Buying books and CDs over the Internet (make) .... popular by the company Amazon.

g The first mobile phones with cameras (sell) .... in Japan.

h Vinyl albums and tapes (replace) .... by CDs, which are now being replaced by mp3.

i The first English dictionary (wrote) .... by Robert Cawdrey in 1604.

j The first mass-produced cars (introduce) .... by the Ford company in the USA.

2 Read the text and underline all the subject, verb and object structures. Then rewrite the text using present simple passive verbs. Leave out any unnecessary words.

How a toy car is made

In the factory, they use a computer to plan the exact shape of the car. They then feed this computer program into a machine, and produce a plastic prototype. Then they produce the actual toy cars in a factory abroad. As far as construction is concerned, they make the bodies of the cars from plastic. They add small electric motors to the cars, and then they paint them. They also attach licence plates. Quality control inspects the cars and then they wrap them and pack them into cardboard boxes. They ship the cars to Britain.

a As a first step, ...*a computer is used to plan the exact shape of the car.*........

b Then .... and ....

....

c The actual ....

d The bodies ....

e Small ....

Licence ....

f At the next stage, ...

g Finally, ... Britain.

3 Complete the text with either the *will* passive or present perfect passive forms of the verbs in brackets.

In recent years many plans **a** (make) <u>have been made</u> for large floating cities with living accommodation for as many as 50,000 people. One such project which **b** (advertise) .... is the Freedom Ship. According to the plans for this project, this huge ship **c** (construct) .... from smaller units, which **d** (take) .... out to sea for final assembly. The ship **e** (power) .... by 100 diesel engines, and the residents on board **f** (carry) ....

around the world continuously. The large number of people on the ship **g** (provide) .... with all kinds of entertainment and sports facilities, and modern recycling methods **h** (use) .... to save energy on board. At the time of writing, this project **i** (not build) ...., and **j** (criticize) .... by some people who say it is too expensive. We shall have to wait and see whether this ambitious plan ever becomes reality.

GLOSSARY

4 Rewrite the sentence using a present perfect passive with *by*. Leave out any unnecessary words.

a Cheaper air travel has made possible the global expansion in tourism.
   The global expansion in tourism has been made possible by cheaper air travel.

b Countries all over the world have experienced a growth in tourism.
   ....

c Millions of tourists have visited the popular Mediterranean resorts since the 1970s.
   ....

d Recently tourists have chosen more distant locations in Africa, Asia and South America.
   ....

e Mass tourism has badly affected some countries.
   ....

f International companies have built large hotels on unspoilt coastline.
   ....

g These developments have disturbed local wildlife.
   ....

h Tourists have damaged coral reefs and other habitats.
   ....

i Such developments have also displaced local people.
   ....

j Some governments have developed the idea of ecotourism to counteract some of these problems.
   ....

5 Read the information about urban development. Then complete the text with the present perfect passive or past perfect passive form of the verbs in brackets.

In many countries in recent years, areas of urban land which were once used for industrial purposes **a** (redevelop) *have been redeveloped* for other purposes. In London, for example, the Docklands **b** (transform) .... since the 1980s. The docks **c** (built) .... in the 19th century when London was a busy port, but by the 1980s, most business **d** (lose) ...., and many docks **e** (close) .... This left large areas of derelict land, and many people without jobs. Since the 1980s, £10 billion (€14.7 billion) **f** (spend) .... on the project. 600 hectares of derelict land **g** (improve) ...., 90 km of new roads **h** (build) ...., 80,000 new jobs **i** (create) .... and 24,000 new homes **j** (construct) .... In addition to this, 100,000 new trees **k** (plant) .... and 130 hectares of parks **l** (create) .... Cultural venues such as the Docklands Arena **m** (open) .... Some local people do not agree with all the things that **n** (do) ...., as houses here are expensive, and most jobs are in media, IT or business. On the other hand, a declining area of the city **o** (give) .... a new lease of life.

GLOSSARY

6A Rewrite each sentence so that it does not contain the words *someone* or *people*.

a Someone built ships with sails more than 5,000 years ago.
Ships with sails were built more than 5,000 years ago.

b Someone constructed a hot-air balloon in 1783.

c People developed the steam ship in the 19th century.

d Someone opened the first successful passenger railway in 1830.

e People started the first passenger airlines after the First World War.

6B Rewrite each sentence so that it includes the agent *by*.

f The Chinese probably printed the first books more than a thousand years ago.

g The Remington company sold the first modern typewriters in the 1870s.

h Edison recorded the first words on a gramophone record in 1877.

i The Lumière brothers created the first modern cinema in France in 1895.

j Valdemar Poulsen invented the tape recorder in 1899.

EXTENSION ACTIVITY

1 How much do you know about history? Write five sentences about famous events in the past, using these verbs: *discover, invent, paint, write, build*.

2 Write a list of five recent news events in your country. Describe what was done at a particular time.

Need more practice? Go to the Review on page 192.

21 causative *have*, verbs with two objects, passive reporting verbs

FORM

have + object + past participle

present simple	I **have my hair cut** once a month.
present continuous	They're **having their house decorated** at the moment.
past simple	We **had the computers checked** last week.
present perfect	Tom **has had his nose altered**.
going to future	I'm **going to have my photograph taken**.

Use causative *have*

● to describe a service eg painting, decorating, haircut, operation, etc that somebody does for us. We do not usually say who performed the action unless this is important.
   I'm going to have my photograph **taken**. (by a photographer = not necessary)
   I'm going to have my photograph taken **by a top fashion photographer**. (important information)

● for unfortunate events eg accident, fire, theft etc.
   Sally **has had** her car **stolen**.

We can use *get* instead of *have* in everyday speech eg *I* **get my hair cut** once a month.
Note: *Get something done* can also mean *manage to do* something.
   Did you **get your project done**?
We also use *get done* for unfortunate events when there is no agent.
   Did anyone **get hurt**?
We can also use *get* instead of *be* in the passive in everyday speech with verbs such as *invite, offer, choose, take, send* etc.
   We **got invited** to Jim's house.   She **got sent** to France on a course.

FORM

Verbs with two possible objects

buy, give, lend, make something for someone, offer, prepare something for someone, promise, sell, send, take something to someone

give	Jim **gave Alan** some **help**.	Jim **gave** some **help** to **Alan**.
take	David **took Susan** a **present**.	David **took** a **present** to **Susan**.

Verbs with two possible objects have two passive forms, but one is more commonly used.
   Alan **was given some help** by Jim.   (more common)
   Some **help was given** to Alan by Jim.
   Susan was taken a present by David.   (more common)
   A present was taken to Susan by David.

FORM

Reporting verbs

believe, expect, know, report, say, think, suppose, understand
Present simple passive + *to do / to be doing* are used for reports about the present.
*The missing painting **is believed to be** in Switzerland.*
*The government **is said to be studying** the proposal.*

Use reporting verbs and *to do / to be doing*

● when there is uncertainty about the report. This is common in news reports.
   The missing painting is in Switzerland.   (= a definite fact)
   The missing painting is believed to be in Switzerland.   (= that's what people believe)

Includes exercises from Units 20 and 21.

1 Complete each sentence using present continuous causative *have*.
   Leave out the words underlined.

   a   What are you doing on Monday?
       In the afternoon a photographer is taking my photograph.
       In the afternoon I ....*am having my photograph taken.*....

   b   What is Anna doing on Tuesday?
       In the morning a hairdresser is cutting her hair.
       In the morning she ....

   c   And what is Alan doing on Wednesday?
       In the afternoon a dentist is taking out a tooth.
       In the afternoon he ....

   d   What is happening at your house on Thursday?
       Some decorators are painting our kitchen.
       We ....

   e   Are you using your car on Friday?
       No, the garage is servicing it.
       No, I ....

   f   And what are Sue and David doing on Saturday?
       Some plumbers are fitting their new central heating.
       They ....

2 Rewrite each sentence so that it contains a past simple causative *have*. Leave out any unnecessary words.

   a   Someone broke Tim's nose while he was playing football.
       Tim ..*had his nose broken while he was playing football.*..

   b   Someone stole Maria's bike last week.
       Maria ....

   c   Someone damaged Mr Grover's car last week.
       Mr Grover ....

   d   Someone took Anna's mobile.
       Anna ....

   e   Someone sprayed paint on our garden wall.
       Our ....

   f   Someone broke into our house.
       We ....

   g   Someone knocked off one policeman's helmet.
       One policeman ....

   h   Someone smashed our windows with a brick.
       We ....

causative *have*, verbs with two objects, passive reporting verbs

3 Rewrite each sentence without the words <u>underlined</u> and using a form of causative *have*. Make any other necessary changes.

> *Cosmetic surgery, which used to be only for film stars, has recently become very popular among the population as a whole.*

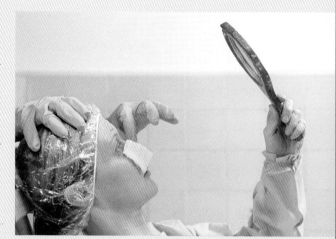

a <u>Surgeons</u> remove people's scars and blemishes.
   People have scars and blemishes removed.

b <u>They</u> also lift people's faces in order to look younger.

c In a recent poll, many people admitted that surgeons had altered their noses.
   In a recent poll,

d <u>Surgeons</u> had also reshaped the eyes of several people.

e <u>Doctors</u> had also thickened one woman's lips.

f Psychologists are worried that so many young people want doctors to change their appearance.
   Psychologists are worried that

g So if you're thinking of <u>asking a doctor to</u> perform an operation, think again.
   So if you're thinking of

h Plastic surgery can also ruin people's lives.

GLOSSARY

4 Rewrite each question so that it contains a form of *get*. Make any necessary changes.

a Did you finish your project in the end?
   Did you get your project finished in the end?

b Was David sent to the head teacher's office?

c Have you done all your homework?

d Did they choose Susan as class representative?

e When are you sorting out the school sports programme?

f Have you organized your revision?

g Was Tony injured playing basketball?

h Were you invited to Maria's party?

5 Rewrite each sentence beginning and ending as shown.

a At the end of her term at college, a multi-national company offered Emma a job in Dubai.
At the end of her term at college, Emma _was offered a job in Dubai_
by a multi-national company.

b It wasn't very well-paid, but they promised her a good position in the future.
It wasn't very well-paid, but she .... in the future.

c They sent her a letter explaining all the details.
She .... the details.

d The company explained that they would give her free accommodation.
The company explained that she .... free accommodation.

e Her parents lent her some money to buy some new clothes and a laptop.
She .... by her parents to buy some new clothes
and a laptop.

f Her fellow students gave her some CDs as a present.
She .... as a present by her fellow students.

6 Rewrite each news item beginning as shown.

a People believe that the Prime Minister is seriously ill.
The Prime Minister _is believed to be seriously ill._

b People think that she is in hospital.
She ....

c People suppose that she is flying to Washington tomorrow.
She ....

d People understand that she is remaining in London.
She ....

e People do not say that she is dangerously ill.
She ....

f People expect her to leave hospital in a few days.
She ....

g People believe that doctors are at her bedside day and night.
Doctors ....

h People know that her illness is a kind of flu.
Her illness ....

i People understand that she is taking antibiotics.
She ....

j People report that she is in good spirits.
She ....

EXTENSION ACTIVITY

1 Write a sentence describing what you have done by these people.
decorator   mechanic   photographer   tailor   burglar

2 Write a sentence describing what you have done in these places.
hairdresser's   garage   dry cleaner's   dentist's   artist's studio

causative have, verbs with two objects, passive reporting verbs

22 modals: ability, obligation (present / future)

ability: *can, can't, cannot*

Can't is the negative, with *cannot* as a formal and written form. There is no third person *-s* form.
Question forms are *Can I, Can you* etc.
Use *can / can't*

- to describe ability or lack of it.
  *Many **animals can see clearly** in the dark. **Human beings can't do** this.*
- to describe what is allowed or not allowed.
  *You **can look** at the animals in the zoo but you **can't touch** them.*
- with a future meaning.
  *Sorry, but I **can't come** to the party next week.*
- with verbs of perception: *hear, see, taste, feel, smell.*
  *What **can you** see?   I **can smell** gas!*

ability: *be able to*

This has the same meaning as *can*.
Use *be able to*

- instead of *can*.
  *Many animals **are able to see** in the dark.*
- when *can* is unsuitable. Because *can* has only present and past forms, we use *be able* to for other tenses, and infinitive form.
  *I **haven't been able to finish** my project.   We **hope to be able to visit** you next month.*

obligation: *have to / has to*

The forms follow *have: I have to, he / she has to* etc; *do I have to, does she have to; I don't have to* etc.
Use *have to / has to*

- to describe what is necessary, a rule, or something we do because other people tell us to.
  *Baby birds **have to learn** how to fly or they won't survive.*
  ***Do we have to buy** another ticket to see this part of the castle?*

The negative form, *don't / doesn't have to*, is used to describe something unnecessary.
  *I **don't have to go** to work tomorrow. There's a holiday.*

obligation: *must / mustn't*

The negative is *mustn't*, with *must not* as a formal and written form. There is no third person *-s* form.
Question form is *must I, must you* etc.
Use *must* to describe something we personally think is necessary and important to do.

- There is sometimes little difference between first person *I must* and *I have to*.
  *Sorry, I really **have to go** now.   Sorry, I really **must go** now!*
- In other contexts, there is a difference.
  *You **must be** more careful!   (= personal opinion of the speaker)*
  *We **have to wear** safety goggles.   (= an 'outside' opinion or rule)*
- We usually use the question form of *have to* for *must*.
  ***Do I have to sit** here?*
- We use *mustn't* when we think an action is against the rules.
  *You **mustn't throw** things in the science lab! It's dangerous!*
- Compare *mustn't* and *don't have to*.
  *You **mustn't use** a pencil.   (it's not allowed)*
  *You **don't have to use** a pen.   (it's not necessary – use a pen or a pencil)*

Use *should, ought to*

● to say what we think is right or correct, or is a good idea in your opinion. This is not as strong as *must*.
  You **should pay** more attention.   You **shouldn't talk** so much.

● to give advice.
  I think you **should study** biology next year.

● in the same way. *Ought to / ought not to* has the same meaning as *should / should not*.

Use *had better*

● to say what we think someone should do. There is only one form *had better / 'd better*. The negative is
  had better not.
  You'd better wear your raincoat. It's going to rain.   **You'd better not wait** too long. You'll be late.

Use *need to*

● with the same meaning as *have to*. *Need to* is not a modal verb.
  You **need to** work harder.   You **don't need to come** tomorrow.
  Do I **need to bring** my dictionary?

Need is a modal verb and has no third person form. It is mainly used in questions and negatives, and is more formal in use.
  Need I say more?   He **need not take** the exam.

....

1 Complete each sentence with *can* or *can't* + the verb in brackets. Use a form of *be able to* if *can / can't* is not possible.

a That shelf is too high. I (reach) ......*can't reach*...... it.

b What's that noise? I (hear) .... something.

c There's something wrong with this door. I (open) .... it.

d I'm really hungry! I (take) .... my lunch break yet.

e Sorry, I (come) .... tomorrow. I'll try and see you next week.

f I really want (use) .... a computer properly.

g Don't push Harry in the water. He (swim) ....

h I feel terrible. I (sleep) .... for the past couple of nights.

2 Complete the sentence with *must* or *mustn't*. They are all strange but true laws.

a In New Hampshire, USA, you ......*mustn't*...... pick up seaweed from the beach.

b In Louisiana, USA, schoolchildren .... call their teachers *Sir* or *Ma'am*.

c In Canada you .... let a llama eat grass in a national park.

d In Italy, a man .... wear a skirt in public.

e In Illinois, USA, you .... use the steering wheel when you drive a car.

f In Michigan, USA, people .... swear in front of women and children.

g In Baltimore, Maryland, USA, you .... take a lion into a cinema.

h In Kentucky, USA, everyone .... take at least one bath every year.

3 Complete the sentence with *mustn't*, or *don't / doesn't have to*.

a You ......*mustn't*...... stand on the desk. You'll break it.

b We .... take an umbrella. I'm sure it isn't going to rain.

c You .... put a stamp on this letter. It says FREEPOST on it.

d We .... forget to take the presents with us when we go.

e In our country children .... go to school on Saturday.

f You .... touch the ball. It's against the rules.

modals: ability, obligation (present / future)

87

4 Complete the text with the verbs in brackets and a form of *can* or *have to*.

Rapid population growth **a** (cause) _can cause_ problems. The government **b** (provide) .... more hospitals, schools and jobs, farmers **c** (produce) .... more food and all the extra people **d** (have) .... homes. In a less economically developed country, the economy **e** (grow) .... fast enough to deal with the problems. Many countries realize that they **f** (control) .... population growth. Some countries believe they can encourage family planning through education and publicity. Other countries believe that they have such a serious problem that they **g** (take) .... special measures to control the number of people. In China, for example, there is a 'one child' policy. Couples **h** (ask) .... permission from the government to marry, and women **i** (be) .... at least 25 years old. The couple then **j** (ask) .... permission to have a child, and are allowed only one.

GLOSSARY

5 Complete the text to give advice on how to deal with a snake bite using *should* or *shouldn't*. Check the factual answers on page 208.

a You ___should___ stop the victim moving too much.

b You .... give the victim a painkiller.

c You .... check the person's temperature, breathing and blood pressure.

d If the snake is dead, you .... keep it for later examination.

e You .... cut into the bite.

f You .... keep the person calm.

g You .... try to suck out the poison with your mouth.

h You .... give them food and drink.

6 Add a comment to each situation, using the pronoun in brackets and an idea from the list with *had better*.

take an umbrella	don't play in the match	check it in the dictionary	leave now
wear a hat	don't wake him up	take some sandwiches	call a taxi

a I think it's going to rain.   (we) _We'd better take an umbrella._

b It's a long way to the station.   (you) ....

c You don't look very well.   (you) ....

d We might get hungry later.   (we) ....

e It's going to be hot today.   (you) ....

f The last train leaves in fifteen minutes.   (we) ....

g He's still asleep.   (we) ....

h That word doesn't look right.   (you) ....

maths

7 Read these test tips for maths. Then complete each sentence so that it contains the word or words in capitals. Leave out any unnecessary words.

a It's important for you to think about all the information given.   NEED TO
You   *need to think about all the information given.*

b Don't worry about spelling, but you should try to be as accurate as you can.   NEEDN'T
You

c It's necessary for you to identify all the necessary steps to solve a problem.   NEED TO
You

d You have to understand technical words, eg equation.   NEED TO
You

e It's vital for you to be able to use methods of multiplication and division.   NEED TO
You

f It's important for you to know when to use an example.   NEED TO
You

GLOSSARY

8 Choose the correct option, A, B, C or D, to complete the sentence.

a Are you any good at athletics? How fast ___D___ you run?
b You _____ take some money with you in case you need it.
c I think that was the last bus. _____ look for a taxi.
d I'm really tired, but luckily I _____ get up early in the morning.
e You _____ look at other students' work. It's against the rules.
f 'My tooth really hurts!' 'I think you _____ go to the dentist's.'
g Sorry, but my train is at 6.00. I _____ leave now.
h You _____ eat so many sweets. They aren't good for you.

a	A *should*	B *must*	C *need*	D *can*
b	A *have to*	B *shouldn't*	C *can*	D *should*
c	A *We needn't*	B *We'd better*	C *We're able to*	D *We don't have to*
d	A *can't*	B *don't have to*	C *had better*	D *shouldn't*
e	A *had better not*	B *needn't*	C *don't have to*	D *mustn't*
f	A *mustn't*	B *needn't*	C *ought to*	D *can*
g	A *have to*	B *shouldn't*	C *mustn't*	D *can*
h	A *can't*	B *don't have to*	C *shouldn't*	D *needn't*

EXTENSION ACTIVITY

1 Make a list of ten things you have to do at school or at work.

2 Give some advice about what you should do if you want to learn a foreign language well.

modals: ability, obligation (present / future)

23 modals: ability, obligation, criticism (past)

past ability: *could, couldn't, was / were able to*

Could / couldn't are past forms of can / can't. Could not is used in formal speech and writing.
Use *could / couldn't*

- to describe past ability.
  *We don't know how fast Ancient Greek athletes **could run**.*
- to describe what was allowed or not allowed.
  *Women **couldn't compete or watch** the ancient Olympic Games.*

See also **Units 22** and **24** for other meanings of *could*.
We can use *was / were able to* in the place of *could / couldn't* to describe past ability in general.
  *He tried hard but **wasn't able to win** the race.*
We use *was / were able* to, not *could / couldn't*, when we mean that we could do something and we actually did it.
  *One runner fell badly, but fortunately **was able to finish** the race.*

past obligation: *had to, didn't have to*

Had to / didn't have to / did you have to etc are past forms of *have to* and *must*.
Use *had to*

- to describe past obligation, for both *must* and *have to*.
  *Athletes who cheated in the Olympic Games **had to pay** for a statue of the god Zeus.*
  *Of course, in ancient times athletes **didn't have to take** drugs tests.*

past necessity: *needed to, didn't need to, needn't have*

Use *needed to* (regular verb) to describe what was necessary.
  *He **needed to stop** for a drink, but he kept running.*
Use *didn't need to* to describe what was not necessary.
  *In ancient Greece, winning athletes **didn't need to work** again.*
The question form is *did you need to* etc.

Use *needn't have* + past participle (a form of modal verb *need*) to explain that someone did something, but what they did was unnecessary.
  *I was worried because I thought that my tickets for the Games wouldn't arrive in time. But I **needn't have worried**. They arrived this morning!*

past criticism: *should have / shouldn't have, ought to have, ought not to have*

Use *should have / shouldn't have* + past participle to criticize a past action.
  *'You started before the gun! You **shouldn't have done** that.'*
  *'But it was an accident!' 'Well, you **should have been** more careful!'*
Use *ought to have / ought not to have* + past participle in the same way.

1 Complete the sentence with *could* or *couldn't*.

a The suitcase was so heavy I .... couldn't .... lift it.

b I learned to play the piano when I was ten but I .... only play one song.

c I have to go home soon, my parents said I .... stay out late.

d We don't know how, but the ancient Egyptians .... move huge pieces of stone to build the pyramids.

e Frank Sinatra .... sing really well but he .... write his own songs.

f He .... do the homework because he lost his book.

g The Britons .... make soap before the Romans.

h 100 years ago, most people .... travel abroad because it was too expensive.

i The class worked hard so they .... leave early.

j When you were younger, ... you play any musical instruments?

2 Complete the comment on the situation with either *didn't need to* or *needn't have (done)* and the verb in brackets.

a I worked fast and finished my project on time, but now our teacher has given the class three more weeks.

(work) .... I needn't have worked .... so hard!

b At least I managed to do it without working at the weekend.

(work) .... the weekend.

c And although I thought I would have to borrow some books, in the end this wasn't necessary.

(borrow) .... any books.

d But I gave up a lot of my spare time when I didn't have to!

(give) .... so much of my spare time.

e I spent a lot of time reading and writing every evening.

(spend) .... reading and writing every evening.

f But I managed to do it on my own, and I didn't ask for any help.

(ask) .... any help.

g And I didn't give up playing tennis.

(play) .... tennis.

h I spent a lot of time using the Internet unnecessarily.

(use) .... so much.

i But it was quite easy in the end, and I did it without thinking too hard!

(think) .... too hard.

j In the end, I worried about it a lot, but this wasn't necessary!

(worry) .... it so much

3 Complete the text with *had to, didn't have to, could* or *couldn't* + the verbs in brackets.

A young chimney sweep

Life for children in Victorian Britain was very different from the life children lead today. Firstly, Victorian children **a** (go) *didn't have to go* to school, and in any case poor families **b** (pay) .... for lessons because they didn't have enough money. So children **c** (find) .... jobs at an early age, starting in the coal mines, for example, at the age of five. The more fortunate children became apprentices, learning a trade and working at the same time. Such children **d** (work) .... for fifty or sixty hours a week, usually for very low wages, and **e** (sign) .... an agreement which kept them with the same master for a number of years. The worst jobs were in factories, where many children under the age of nine were employed. Children were also employed to clean chimneys, and known as 'chimney sweeps'. These children **f** (climb) .... up chimneys and clean them. They **g** (be) .... small, or else they would get stuck in the chimney. Using children to do this job was banned in 1840, but employers then **h** (use) .... special brushes, which were expensive, and so they continued to use children. The employers **i** (pay) .... a small fine if they were caught. After the Factory Act of 1833, employers in textile factories **j** (employ) .... children under the age of nine, though children aged nine to 11 **k** (work) .... eight hours a day. However, nothing changed in coal mines and in other factories, where employers **l** (put) .... children to work in dangerous and dirty conditions. It wasn't until 1847 that employers **m** (limit) .... the working day to ten hours, for both children and adults.

GLOSSARY

4 Comment on the situation saying what the person *should have done* or *shouldn't have done*. Use the verb in brackets.

a The ancient Greek philosopher Aristotle said that a heavy object always falls faster than a light object, but he didn't conduct an experiment to prove it, and in fact he was wrong. (conduct) .... *He should have conducted an experiment.*

b The English scientist Francis Bacon wanted to find out whether snow would preserve a dead chicken. He spent a long time in the cold doing this, and then died of a chill. (wear) ....

c Scientists often test things on themselves or their students. In the case of von Liebig, a German chemist, he dropped acid onto the arms of his students to see what would happen. Unfortunately the acid burned their skin very badly. (test) ....

d Other scientists injure themselves by accident. Pierre Curie carried radioactive substances in his trouser pockets. This burned holes in his pockets and injured his legs. (carry) ....

e Another problem is that of fame. In some cases, scientists have their work done for them by others. The astronomer William Herschel made many important discoveries, but he was helped a lot by his sister Caroline. Unfortunately, he didn't mention this to other scientists. (told people) ....

f Other scientists get into political trouble. The French chemist Lavoisier discovered how oxygen is used in burning, and in rusting. However, the French revolutionary authorities arrested him because he was also a tax collector, and in 1794 he was executed. (execute) ....

history

5 Complete the text with *could, couldn't, had to, didn't have to, didn't need to, needn't have, should have* or *shouldn't have* and the verbs in brackets. Not all are used in the text.

History contains a lot of stories about people who **a** (be) ...*should have been*... a little bit more careful. In 1576 the explorer Sir Martin Frobisher sailed to the north of Canada trying to find a way to Asia. Unfortunately, he **b** (find) .... it, but during the voyage, his men landed on Baffin Island as they **c** (look for) .... food and shelter. Here he discovered some rocks which he thought contained gold. When he returned to England he showed the piece of rock to people who agreed that it was gold, and Frobisher returned to the island with a larger ship. It was a difficult journey, as the ship **d** (avoid) .... huge icebergs. On the island there were polar bears which **e** (kill) .... a man quite easily. And Frobisher was worried that someone else would get to the gold first. Perhaps he **f** (tell) .... so many people about his discovery, he thought. But he **g** (worry) .... about his secret. He found the place again, and his men **h** (work) .... in the freezing weather to dig for the gold. They returned to England again, and this time he **i** (stop) .... his discovery from becoming generally known. More and more people wanted to go to Baffin Island, and the next year the ships came back with hundreds of tonnes of gold. Unfortunately, this is where things went wrong. When Frobisher tried to sell the gold, he discovered that perhaps he **j** (show) .... it to more people in the first place. The people he had showed it to had been wrong. They **k** (tell) .... the difference between gold and iron pyrite, a compound of iron and sulphur. Everyone laughed at Sir Martin and his men, and he **l** (admit) .... that he had made a mistake.

that's why they call it Fool's gold

GLOSSARY

EXTENSION ACTIVITY

1 Think about your first school. Make a list of thing you had to do, or didn't have to do.

2 Make a list of things that famous people in the past should or shouldn't have done.

*Need more practice? Go to the **Review** on page 192.*

modals: ability, obligation, criticism (past)

24 modals: possibility, uncertainty, certainty (present / future)

possibility and uncertainty

Use *may, might, could* + bare infinitive

- to describe things that will possibly happen.
  *The next earthquake **may** / **might** / **could happen** tomorrow.*

Use *may not* and *might not* + bare infinitive

- to describe things that will possibly not happen in the future.
  *The next earthquake **may not** / **might not happen** for another fifty years. It's impossible to predict exactly.*

possibility

Use *can* + bare infinitive

- to describe a possibility in general, but not with a future time reference.
  *During an earthquake, people **can suffer** injuries when parts of buildings fall into the street.*

certainty

Use *will* + bare infinitive

- when we are certain something will happen in the future.
  *During a strong earthquake, some older buildings **will collapse**.*

Use *must* + bare infinitive

- when we are certain something is true (usually with *be*), or when we suppose what a situation is like.
  *I've never been in an earthquake. **It must be** really frightening.*
  (= I'm certain of that.)
  *You've done a lot of work. You **must feel** really tired!*
  (= I'm sure you do.)

negative certainty

Use *can't* + bare infinitive

- when we are certain something is **not** true (usually with *be*) or impossible.
  *That **can't be** an earthquake! We don't have earthquakes here!*
  *You **can't know** the answer already! That's impossible!*

1 Complete the sentence with *may* or *may not*.

a They sky looks a bit grey. It ....*may*........ rain later.

b I don't think the new secretary likes her job. She .... stay very long.

c If you leave right now, you .... be on time.

d In the future when technology has improved, it .... be possible to build a spaceship that can travel to distant planets.

e I'm not sure if Sue's at home today. She .... have come back from her holiday yet.

f The Prime Minister .... fly to India later this week for talks on reducing global warming.

g I .... go to the party because I'm not feeling very well.

h According to astronomers, there .... be intelligent life on other planets. We don't know because we haven't travelled very far into space yet.

i Jarek .... have an mp3 player. Ask him if you can borrow it.

j Juan .... pass his exams if he revises every day.

2 <u>Underline</u> the correct form.

a Even if you don't live in a Mediterranean country, you *can* / <u>*might*</u> already know about earthquakes.

b They *can* / *might* be frequent in some countries, though most are too small to be noticed by humans and you *may not* / *cannot* even notice when one occurs.

c Earthquakes are the result of movements of the Earth's tectonic plates, though human activity *may* / *will* be responsible.

d Most earthquakes happen at depths of 20 or 30 km, though they *will* / *can* be as deep as 600 km.

e What is it like to experience an earthquake? If the tremor is very small you *might* / *couldn't* feel nothing at all.

f In a stronger tremor, there is more movement, and so the furniture in the room *can* / *will* move.

g Tall buildings *will* / *may* definitely move a little, and, depending on how well the building is constructed, cracks *will* / *might* appear in the walls.

h In a major earthquake, the building *could* / *can* collapse completely, though with modern earthquake-proof buildings, this is unlikely.

3 Rewrite the sentence so that it contains the word in capitals.

a I'm sure you know the difference between a solid and a gas!   MUST
   You must know the difference between a solid and a gas!

b If a substance does not contain hydrogen, then we are sure that it isn't an acid.   CAN'T

c If we put some litmus paper in a solution and it turns red, then we are sure that the solution is an acid.   MUST

d If we add a substance to a red cabbage solution and it stays red, then we are sure the substance isn't an alkali.   CAN'T

e If we add a substance to a red cabbage solution and it turns green, then the substance is sure to be an alkali.   MUST

f If we put some litmus paper in a solution and it turns red, then we are sure that the solution isn't an alkali.   CAN'T

g If it's not an acid, or an alkali, then it's sure to be neutral.   MUST

h If we use a universal indicator to check a substance, and it turns purple, then we are sure that the substance isn't an acid.   CAN'T

4 Rewrite each sentence so that it begins as shown and contains the word in capitals.

a If the world becomes warmer, as some scientists predict, it is possible that Europe will change dramatically over the next century.   COULD
   If the world becomes warmer *as some scientists predict, Europe could change dramatically over the next century.*

b It is possible that there will be no snow-covered mountains in Europe by then.   MIGHT
   There

c And it's possible that areas in the south of Europe will become deserts.   COULD
   And areas

d It's also possible that heavy rain will become normal in northern Europe.   MIGHT

e While it's possible that southern Europe will be always short of water.   COULD
   While southern Europe

f It's possible that there will be some benefits for some people.　　　MIGHT

There _____

g It's possible that summers will become longer, and hotter, and winters will become

warmer.　　　COULD

Summers _____

h On the other hand, it's possible that some species of plants and animals will become

extinct.　　　MIGHT

On the other hand, some species of plants and animals _____

---

5 Choose <u>all</u> the possible answers, A, B or C, for each gap.

Most of us enjoy a good night's sleep, but we **a** _A, B_ not realize just how important sleep is. Everyone knows that without sleep for a night or two, a person **b** _____ find it hard to think well. After three nights without sleep, you **c** _____ start to see things, and you **d** _____ begin to lose your sense of reality. In experiments, rats which are not allowed to sleep **e** _____ actually die, which seems to prove that sleep **f** _____ be very important. We know that children who do not sleep enough can fail to grow properly, as growth hormones **g** _____ be active while the body is asleep. Lack of sleep **h** _____ also damage the immune system, so you **i** _____ fall ill more often. Scientists don't know exactly what sleep is for and why humans need so much of it, but they believe that it **j** _____ give the body a chance to repair muscles and replace cells. It **k** _____ also give the brain the opportunity to organize memory, and some experts believe that dreams **l** _____ help in this process. The brain also needs to rest, so sleep **m** _____ give the brain a chance to 'recharge' its batteries. Obviously, sleep **n** _____ also be related to the fact that there are hours of darkness when our activities are limited. Another possible reason for sleeping is that if we didn't sleep and save some energy, we **o** _____ have to eat a lot more food.

a	A *may*	B *might*	C *must*	**i**	A *might*	B *must*	C *could*
b	A *can*	B *will*	C *must*	**j**	A *might*	B *can't*	C *will*
c	A *can*	B *could*	C *might*	**k**	A *might*	B *could*	C *may*
d	A *can't*	B *must*	C *could*	**l**	A *could*	B *can't*	C *may*
e	A *might*	B *can*	C *will*	**m**	A *might*	B *can*	C *can't*
f	A *will*	B *must*	C *can't*	**n**	A *must*	B *can*	C *can't*
g	A *can*	B *can't*	C *may*	**o**	A *can't*	B *will*	C *might*
h	A *can*	B *may*	C *could*				

GLOSSARY

EXTENSION ACTIVITY

1 Make some predictions about how your life could change in the next 20 years.

2 What do you think it must be like to be an astronaut? Use these ideas: *food, feelings, sleep, washing, how you spend the time, training.*

*Need more practice? Go to the **Review** on page 192.*

social studies

modals: possibility, uncertainty, certainty (present / future)

25 modals: possibility, uncertainty, certainty (past)

Use *could*, *may*, *might* + *have* + past participle

- to describe things that possibly happened in the past.
  *I don't know where my bag is. I suppose someone else **might have taken** / **could have taken** it by mistake.*
  *Scientists now believe that ice **may have shaped** the surface of the planet Mars.*

Use *could*, *might* + *have* + past participle

- to make a contrast between what was possible in the past and what actually happened.
  *That was a stupid thing to do! You **might have hurt** someone.*
  *It was lucky you didn't light the gas. It **could have exploded**.*

- to criticize someone's actions.
  ***You might have told me** the bus left at 3.00! I missed it!*

Use *can't have* + past participle

- when we are certain something was not true.
  *I still haven't heard from Peter. He **can't have got** my message.*

Use *must have* + past participle

- when we are certain something was true.
  *Congratulations on your exam results. You **must have been** really pleased when you heard the news.*
  *After the volcanic eruption on the Greek island of Santorini in about 1650 BC, there **must have been** a huge tsunami.*

Use *could*, *may* and *might* and *could have*, *may have*, *might have*

- in conditional sentences, when the results are not certain.
  *If you **heat** the solution too quickly, it **may** / **might** / **could** explode.*
  *If we **found** water on Mars, we **could use** it to make rocket fuel.*
  *If the dinosaurs **had survived**, they **might have stopped** mammals developing.*
  *If you **hadn't reminded** me about the party, I **might have forgotten** all about it.*

1 Complete the comment using the word in capitals.

a You almost dropped the computer and you nearly damaged it.   COULD
You   *could have damaged the computer!*

b You weren't careful when you were carrying it.   MIGHT
You

c It would have been a good idea to ask for help!   MIGHT
You

d You pulled out the sheet of paper and you nearly broke the printer.   COULD
You

e You opened an e-mail and the computer nearly got a virus.   COULD
The computer

f Why didn't you check the name of the sender!   MIGHT
You

g The computer almost crashed and you would have lost all your work.   COULD
You

h That was nearly a very serious problem.   COULD
That

i You didn't tell me you hadn't used a computer before!   MIGHT
You

j You didn't turn the computer off when you finished!   MIGHT
You

2 Complete the sentence using the word in capitals.

a Don't go near the edge. You'll fall!   COULD
If you   *go near the edge you could fall*

b You rescued me and I didn't drown.   MIGHT
If you

c Nobody saw Tom come in late, and he didn't get into trouble.   COULD
If somebody

d Run a bit faster! Maybe you'll win the race!   MIGHT
If you

e Maria's explanation wasn't detailed. We didn't believe her.   MIGHT
If Maria's

f Don't lift such heavy weights. You'll hurt yourself!   COULD
If you

g Put your wallet in your pocket! Perhaps someone will steal it!   COULD
If you

h Lucky you didn't drop the plates and break them!   COULD
If you

i Phone him and perhaps he'll still be at home.   MIGHT
If you

j United didn't score an early goal, and they didn't win.   MIGHT
If

3 Rewrite the sentence using the word in capitals.

a Some people think it is possible that the ancient Egyptians crossed the Atlantic.   MIGHT

   The ancient Egyptians might have crossed the Atlantic.

b They think it is possible that the Egyptians traded with America more than 3,000 years ago.   COULD

c Traces of tobacco have been found in Egyptian mummies and it's possible that this came from Central America.   MAY

d The discovery of silk in mummies also suggests that it's possible the Egyptians traded with China.   COULD

e And because there are pyramids in Central America, it's possible that the Mayas got the idea for building pyramids from Egypt.   MIGHT

f On the other hand, as Egyptian pyramids and Maya pyramids are so different, it's possible that the two civilizations had similar ideas.   MAY

g There has even been a claim that it was possibly aliens from another planet who built the Mayan pyramids.   MIGHT

h According to this theory, it's possible that the aliens used the pyramids as landing places for their flying saucers.   COULD

4 Rewrite the sentences about the conquests of the Spanish in South America using the word in capitals. Leave out 'I imagine…'

a I imagine the local people were shocked when they saw the Spanish armies.   MUST

   The local people must have been shocked when they saw the Spanish armies.

b I imagine they didn't know where the Spanish came from.   CAN'T

c I imagine they soon realized that they were enemies.   MUST

d I imagine they weren't aware of the invaders' intentions.   CAN'T

e I imagine they wondered whether they were gods.   MUST

f I imagine the Spanish didn't expect to beat the local people so easily.   CAN'T

g I imagine they thought they would be killed.   MUST

h I imagine they didn't realize what the Incas were like.   CAN'T

i I imagine the local people gave up when faced by horses and guns.   MUST

j I imagine the Spanish didn't expect to find so much gold.   CAN'T

5 Rewrite the two sentences as one *if*-sentence, containing *could have (done)* or *might have (done)*. Leave out any unnecessary words.

a The Trojans took the wooden horse into Troy. If they hadn't, perhaps they would have won the war.

If the Trojans hadn't taken the wooden horse into Troy, they might / could have won the war.

b Alexander the Great died at an early age. If he hadn't, perhaps he would have conquered the whole world.

c The Romans spent a lot of time fighting among themselves. If they hadn't, perhaps their empire would have lasted longer.

d The medieval Europeans didn't know that America existed. If they had, perhaps they would have gone there sooner.

e The Aztecs thought the Spanish used magic powers. If they hadn't, perhaps they would have beaten them.

f The Spanish didn't succeed in invading Britain in 1588. If they had, perhaps they would have then conquered all of Europe.

---

history

6 Read the text. Then write eight sentences explaining what people think might have happened to the Mayas.

Nobody is quite sure what exactly happened to the Mayan civilization. We know that in 900 AD their cities were still prosperous, but a hundred years later they had been abandoned. A number of theories have been put forward to explain this. One theory is that the Mayan ruling class died out because rulers did not work and so became unhealthy, and there was nobody to tell the farmers what to do. Another idea is that farmers were unable to grow enough food to support large populations in cities. Other people believe that a natural disaster, such as an earthquake, occurred, the cities were destroyed, and the people never moved back. Or perhaps another Mexican people conquered the Mayas, and destroyed their cities. Another theory is that there was a revolution, in which the farmers killed their rulers. Some experts believe that an epidemic of some kind caused the disappearance of the Mayas. Others think that the Mayan cities suffered from an environmental disaster, caused by drought or overproduction. Finally, some people believe that the people abandoned their cities because their priests told them to do it.

a *The Mayan ruling class might have died out because rulers did not work.*

b

c

d

e

f

g

h

GLOSSARY

modals: possibility, uncertainty, certainty (past)

EXTENSION ACTIVITY

Make two comments about each situation, saying what might have happened.

Your wallet is missing. A friend hasn't called you for several weeks.
Your English teacher hasn't arrived for the class.

26 modals: request, permission, offer, suggestion, advice, *will* as obligation

requests

A request is a way of politely asking someone to do something. The kind of request we use depends on where we are, who we are talking to, and what we want the person to do. Some forms are considered to be more polite than others.

Polite	Can you help me with the computer?
More polite	Could you help me with the computer?
	Would you help me with the computer?
	Do you think you could help me with the computer?
	Could you possibly help me with the computer?
	Do you mind helping me with the computer?
	Would you mind helping me with the computer?
Responses	Sure. / Of course. / No problem.

asking permission

We ask permission when we want to be allowed to do something. Some forms are considered to be more polite than others.

Polite	Can I leave early?	Yes, you can. / No, you can't.
More polite	Could I leave early?	That's all right. / Sorry, no.
	Do you think I could leave early?	
	May I leave early?	
	Do you mind if I leave early?	
	Is it all right if I leave early?	

making offers

We make an offer when we ask if someone wants us to do something, or say that we will do it.

> Shall I turn on the light? Yes, please.
> I'll turn on the light. Thanks.

Making an offer can also mean asking someone if they want something.

> Would you like a glass of water? Yes please. / No thanks.

making a promise

> I'll be back in five minutes. I won't do it again, I promise.

making suggestions and giving advice

A suggestion is an idea about what we or other people could do.

Let's go to the library and look it up.	Good idea.
How about going to the library and looking it up?	
Shall we go to the library and look it up?	
Why don't we go to the library and look it up?	(Why don't you, doesn't she, etc)
We could go to the library and look it up.	

Giving advice involves telling another person what they should do.

I think / I don't think you should make a decision now.
You shouldn't make a decision now.
If I were you, I wouldn't make a decision now.
I'd make a decision now, if I were you.

will as obligation

In formal language and writing we can use *will* to describe a rule.

> All students **will wait** outside the examination room until told to enter.

1 <u>Underline</u> the correct form.

a I have an appointment at the dentist's at 4.00.
Would I / <u>May I</u> leave half an hour early?

b John, you're nearest the window. *Could you /*
Could I open it please?

c *Would you mind taking / Do you mind if I take* this
note to the teachers' room for me?

d Those books must be heavy. *Shall you / Shall I*
carry some of them?

e If I were you, *I wouldn't leave / you shouldn't leave*
your bag by the door.

f *I don't think you should spend /*
Why don't you spend so much time
playing computer games.

g *Do you think I could explain / Do you think*
you could explain what this means?

h I haven't got time to explain now. *Let's ask / Why*
don't you ask me again tomorrow?

i *Would you like / Do you mind* more paper?

j *Can you / May you* let me have your project
tomorrow?

2 Choose the correct form, A, B or C, to complete the sentence.

a ......*B*...... sit here, or do you want me to sit somewhere else?

b I'm sorry I haven't got my homework. .... forget it again.

c I don't think you've understood this. .... look at Unit 12 again.

d Good morning, welcome to our school. .... help you?

e We need to talk about our group presentation for Friday. ....
meet after school tomorrow?

f Your leg is certainly badly bruised. I wouldn't carry on playing, ...

g That's not a very nice way to talk to other people. .... speak like that.

h Mrs Allan is leaving at the end of term. .... buy her a present.

i I can't talk to you at the moment, I'm busy. .... wait outside for
a few minutes?

j I don't think I can do this on my own. .... helping me?

I can't talk to you at the moment,
I'm busy.

a A *Could you*   B *Shall I*   C *Why don't we*
b A *Do you mind if I* B *If I were you I wouldn't* C *I won't*
c A *If I were you*   B *Do you think I could*   C *I think you should*
d A *May I*   B *Would you mind*   C *Let's*
e A *How about*   B *Why don't we*   C *If I were you, I'd*
f A *you shouldn't*   B *shall I*   C *if I were you*
g A *I don't think you should* B *Is it all right if I* C *Would you mind*
h A *Let's*   B *Do you mind if I*   C *How about*
i A *If I were you I'd* B *Do you think you could* C *May I*
j A *Would you like*   B *I think you should*   C *Do you mind*

3 Complete each sentence with one suitable word.

a I've got an idea. .....*Shall*..... we record the
conversation on tape?

b Do you think you .... go next door
and borrow a piece of chalk?

c If I .... you, I'd pay more attention.

d Would you .... carrying this?

e Perhaps playing football isn't such a good idea.
How .... going to the gym instead?

f It's cold. .... I close the window, please?

g Is it all right .... we go and work in the
library?

h I .... leave your books on top of the
radiator, if I were you.

i I know, ... ask Mr Jones to help us.

j You waste a lot of time when you work with Helen.
I think you .... work with someone else.

4 Match sentences **1** to **10** with sentences **a** to **j**.

a Giving up maths is quite an important decision. ___9___

b Could you possibly give me a hand with these books?

c Well done, you've worked very hard for the past hour.

d I think we should get together and talk about our presentation before we do it in class.

e You've done a lot of work, and I think you are ready for the exam.

f Would you mind staying behind for a few minutes?

g I've got a really bad headache.

h We've kicked the ball into one of the gardens over there.

i I'm sorry I behaved so badly.

j You should be able to see the cells if you use the microscope properly.

1 I don't think you should worry about it.
2 I think you should have another look.
3 I won't do it again.
4 I'd like to have a word with you about something.
5 Yes of course. Where do you want me to put them?
6 Shall I climb over the wall and get it?
7 Would you like a break now?
8 May I go out for a few minutes?
9 If I were you, I'd talk to your parents about it.
10 Why don't we meet before school tomorrow?

5 Rewrite the sentence so that it contains the word in capitals.

a Do you mind if I keep my coat on?   RIGHT
   Is it all right if I keep my coat on?

b Do you want me to give out the books?   SHALL

c If I were you, I'd buy a dictionary.   SHOULD

d Can you share with Mary?   MIND

e Why don't we play volleyball for a change?   HOW

f I promise not to forget my homework.   WON'T

g Could you explain what this means?   DO

h I think you should read it again.   IF

i Do I have your permission to leave the room?   MAY

j I wouldn't touch that if I were you.   DON'T

6 Rewrite each sentence so that it begins as shown and has the same meaning.

a Do you want to go to lunch now?
Would ...*you like to go to lunch now?*.........

b Could you collect in the homework please?
Do you think ....

c Let's have another look at the table on page 218.
Why ....

d I think you should revise all of Unit 6.
If ....

e Would you like me to explain it again?
Shall ....

f Would you mind staying behind for a moment?
Can ....

g May I sit near the front, please?
Is ....

h We could look for the information on the Internet.
How ....

the arts

7 Complete the dialogue with the words in brackets and the phrases on page 102.
More than one answer may be possible.

Antonia: I need to know the plot of Antony and Cleopatra for English. **a** (you / tell me) *Could you tell me?*

Martine: OK. **b** (you / make notes / so you don't forget?) ....

Antonia: That's a good idea. So, what's it about?

Martine: Antony is a general in the Roman Army, and Cleopatra is the Queen of Egypt.

Antonia: c (speak / more slowly?) .... I can't write very quickly.

Martine: OK. Antony is in love with Cleopatra, but the Romans don't approve of their relationship. While in Egypt, he hears that his wife has died and an enemy of Caesar, Pompey, is building an army to take power. **d** (speak / more slowly?) ....

Antonia: No, that's fine. **e** (you / what happens next?) ....

Martine: OK. Antony goes back to Rome and marries Caesar's sister Octavia, to show he is still loyal to the Empire. Pompey and Caesar agree not to fight, and Antony and his new wife go to Athens. But Caesar breaks his promise, fights Pompey and wins. When Antony finds out about Caesar, he sends Octavia back to Rome and returns to Egypt, where he recruits an army and prepares to fight Caesar. **f** (tell you / who wins?) ....

Antonia: Yes, please.

Martine: Antony wins a few battles but he thinks that Cleopatra has betrayed him, and he vows to kill her. She is so scared that she pretends to have committed suicide, and when Antony hears this, he stabs himself.

Antonia: g (stop please?) .... That's a really horrible story!

Martine: h (read the play) .... The language is a bit difficult but it's very beautiful. **i** (we / go to the library?) ....

Antonia: OK, **j** (we / go now) .... Thanks for your help.

GLOSSARY

modals: request, permission, offer, suggestion, advice, *will* as obligation

EXTENSION ACTIVITY

Write examples of: *a request, asking permission, making an offer, making a promise* and *giving advice.*

27 countable and uncountable

- most nouns add –s to form the plural
- there are irregular nouns like *man / men, knife / knives, life / lives, loaf / loaves, person / people, child / children, mouse / mice*
- some nouns like *sheep, fish, aircraft* do not normally add plural *-s*
- some nouns are always plural and have no singular form: *clothes* (*cloth* is a material), *belongings, congratulations, goods, stairs, surroundings, thanks*
- many nouns are uncountable, and do not have plural *-s*, or have a different meaning when countable or uncountable. Uncountable nouns normally use a singular verb.

countable	*trees*	**uncountable**	*electricity*
countable	*woods* (small forests)	**uncountable**	*wood* (material)

- many nouns have an uncountable general meaning, and a countable particular meaning which can have plural *-s*

general	*Few people are in favour of war.*
particular	*There have been several wars between the two countries.*

- most uncountable nouns are things which we clearly cannot count. We use zero article, or *some*.

Gas, liquid, material	*air*	*water*	*iron*	*paper*
Grains etc	*rice*	*sugar*	*flour*	*coffee*
Abstract ideas	*health*	*time*	*fun*	*peace*
Feelings	*anger*	*pity*	*courage*	*boredom*
Activities	*travel*	*work*	*research*	*behaviour*

Other common nouns which do not normally have plural *-s*, and use a singular verb:

accommodation, advice, cash, clothing, equipment, experience, furniture, hair, information, knowledge, luggage, money, rubbish, scenery, traffic, weather, work

- note changes of meaning when uncountable nouns are used as countables with **a / an** (see **Unit 31**), and can have plurals

  *The doctor had many years of **experience**. (knowledge of life)*
  *Helen had **a bad experience** at her last school. (something that happens to you)*
  *Many people here are looking for **work**. (jobs)*
  *This is **a work** of 1926. (a work of art: a painting etc)*
  *Can you buy **a paper**? (a newspaper)*
  *We had **a good time** last night. (when you do something)*
  *There is **a hair** in my soup! (a single one)*

Other countables with specific meaning:

an iron	an object used to make clothes smooth
a coffee, a beer etc	a cup or glass etc of a liquid

- some uncountable nouns have a different countable word

bread – a loaf	*luggage – a bag, a case*
money – a note, a coin	*work – a job*
travel – a journey, a trip	*accommodation – a room, a flat etc*

- many uncountable nouns have a scientific or technical use in countable form. Always use your dictionary to check which meaning is being used.

  ***Sugars** are also classified by the number of carbons they contain.*

singular nouns ending in -s plural

Some nouns end in a plural *-s* but have no singular, and have a singular verb.

*the **news**   **mains** electricity   **mathematics / physics / economics***

1 <u>Underline</u> the correct form.

a There are more than a thousand <u>*sheep*</u> / *sheeps* on this farm.

b Please accept my *thank* / *thanks* for your beautiful present.

c Helen is the only *person* / *people* I know with three cars.

d There are two *knife* / *knives* in the top drawer.

e Alan hurt his leg when he fell down the *stair* / *stairs*.

f Kate decided to change her style and bought new *cloth* / *clothes*.

g Paul found his *belonging* / *belongings* outside in the street.

h Would you like to try a chocolate *mouse* / *mice*?

i World Airways has bought 20 new *aircraft* / *aircrafts*.

j We have already sent the *good* / *goods* you ordered.

2 Complete the sentence with a word from the list in either singular or plural form as necessary. You can use a word more than once. One word is not used.

| advice | hair | information | iron | journey |
| knowledge | ~~salt~~ | travel | wine | wood |

a Some doctors say that it is dangerous to put too much ___Salt___ on our food.

b If you want to be an explorer, you have to enjoy _____ . That's obvious.

c Until the 19th century, ships were built using different kinds of _____ .

d The body of an armadillo is completely covered in _____ .

e There are many organizations that give school leavers _____ about careers.

f The first electric _____ , in the late 19th century, had no temperature control.

g In chemistry, solutions of _____ in water are called electrolytes.

h The _____ of France are famous throughout the world.

i Discoveries made in physics in the 20th century have given us new _____ of the universe.

j The Internet is a good source of _____ , though not all of it is accurate.

3 Rewrite each sentence so it contains a word from the list.

| ~~accommodation~~ | clothing | equipment | furniture |
| rubbish | scenery | weather | work |

a The students' rooms were of a very high standard.
   The students' accommodation was of a very high standard.

b The rain and snow and high winds have been very bad this year.

c The chairs and tables and cupboards are arriving tomorrow.

d There are a lot of bottles and bits of paper at the edge of the sports field.

e The new things we use cost a lot of money, so look after them.

f The jobs in the factory were very difficult.

g The mountains and lakes and rivers in this country are very beautiful.

h Most of the coats and shirts and trousers were destroyed in the fire.

27

countable and uncountable

107

4 Choose the correct form, A or B, to complete the sentence.

a Martin had some very strange ___B___ when he stayed in the old castle.
A *experience*   B *experiences*

b I've always enjoyed _____ , which is why I have worked abroad a lot.
A *travel*   B *journey*

c The teacher was upset at the children's _____
A *behaviour*   B *behaviours*

d Some people think that if they don't eat _____ , they will lose weight.
A *bread*   B *loaf*

e The computer printer has run out of _____
A *paper*   B *papers*

f In this part of the country, it isn't easy to find a _____
A *work*   B *job*

g Can you take my _____ upstairs, please?
A *luggage*   B *luggages*

h Kate is earning a lot of _____ in her new job.
A *money*   B *moneys*

5 Complete the sentence with a singular or a plural form of *be*.

a The news ___*is*___ on Channel Five at nine o'clock.

b These loaves _____ really fresh.

c I think that maths _____ the most difficult subject.

d The coffees you ordered _____ on the table over there.

e The works of Shakespeare _____ still popular.

f Everyone says that money _____ hard to come by these days.

g The people I know _____ all on holiday at the moment.

h The traffic _____ really terrible this evening.

6 Answer the questions about the text below. Letters in the questions refer to the nouns lettered in the text.

Energy is never created or destroyed

If you turn off **a a light** at the switch, **b the room** goes dark immediately. **c Light** doesn't stay as light for very long after leaving **d the lamp**, so the light in the room has to be continually replaced. What happens to **e the energy** that leaves the lamp?

The hot lamp loses energy to the surrounding **f air** – this is carried away by a **g convection current**. The light and infra-red **h radiation** are absorbed by the walls and other surfaces, causing them to warm up. All the energy from the lamp spreads out into the room, causing a very small **i temperature rise**. Almost all the energy that we take from sources such as **j electricity, gas, coal** and **petrol** ends up as **k heat**

in our surroundings – in the buildings that we live in, the air and the outdoors. We cannot get this energy back very easily; it is much easier to obtain more energy from a fuel or electricity than to extract the energy from the air and the **l ground** outside.

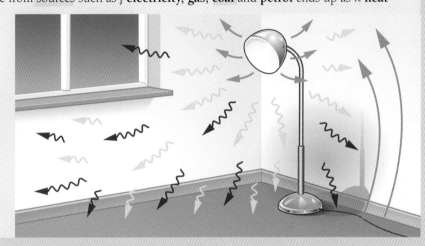

Circle the correct answer.

a a light (a) means   **A** *light in general*   **B** *a lamp, something that makes light*

b light (c) means   **A** *light in general*   **B** *a lamp, something that makes light*

c Which of these nouns can we make plural?

    A the room (b)   **B** light (c)   **C** the lamp (d)   **D** the energy (e)

Complete these sentences with a singular or plural form of one of the nouns in the text.

d .... all over the country will fall rapidly tomorrow, and there is a danger that the demand for .... may cause power cuts in some places.

e .... is made up of nitrogen, oxygen, carbon dioxide and a number of other ....

f People in London reported seeing numbers of unusual .... in the sky, and many believed they were UFOs.

GLOSSARY

EXTENSION ACTIVITY

1 Make a list of nouns from this unit that are uncountable in English, but plural in your language.

2 Correct the errors in these sentences.
Jane had her hairs cut last week. She looks fantastic.
I'm looking for an accommodation near the college.
I'll give you an advice. If I were you, I wouldn't take that job.

*Need more practice? Go to the **Review** on page 192.*

28 noun + noun, 's or of

noun + noun

Nouns are often used before other nouns as adjectives. The noun that comes first does not have plural -s. This is called a compound noun.

power station   (a building that contains machines that produce power)
export earnings   (earnings from exports)

A noun as adjective often explains

- what a thing is part of   **a computer screen**
- where the thing is found   **the bathroom window**
- what a thing is for   **a bottle opener**
- what type of thing it is   **a seat belt**
- what a thing contains   **a teapot**

Words which are always plural eg *clothes*, *news*, keep the plural form in compounds.

a clothes brush   **a news broadcast**

Two short nouns usually join together as one word, eg *teapot*. Other compounds are written as two words, eg *a bottle opener*, or may have a hyphen, eg *a bus-stop*. Check in a dictionary as the use of hyphens varies greatly.

A noun can have two nouns as adjectives.

shop window displays   **Christmas tree lights**

possessive apostrophe, of

Use the apostrophe and -s at the end of a singular noun or name to show that something belongs to someone, eg *Helen's bike*.

Use only an apostrophe after a plural –s, eg *the junior girls' team*.

With names ending in -s, use either an apostrophe, or an apostrophe with -s.

St James' Park   **St James's Park**

We generally use *of* when we describe one thing belonging to another.

the bottom of the sea   **the rotation of the Earth**

Note that usage varies, and other forms are possible, depending on the context. When you are uncertain, use *of*.

the sea bottom   **the Earth's rotation**

Note: the apostrophe is also used in **contractions**, eg *it isn't*. This is not a possessive apostrophe.

1A Explain what each thing is for.

   a a bottle opener .... *It opens bottles.* ....

   b a pencil sharpener ....

   c a coffee maker ....

   d a lawn mower ....

   e a dishwasher ....

1B Make a noun + noun compound.

   f a strap you find on a watch ....

   g a hole where you put a key ....

   h a racket for playing tennis ....

   i a light you find in the street ....

   j a book you get from the library ....

2 Rewrite each phrase underlined as a noun + noun compound. You may have to change plural and singular forms.

   a The Eastern Highlands are a <u>range of mountains</u> running along Australia's east coast.

       ..... *a mountain range* ....

   b Temperatures in <u>areas of desert</u> can reach 50°C in summer.

       ....

   c Aboriginal peoples are thought to have come to Australia from Southeast Asia around 50,000 years ago when <u>levels of the sea</u> were much lower.

       .... (leave out *the*)

   d Over a third of Australia's <u>income from exports</u> comes from agricultural products.

       ....

   e Australia is still the largest <u>exporter of wool</u> in the world.

       ....

   f The most important area for <u>the farming of beef</u> is the northern state of Queensland.

       .... (leave out *the*)

   g Crops are watered with <u>systems of irrigation</u>.

       ....

   h Australia is also rich in <u>resources of minerals</u>.

       ....

   i Minerals produce high <u>earnings from exports</u>.

       ....

   j Sydney is the largest city and has an important <u>district for business</u>.

       ....

noun + noun, 's or of

3 Rewrite the <u>underlined</u> words as a phrase with *of*. You may have to change plural and singular forms.

The **a** <u>air temperature</u> in a cloud determines **b** <u>rain and snow formation</u>. In tropical areas where the **c** <u>cloud temperature</u> is mainly above 0°C, rain is formed by a process called *coalescence*. The clouds are made up of millions of **d** <u>water droplets</u>, and as these droplets collide, they form larger droplets. Gradually the **e** <u>droplet size</u> increases until they are too heavy to be kept in the air by **f** <u>air currents</u>, and fall as **g** <u>raindrops</u>. In cooler areas, clouds may stretch up into air which is below freezing. These clouds are a mixture of water droplets lower down, and **h** <u>ice crystals</u> and special supercooled water droplets higher up. The supercooled droplets exist as water even though the temperature is below freezing. As well as coalescence at the bottom, a process called *accretion* happens higher up in these clouds. The ice crystals attract the supercooled droplets, which freeze onto them. As the crystals grow and stick to others, **i** <u>snowflakes</u> form. When they become too heavy to be held up, they fall.

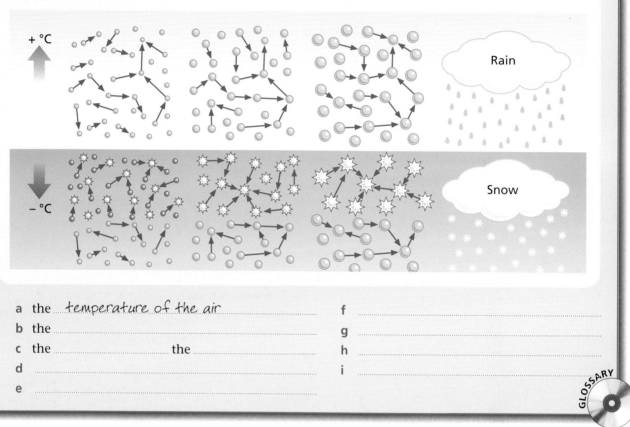

a   the   *temperature of the air*

b   the ....

c   the .... the ....

d   ....

e   ....

f   ....

g   ....

h   ....

i   ....

GLOSSARY

4 Make a noun + noun compound using two of the words. You may have to change a word from plural to singular.

a   the same temperature as there is in the room   *room temperature*

b   fumes which come from exhausts

c   salts which come from minerals

d   chemicals present in food

e   generations which will exist in the future

f   disease suffered by the heart

g   a solution of salt

h   pollution carried in the air

i   change in the climate

j   a bill you receive for your use of electricity

5 Use some of the words to make a two- or three-word compound. You may have to change a word from plural to singular.

a   a window in which things are displayed in a shop .... *shop window* ....

b   a ticket you buy so that you can travel on a bus ....

c   a key you use to open the front door ....

d   a chain you use as part of a bicycle ....

e   a directory which contains a list of telephone numbers ....

f   a case in which you can put your glasses ....

g   an engineer who knows how computers work ....

h   a shelf on which you put books ....

i   a bell which rings when there is an alarm ....

j   a bus which takes children to and from school ....

---

the arts

6   Put in eight more missing possessive apostrophes, not counting the example.

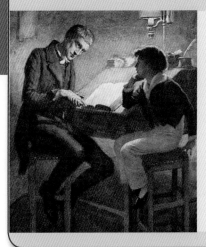

David Copperfield, the novel by Charles Dickens, is a story of one boy's struggle after losing his parents. Davids father dies when he is young, and his mother remarries. His stepfather, Mr Murdstone, treats David unkindly, and he can only find happiness with the Peggoty family, his nurses relatives. At school, at first he is unhappy but then wins his friends respect. However, when his mother dies, his stepfather sends him to work in a factory in London, where the other boys make fun of him. David runs away and walks to his aunts house in Dover. Here he grows up happily, goes to school and becomes a clerk in a lawyers office in London. He falls in love with Dora, his employers daughter, and when his aunts money is lost in a bad investment, he works writing reports of parliament for the newspapers. Many parts of the story follow the events of Dickens own life.

GLOSSARY

EXTENSION ACTIVITY

1   Make a compound noun from each description.

a lamp you have on your desk   *a desk lamp*

a handle on a door ....

a jug that contains water ....

a book you use for writing exercises ....

the door at the front of the house ....

a room where computers are used ....

2   Explain what these words mean. Check in a dictionary.

a bus stop   a dog trainer
a football shirt   kitchen paper
a news report   a coffee maker

noun + noun, 's or of

29 articles (1)

Use indefinite article *a / an*

- when first describing something, or making a general statement about something not known or without any details. Use *an* when the word following begins with a vowel.
  *Suddenly **a man** appeared outside the window.*
  *That is **an interesting** point.*

- to give an example.
  ***A thermometer** is used for measuring temperature.*

- to describe one of a class of things or people.
  *Paula is **an Italian**.   She's **a teacher**.*
  *It's **a racing bike**.*

- for rates and speeds etc.
  *Some people can cycle at **50 km an hour**.*
  *Phil earns €**500 a month**.*

Use definite article *the*

- with things or people already mentioned.
  *First, I take a test tube. Then into **the** test tube I pour 50 cc of water.*

- when a noun is made definite by details following it.
  *That man outside was **the man that the police were looking for**.*

- when we definitely know what is being talked about.
  *Are you going to **the post office**? Can you get me some stamps?*
  *Pass me **the salt**, please.*

Use zero article

- to describe something general or uncountable.
  ***Love** makes the world go round. **Water** boils at 100°C.*
  *Some people believe that **men** and **women** think differently.*

- with proper names, though these can begin with **the** if they have details following them.
  ***Kate** lives in **Manchester** in a little street called **Green Street**.*
  *This is **Mary Smith**. She is **the Mary Smith I told you about**.*

- with general examples, countable or uncountable.
  ***Doctors** often have to work more than a hundred hours a week.*
  ***Water** is a scarce resource in many parts of the world.*

Note that article use depends on context. **Unit 30** contains more examples of how to use *a / an*, *the* and zero article.

1 <u>Underline</u> the correct word.

a I don't like that coat. *The* / *A* colour is horrible.

b He doesn't like going to see *the* / *a* dentist.

c She asked for *the* / *a* cup of coffee, but she got tea instead.

d *The* / *A* laboratory is a place where scientific experiments are done.

e I don't believe he's *the* / *a* policeman, he looks too young!

f She is *a* / *an* intelligent woman.

g I went to *the* / *a* bank today and they said I didn't have any money!

h Who left *the* / *a* door open?

i *A* / *An* hotel is more expensive than a / an youth hostel.

j *The* / *A* film starts at half past seven.

2 Choose the correct form, A, B or C, to complete the sentence.

a If you want to be healthier, think carefully about ....*B*.... you eat.
   A *food*   B *the food*   C *a food*

b If you don't enjoy .... , do something else.
   A *the exercise*   B *an exercise*   C *exercise*

c Try learning ....
   A *a new sport*   B *new sport*   C *the new sport*

d Sometimes the food you eat is less important than ....
   A *food you don't eat*   B *a food you don't eat*   C *the food you don't eat*

e Do you eat enough .... ?
   A *fruit and vegetables*   B *the fruit and vegetables*   C *fruit and the vegetables?*

f There is a saying, '............. a day keeps the doctor away.'
   A *The apple*   B *A apple*   C *An apple*

g .... chocolate cake should only be eaten occasionally.
   A *The piece of*   B *Piece of*   C *A piece of*

h Stress also makes .... unhealthy.
   A *the people*   B *people*   C *a people*

i If you've had .... , try and do something nice for yourself.
   A *the bad day*   B *bad day*   C *a bad day*

j You could visit a friend or go to ....
   A *cinema*   B *the cinema*   C *a cinema*

3 Complete the text with *a / an* or *the*.

Memo checklist

a ....The.... word *memo* is short for *memorandum* and it means **b** .... note to help as **c** .... reminder.

It is only used within **d** .... business and so there is no need for **e** .... full external address of **f** .... person you are sending it to. However, you might need to show **g** .... internal office address, eg room number and building.

There are usually just spaces for **h** .... names of the person sending and the person receiving **i** .... memo. However, copies might be sent to other people in **j** .... company for reference.

The subject is clear from **k** .... heading and **l** .... text is brief.

There is no formal signature. Sometimes **m** .... originator will sign their name freehand at **n** .... bottom.

Business letter checklist

o .... language used in **p** .... business letter tends to be formal eg 'We regret to inform you …'

q .... letterhead includes **r** .... full address and telephone number of **s** .... business.

t .... address of **u** .... recipient is also included in full on **v** .... left-hand side above **w** .... text.

Everything is left justified (starts at **x** .... left-hand edge) except **y** .... letterhead.

Letters starting 'Dear Sir' end in 'Yours faithfully'. If you start with **z** .... name of the person you are writing to, for example 'Dear Mr Brown', you end **1** .... letter with 'Yours sincerely'.

2 .... date and any reference number are shown at **3** .... top of **4** .... letter.

---

4 Complete the text with *a / an*, *the* or leave blank for zero article.

science

Energy

a ....–.... waves are vibrations that transfer energy from place to place without **b** .... matter (solid, liquid or gas) being transferred. For example, think of **c** .... Mexican wave in **d** .... crowd at **e** .... football match. **f** .... wave moves around **g** .... stadium, while each spectator stays in their seat, only moving up then down when it's their turn.

Some waves must travel through **h** .... substance. This substance is known as **i** .... medium, and it can be solid, liquid or gas. **j** .... sound waves and seismic waves are like this. As the waves travel through it, **k** .... medium vibrates.

Other waves do not need to travel through **l** .... substance. They may be able to travel through **m** .... medium, but they do not have to. **n** .... visible light, infrared rays, and microwaves are like this. They can travel through **o** .... empty space.

GLOSSARY

Glaciers

5 Complete the text with *a / an*, *the* or leave blank for zero article.

Most of **a** the world's glaciers are found near **b** _____ Poles, but **c** _____ glaciers exist on all of **d** _____ world's continents. **e** _____ glaciers need **f** _____ special kind of climate. Most are found in **g** _____ areas of high snowfall in winter and cool temperatures in summer. These weather conditions ensure that **h** _____ snow that falls in the winter isn't lost by **i** _____ melting, or **j** _____ evaporation in summer. Such conditions typically occur in polar and high alpine regions. There are two main types of **k** _____ glaciers: **l** _____ valley glaciers and **m** _____ continental glaciers or ice sheets. **n** _____ glaciers depend on **o** _____ snow or **p** _____ freezing rain to survive. In Antarctica, for example, although **q** _____ temperature is low, there is little snow or rain, and this causes **r** _____ glaciers there to grow very slowly.

A glacier forms when **s** _____ snow builds up over time, turns to **t** _____ ice, and begins to flow outwards and downwards because of **u** _____ pressure of its own weight. **v** _____ buried layers slowly grow together to form a thickened mass of **w** _____ ice. **x** _____ thickness of **y** _____ glacial ice usually makes it seem a little blue in colour.

GLOSSARY

6 Complete each sentence with *the, a / an* or zero article.

a Last week at school we learned how to make ___a___ barometer.
b This is _____ cardboard which we used to make our barometer.
c And this is _____ bottle we used. We attached the cardboard to it.
d We made _____ measuring scale and attached it to the side of the bottle.
e This is _____ bowl we also used as part of our barometer. We filled the bowl with water, and filled the bottle three quarters full, and then turned the bottle upside down in the bowl.
f The pressure of air has an interesting effect on _____ water you put in the bowl.
g The pressure makes _____ water in the bottle rise.
h We used _____ measuring scale on the side of the bottle to measure the air pressure.

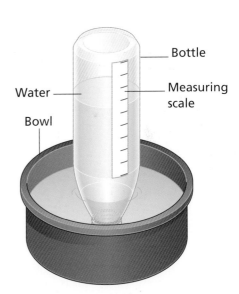

Bottle
Water
Measuring scale
Bowl

EXTENSION ACTIVITY

1 Does your language have definite, indefinite and zero articles that work in the same way as English articles? Look at all the examples on page 114 and translate them. What are the differences?

2 Check that you have the correct answers to Exercise 1, and then translate the sentences.

geography

29

articles (1)

117

30 articles (2)

Use indefinite article *a / an*

● to mean *one*.
   What would you like to eat?   *Can I have **a banana**?*

● to refer to large whole numbers, fractions, weights and distances.
   a hundred   *a million*   *a third*   *a fifth*
   *two and **a** half*   *a kilo*   *a metre and **a** half*

● with *a headache*, *a cold* etc.
   *I've got **a headache** / **a toothache** / **an earache**.*   *Have you got **a cold**?*
   Note that most illness words use *zero article*.
   *I've got **flu**.*   *She's suffering from **appendicitis**.*

● in the expressions *what a...!*, *such a...!*
   We use *what a* ... when we are surprised or impressed by something.
   ***What a** fantastic idea!*   ***What a** great bike you have got!*
   We use *such a* ... for emphasis with singular nouns.
   *This is **such a** difficult problem!*   *Thanks, you've been **such a** good friend.*

● to describe one example of a set of things.
   *That's **a Picasso**. (a work of art)*
   *This is **a Robbie Williams song**.*

Use definite article *the*

● with nationality adjectives that refer to all the people of that nationality, eg *Chinese, Japanese, French, Spanish, British, Swiss*.
   ***The French** drink a lot of wine.*
   ***The Swiss** are famous for their banks.*

● with plural nationality nouns in same way, eg *Russians, Americans, Poles, Greeks, Turks*.
   ***The Russians** and **the Poles** are used to cold weather.*

● with a singular noun to describe a class of things.
   ***The car** has taken over our cities.*

● with the names of shops and places with a general reference.
   *Anna's at **the** cinema / **the** supermarket / in **the** garden / in **the** mountains / at **the** beach etc.*

● with some familiar objects when we think of them as the only one.
   *One moment **the** Sun was shining in **the** sky. Then **the** Moon seemed to rise out of **the** sea.*

● with the names of oceans.
   *They crossed **the Pacific** in a small boat.*

Use zero article

● to talk about school subjects, such as geography, history etc.
   *If you want to study **physics**, you have to be good at **maths**.*

● to refer to days, months or parts of the day.
   *I'll see you **on Monday at midday**.*   *School begins **in September**.*

● with continents, countries, lakes, mountains etc. When plural, we use *the*.
   *Lake Geneva borders **France** and **Switzerland**.*
   *From here you can see **the Alps**.*

● with *at home, at school, in hospital, in prison, in bed* when we speak in general.
   *David isn't **at school** today. He's **in bed at home**.*
   But when referring to something other people know about, eg a specific place, building etc, we use *the*.
   *The bus stops **outside the school**.*   *Leave the towels **on the bed**.*

● with *such* ... for emphasis with plural or uncountable nouns.
   *You are **such noisy children**!*   *This is **such wonderful ice cream**!*

1 Underline the correct option. This may include a space (--) for zero article.

a *The* / -- Republic of Slovenia lies at *a* / *the* heart of *the* / -- Europe.

b It is where *the* / -- Alps face *the* / -- Pannonian plains and *the* / -- Mediterranean meets *the* / -- Karst region.

c To the north is *the* / -- Austria and *the* / -- Hungary is to *the* / -- east.

d To the south is *the* / -- Croatia and to the west is *the* / -- Italy.

e *A* / *The* / -- weather here is ideal for *the* / -- holidays.

f There are approximately 2,000 hours of *a* / *the* / -- sunshine per year, and there is plenty of *the* / -- snow in winter.

g There are many woods and forests covering more than half of *a* / *the* / -- country.

h In *the* / -- Kocevje area in one of *a* / *the* / -- oldest forests in *the* / -- Europe, it is possible to walk among the trees for days.

2 Complete the text with *a / an*, *the* or leave blank for zero article.

a ....─............ people often say they have flu when all they have is .... cold and .... slight temperature.

b .... full name of flu is .... influenza.

c .... real flu is caused by .... virus.

d There are many different kinds of .... flu virus.

e They give you .... high temperature, aching muscles and .... headache.

f They also give you .... cold shivers and .... feeling of .... tiredness.

g You may also get .... cough.

h There is no treatment as .... antibiotics cannot kill .... viruses.

i You should go to .... bed and rest.

j If you go to .... school and mix with others, you will spread .... virus to them, so it is better to stay at .... home until you feel better.

3 Complete the text with *a / an*, *the* or leave blank for zero article.

Equity Travel School Tour Specialists

Equity has been arranging **a** _____–_____ educational tours since 1991 and our Directors and Managers have many years' experience in **b** _____ school travel, making us true specialists in **c** _____ field.

Youth and School Group Travel

We know and understand **d** _____ special requirements of schools and youth organizations and can meet your needs. You will receive **e** _____ high-quality educational tour, with unrivalled personal service and excellent value for **f** _____ money.

Educational Tours

All our tours have **g** _____ educational value and many have been specifically designed to comply with **h** _____ requirements of **i** _____ UK National Curriculum.

We organize tours to **j** _____ wide range of countries in **k** _____ Europe, and also offer tours in **l** _____ USA, **m** _____ South Africa, and other parts of the world.

Study Tours

History tours, geography tours, **n** _____ language courses and cookery courses are all available in our study tours programme, specially designed for **o** _____ school groups.

World Wide – USA, South Africa, China and India

There is **p** _____ special brochure of tours to **q** _____ New York and Washington, **r** _____ West Coast of America, South Africa (visiting big game parks), China (visiting **s** _____ Great Wall) and **t** _____ Golden Triangle in India (visiting Delhi, Agra and Jaipur).

---

4 Look carefully at each line. If the line has an article (*a / an* or *the*) which should not be there, write the article and the word following in the space. Put a tick ✓ in the space if the line has no errors.

A hurricane is a fast-moving storm moving in a circle measuring between	a _____✓_____
60 and 1,000 miles in diameter. It forms over a warm water far out at sea.	b _a (warm)_
It begins as a group of strong thunderstorms moving across the ocean,	c _____
usually known as a tropical wave. The weather conditions must be just right	d _____
to turn a tropical wave into a hurricane, and the less than five per cent of them ever	e _____
become the real hurricanes. A tropical wave that begins to spin around a centre	f _____
of low pressure is called a tropical depression. The tropical depressions have	g _____
a maximum wind speeds of less than 65 km per hour at the ocean's surface.	h _____
When the winds reach 65 km per hour or greater, the storm changes	i _____
into a tropical storm, and the meteorologists give it a name. When these winds	j _____
reach 120 km per hour or greater, a hurricane is formed. Each hurricane has	k _____
an area in the middle called an eye. In the eye there is the low pressure and	l _____
the winds are calm. The eye is surrounded by severe thunderstorms with high	m _____
winds and a heavy rain. Hurricanes are called typhoons when they occur	n _____
in the western Pacific Ocean, and cyclones in the Indian and southern	o _____
Pacific Oceans. The name hurricane is used for storms in the North Atlantic	p _____
and in other parts of the Pacific. Most hurricanes occur between the June 1st	q _____
and 30th November.	

GLOSSARY

social studies

5 Complete the text with *a / an*, *the* or leave blank for zero article.

Do exams make pupils lose interest?

a ....—........ children could be turned off their favourite subjects for
b .... life if they are pushed too hard to take c ....
exams, d .... psychologists are warning. e ....
study of 11-year-olds found that those who had taken exams to win
f .... school places rapidly lost g .... interest in their
school work after h .... exams were over. Other children, who
did not take i .... same kind of tests, did not have j ....
same experience. In this study, k .... group of researchers
measured l .... motivation of children in m .... science,
n .... English and o .... maths. Before p ....
exams q .... children all appeared very motivated, but as soon as
r .... exams were over, that changed, and their motivation went
down. Motivation stayed s .... same among another group who
took normal school tests. Researchers think it is possible that some children
can be put off t .... subject permanently by an exam.

Silence exam

6 Complete the text with *a / an*, *the* or leave blank for zero article.

Apple Computer was founded in Los Gatos, California on 1 April, 1976 by Steve Jobs, Steve
Wozniak and Ronald Wayne, to sell a .....*the*..... Apple I personal computer kit at $666.66.
They were hand-built in Jobs' parents' garage, and b .... Apple I was first shown to
c .... public at d .... Homebrew Computer Club. Jobs and Wozniak,
e .... two Steves, had been f .... friends since 1971. Jobs managed to interest
Wozniak in assembling g .... personal computers and selling them. Jobs approached
h .... computer store, which ordered 50 units and paid $500 for each unit. Jobs then
ordered components from Cramer Electronics, i .... company making electronic parts.
    Using j .... number of methods, including borrowing space from k ....
friends and family and selling l .... things including m .... Volkswagen Type
2 bus, Jobs managed to secure n .... parts needed while Wozniak and another friend,
Ronald Wayne, assembled o .... Apple I. The computers were delivered in June, and paid
for on delivery. Eventually 200 Apple I computers were built.
    p .... Apple II was first sold in q .... 1977 . It was popular with
r .... home users and was occasionally sold to s .... business users, particularly
after t .... release of u .... first computer spreadsheet, called *VisiCalc*.

EXTENSION ACTIVITY

1 Look at all the examples on page 118 and translate them. Does your language use these articles in the same way? What are the differences?
2 Check that you have the correct answers to Exercise 1, and then translate the sentences.
Need more practice? Go to the ***Review*** *on page 192.*

articles (2)

31 quantity: *some, any*

Use *some*   (See also **Unit 27**)

- with plural countable nouns, and uncountable nouns in positive sentences.
  *There are **some books** in that cupboard.*
  *I need **some advice**.*

countable	a book	some books	
uncountable	some money	some advice	some milk

- in questions that are invitations, offers or requests.
  *Would you like **some pizza**?*
  *Could you give me **some advice**?*

- in questions when we expect the answer *yes*.
  *Have you got **some homework** to give me?*

- to mean 'not all'.
  ***Some of the people** / **Some people** were drowned, but **others** survived.*

Use *any*

- with plural countable nouns, in questions and negatives.
  *Are there **any** books in that cupboard?   There aren't **any** books in this one.*

- with uncountable nouns in questions and negatives with a singular verb.
  ***Is there any information** about this subject?*
  ***There isn't any water** left.*

- to mean 'whichever one you like'.
  *You can borrow **any books** you need from the library.*

uncountable (mass) nouns   (See also **Unit 27**)
Use a singular verb with:

Things we eat	bread, chocolate, food, fruit, meat, spaghetti
Other words	accommodation, advice, behaviour, damage, education, furniture, grass, hair, help, information, jewellery, knowledge, luggage, money, news, rubbish, shopping, traffic, weather, work

People uses a plural verb.
  *There are **some people** waiting for you.*
It also has a different countable meaning with plural -*s*.
  ***The peoples** of the world want peace.*

countable versions of uncountable nouns
Many uncountable nouns have a countable version. Always use a dictionary to check the meaning.

a chicken (an animal)	some chicken (food)	a coin, a note (money)	some money
a glass (container)	some glass (substance)	an iron (for ironing)	some iron (material)
a paper (a newspaper)	some paper (material)		
a tea, two teas etc (a cup or glass)	some tea etc (a liquid)		

partitives
A partitive is a noun + *of* which makes a countable version of an uncountable.

a slice of bread	a sheet of paper	a bar of chocolate / soap
a packet of rice	a can of cola	a tube of toothpaste
a cup of tea	a bottle of water	a loaf (of bread)

1 Use the prompts to make a question with *there … any*, using a singular or a plural verb. Check the factual answers on page 208.

a be / oxygen on Mars?   *Is there any oxygen on Mars* ?
b be / cheese on the Moon?   _____ ?
c be / mammals with beaks and webbed feet? _____ ?
d be / weather on other planets?   _____ ?
e be / fish that can walk on land? _____ ?
f be / birds that can't fly?   _____ ?
g be / water on the Moon?   _____ ?
h be / apes that can be taught to speak? _____ ?
i be / oil or coal on the Moon?   _____ ?
j be / living dinosaurs left on Earth? _____ ?

2 Rewrite the sentence to make a statement with *not … any* beginning as shown. Then decide if each statement is *True* or *False*. Check the factual answers on page 208.

a Cars don't use water as fuel.
   There *aren't any cars that use water as fuel*

b Mammals don't lay eggs.
   There _____

c Polar bears don't live in the Antarctic.
   There _____

d Alien beings don't exist in our galaxy.
   There _____

e Britain is a country without volcanoes.
   There _____

f It never rains in the Sahara desert.
   There _____

3 Complete each sentence with *a / an*, *some* or *any*.

a My shirt is dry now, but I need _____*an*_____ iron to press it with.
b Would you like _____ chicken? And how about _____ potatoes?
c I can't print off my project because I haven't got _____ paper.
d Have you got _____ money for the machine? I didn't bring _____
e Sorry I didn't come to the party. I had to finish _____ work.
f I'd like to drink some water, but I can't find _____ glass.
g Could you buy me _____ paper on your way home? I want to read the sports news.
h I need _____ advice about which subjects to do next year.
i I'm really hungry. Can you make me _____ meat sandwich?
j Excuse me, could you give me _____ information about the trains to Rome?

quantity: some, any

4 Complete each sentence about endangered species with *a* / *an*, *some*, or *any*.

a When the last member of ___*a*___ species dies, we say that the species has become extinct.

b There aren't _____ dinosaurs left alive because they died out millions of years ago.

c _____ plants, birds and animals are still in danger from human beings.

d This is often because human beings destroy the habitats of animals, so that they don't have _____ food to eat.

e When _____ animal or a plant becomes extinct, this can affect the plants and animals which depend on it for food.

f For example, there aren't _____ dodos left alive.

g This bird once lived on the island of Mauritius where there weren't _____ animals to eat it.

h It couldn't fly, and was _____ easy meal for dogs and rats brought to the island by Europeans in the 16th century.

i Within a hundred years, the dodo became extinct, and although we still have _____ paintings of dodos, there aren't _____ preserved examples.

j Scientists have recently found _____ bones on the island, but nothing else is left of the dodo.

GLOSSARY

5 Complete each sentence with a word from the list.

bar	can	carton	cloud	~~crowd~~
packet	piece	sheet	slice	tube

a Suddenly at the end of the street, a ___*crowd*___ of people appeared, shouting and waving flags.

b When I opened the _____ of cola, it sprayed out onto my shirt.

c We both felt hungry, and luckily I had a _____ of biscuits in my bag.

d If you go to the supermarket, could you buy a _____ of toothpaste?

e There was a sudden explosion, and then all they saw was a _____ of dust.

f Anna always eats a _____ of chocolate on her way to school.

g Shall I cut another _____ of bread for you?

h Can I give you a _____ of advice? Spend more time on your work.

i David took a _____ of paper from his bag, and started writing.

j When I try to open a _____ of milk, I wish it still came in bottles!

6 Complete the sentence to make a summary statement with *some* (meaning *not all*), and *others*.

a Mountain ranges vary in age. The Alps are only 15 million years old, but the Urals and the Appalachians are over 250 million, and the Highlands of Scotland are 400 million years old.

Summary: *Some mountain ranges are* .... only 15 million years old, while ....*others are* .... 400 million years old.

b Pine trees depend on birds to spread their seeds. The monterey and pond pine, however, depend on forest fires, which release the seeds from the cone.

Summary: .... to spread their seeds, while .... to release the seeds from the cone.

c Frogs jump from place to place using their powerful back legs. Asian gliding tree frogs (*Rhacophorus reinwardtii*), however, 'fly' from tree to tree for as much as 12 metres using their webbed feet as parachutes.

Summary: ....

.... using webbed feet as parachutes, while ....

....

Asian gliding tree frog

d Rivers generally flow into a larger river or a lake, or flow to the sea, but in some desert regions, they simply evaporate in the desert and disappear.

.... evaporate in the desert and disappear, while .... into rivers, lakes or into the sea.

e The difference in sea level between high tide and low tide varies from place to place. It can be almost nothing, while in Alaska and eastern Canada the difference can be as great as 10 to 15 metres.

Summary: .... the difference in sea level between high tide and low tide can be almost nothing, while .... as great as 10 to 15 metres.

GLOSSARY

EXTENSION ACTIVITY

1 Look at all the examples on page 122 and translate them into your own language. Underline any problem examples.

2 Check that you have the correct answers to Exercise 5, and then translate the sentences.

quantity: *much, many, few, little, enough*

Use *how many*
- to ask questions about quantity with countable nouns.
  How many tigers are there in the world today?

Use *how much*
- to ask questions about mass with uncountable nouns.
  How much water is there on Earth?

Use *not many*
- to make a negative statement about quantity of countables.
  *There **aren't many tigers** left in the world today.*

Use *not much*
- to make a negative statement about mass of uncountables.
  *If we want to save the tiger, there **isn't much time** left.*

Use *many* and *much*
- in positive statements in formal or written language.
  ***Many people** hunt wild animals for sport. **Much damage** has been caused by this kind of hunting.*

Use *a few*
- to talk about a small number of countable nouns in a positive way.
  *We managed to see **a few tigers** in the distance.*

Use *a little*
- to talk about a small amount of an uncountable noun in a positive way.
  *There is **a little water** left in this bottle.*

Use *a lot (of), lots (of)*
- to talk about a large number of countables or a large amount of an uncountable.
  *We saw **a lot of** / **lots of animals** close up and took **a lot of** / **lots of photos**.*
  *There was **a lot of** / **lots of rain** last month.*

Use *few, very few, only a few*
- to talk about countables in a negative way.
  *Unfortunately **few conservationists** believe that tigers in the wild have a future.*
  *Experts believe that within fifty years there will be **very few** remaining.*
  *Unfortunately, there are **only a few** biscuits left.*

Use *little, very little, only a little*
- to talk about uncountables in a negative way.
  *There is **little hope** that tigers will survive, as they have **very little** space for their natural habitat.*
  *I'm afraid there is **only a little** water left.*

Use *too many*
- with countables to talk about more things than are necessary or possible.
  *There are **too many stars** for scientists to count.*

Use *too much*
- with uncountables to talk about a greater quantity than is necessary or possible.
  *Some plants are damaged by **too much sunlight**.*

Use *enough (of)*
- for countables and uncountables when we say that the quantity or number is sufficient.
  *Have we got **enough food**?*   *Have we got **enough**?*
  *There are **enough plates** for everyone.*   *We've got **enough (of them)**.*

Use *not enough*
- for countables and uncountables when we say that the quantity or number is not sufficient.
  *There is **not enough information** about this problem, and there are **not enough scientists** working to try and find a solution.*

Use *plenty of*
- for countables and uncountables when we say that the quantity or number is more than enough.
  *Don't worry, we have **plenty of time**.*   *I've got **plenty of pens** if you need one.*

1 Complete the question with *how many* or *how much*. Check the factual answers on page 208.

a ___How many___ active volcanoes are there throughout the world?

b _____ oxygen is in the air?

c _____ fish are there in the sea?

d _____ water is there on Earth?

e _____ kinds of clouds are there?

f _____ teeth does an adult human have?

g _____ does the Earth weigh?

h _____ oil is used in the world every day?

2 Complete the sentence with *aren't many* or *isn't much*.

a There ___isn't much___ rain in the Sahara Desert.

b There _____ giant pandas left in the world.

c There _____ snow in countries near the Equator.

d There _____ unexplored places left on Earth.

e There _____ people living in the Antarctic.

f There _____ light in the ocean below 200 metres.

g There _____ iron in the human body.

h There _____ mountains on Earth higher than 7,000 metres.

3 Complete each sentence so that it contains the word or words in capitals. Make any necessary changes.

a Not many people have travelled deeper than 10,000 metres under the sea. **A FEW**
___Only a few___ people have travelled deeper than 10,000 metres under the sea.

b In fact there are only one or two ways of doing this. **FEW**
In fact there are _____ of doing this.

c Divers could not survive at such depths. **NO**
_____ could survive at such depths.

d Some people have descended this far in underwater vessels called bathyscaphes. **A FEW**
_____ have descended this far in underwater vessels called bathyscaphes.

e They cannot remain under water for many hours. **A FEW**
They can remain under water for _____

f There are many problems involved with descending into deep water. **LOT**
_____ problems involved with descending into deep water.

g There is some light up to 200 metres, but at 10,000 it is completely dark. **NONE**
There is some light up to 200 metres, but at 10,000 _____

h There are not many creatures that live at such a depth. **FEW**
_____ creatures that live at such a depth.

A bathyscaphe is used to descend deep into the sea.

quantity: *much, many, few, little, enough*

4 Complete the sentence with *few* or *little*.

a ......*Few*...... people think that there are other planets in our solar system with human life just like our own.

b In fact, there is .... reason to believe that life of any kind exists on other planets.

c There are a .... indications that microbes may exist, or may have existed on Mars.

d However, there is .... real proof of this.

e There are a .... traces of methane in the Martian atmosphere, and some scientists believe that this could have a biological origin.

f Unfortunately, there is .... agreement among scientists about this.

g Analysis of the Martian soil suggests that water exists on Mars, and there are a .... areas where scientists believe ice forms and melts.

h Other scientists argue that there is .... chance of finding any life at all on Mars.

---

5 Complete the text with *many*, *much*, *few*, *lots*, *none* and *little*.

a ......*Many*...... people nowadays try to follow a healthy diet, although not b .... experts agree about what this is. In fact c .... of people assume that 'diet' is something connected with losing weight. Diet simply refers to the kind of food and how d .... of it we eat. There are very e .... foods that we can describe as completely 'unhealthy', and not f .... foods have zero nutritional value. However, if you eat g .... of chocolate and fried food and take h .... exercise, then your diet would probably be described as 'unhealthy'. i .... experts recommend that we all eat j .... of fruit and vegetables, and eat very k .... fatty food.

People are often surprised when they discover how l .... fat there is in popular fast foods such as burgers and pizzas, or how m .... calories there are in soft drinks. Unfortunately n .... of us can resist this kind of food, and there are not o .... people who are prepared to give up chocolate or chips. There are p .... easy answers to the question 'what is a healthy diet?'. However, if we eat q .... of different kinds of food, drink r .... of water, and make sure we take s .... of exercise, then we will be going in the right direction. After all, t .... of us are perfect!

GLOSSARY

6 Complete the sentence with <u>one</u> word so that it means the same as the first sentence.

a What is the total amount of salt contained in the world's oceans and seas?

How ......*much*...... salt is there in the world's oceans and seas?

b We don't know very much about the deep oceans.

We know very .... about the deep oceans.

c Water covers a large part of the Earth's surface.

.... of the Earth's surface is covered by water.

d There seems to be more than enough food for everyone in the world in the oceans.

There seems to be .... of food for everyone in the world in the oceans.

e In fact, large amounts of the food we eat come from the oceans.

In fact, a .... of the food we eat comes from the oceans.

f It's impossible to swim in the Dead Sea because of the large amount of salt in it.

You can't swim in the Dead Sea because it contains too .... salt.

g There is a shortage of fish in some parts of the world.

There aren't .... fish in some parts of the world.

h The Sargasso Sea contains large amounts of seaweed.

There is .... of seaweed in the Sargasso Sea.

i There are areas near the Equator where the wind does not blow very much.

There are areas near the Equator where there is not .... wind.

j Pollution affects nearly every one of the world's ocean areas.

There are .... areas of the world's oceans not affected by pollution.

---

7 <u>Underline</u> the correct option.

In geography, a desert is an area which receives a *few / little* rain and which loses a b *few / lot* of its moisture through evaporation. c *Many / Much* polar regions can be called deserts, but most of us think of a desert as being a sandy, rocky area with d *not enough / few* water. e *Lots / Lot* of deserts consist of sand dunes or bare rock, and f *many / much* are near mountain ranges, which take away the moisture from clouds. Others are far away from the sea or other water, so receive g *few / little* moisture. Although we might assume that very h *few / lots* kinds of life live in deserts, in fact there are i *lots / many* of plants, animals and insects in these regions. j *Lots / Many* desert plants store water in their leaves or roots, and some desert plants can live for k *lots / many* years. Some desert animals live underground. They spend l *little / a few* time in the sun and only come out at night. There are m *enough / lots of* insects, scorpions and spiders as well as reptiles, such as snakes, lizards and tortoises, in deserts. They need to spend n *much / many* hours in the sun to generate body heat, so they have o *few / little* difficulty living in high temperatures. However, p *few / little* of them can bear extreme sunlight, so they tend to move from one area of shade to another.

GLOSSARY

EXTENSION ACTIVITY

1 Write a list of *how much* and *how many* questions, and ask someone else in the class.

2 Write eight true sentences about your country, city or town using *not many* and *a lot of / lots of*.

geography

quantity: *much, many, few, little, enough*

33 quantity: *none, all, each, every*

Use *no*

- with a noun to describe zero quantity or mass.
  No animal can live for long without water.

Use *none of*

- to mean 'not one' of a group.
  None of the students had done the work.

Use *none*

- to mean 'not any', or 'not one' with countables or uncountables .
  Countable   *We looked for some chairs, but **there was / were none** free.*
  Uncountable *I thought we had some milk, but **there is none** left. (singular verb)*

Use *all (of)*

- with a plural noun and verb, often in contrast with *some*.
  ***All animals** need water to live.*
  ***Not all** the cabbages were eaten. **Some** were left.*

- after *be* or an auxiliary verb.
  *You are **all** wrong.   You have **all** made a mistake.*
  *You must **all** be more careful.*
  Note: *all of* has the same meaning.
  *Wild rabbits have eaten **all of our** / **the** cabbages.*

- as a pronoun at the beginning of a sentence.
  ***All** I could see was hundreds of hats.*
  Note: *everything* is more usual as an object.
  *I want to know **everything** that happened.*

Use *most (of)*

- to mean 'nearly all'.
  ***Most mammals** have hair.*
  *Wild rabbits have eaten **most of our** / **the** cabbages.*

Use *each (of)*

- to mean the separate members of a group.
  *We put 50 cc of water in **each test tube.***
  Note: *each of* is also possible.
  *We put 50 cc of water in **each of the test tubes** / **each of them**.*

- with *one*.
  *There were five test tubes, and we put 50 cc of water in **each one**.*

- after a subject or at the end of a sentence.
  *The members of the team **each** received a medal.*

Use *every*

- with a singular noun, to mean all the members of a group together.
  ***Every person in the class** took part in the play.*

Use *whole*

- to mean 'all of something'.
  *You'd better tell me **the whole story** from the beginning.*
  ***The whole class** clapped and cheered.*

Use *both (of)*

● to refer to two things, with a plural noun and verb, as in these sentences:
. **Both books** *were written in 1986.* (plural noun + verb)
You are **both** *wrong.* (after *be*)
You have **both** *made a mistake.* (between auxiliary and participle)
You must **both** *be more careful.* (between modal and verb)
Both of the pencils *were broken.* / **Both of my pencils** *were broken.* (*both of* + *the* + plural noun / possessive)
Both of you *are wrong.* (*both of* + pronoun)

Use *either (of)*

● to mean 'this or the other', with a singular noun and verb.
There are two methods. **Either method** *will give results.*
● with *the* + plural noun. *Either of* is a pronoun form.
Either of the methods *will give results.*
You can use **either of them**. (*either of* + pronoun)

Use *neither (of)*

● to mean 'not this or the other'.
These are incorrect answers. **Neither** *is correct.*
● with *the* + plural noun. *Neither of* is a pronoun form.
Neither of the answers *is correct.*
Neither of them *is correct.* (*neither of* + pronoun)

· ·

1 Put *most*, *all*, or *no* in each space, according to your opinion. Check the factual answers on page 208.

a ......All........ birds have feathers, and they are the only animals that do.
b .... animals (roughly 85%) eat plants or their products, such as seeds.
c .... mammals have hair that is naturally blue or green in colour.
d .... reptiles are 'cold-blooded' and need heat from the Sun to live.
e .... mammals give birth to live young, but a few, such as the duck-billed platypus, lay eggs.
f .... mammals, other than bats, can really fly.
g .... animals, but not apes and monkeys, are colour-blind.
h .... birds lay eggs with hard shells made mostly of calcium carbonate.
i There are .... reptiles in the Arctic or Antarctic.
j .... birds, except penguins, ostriches and some others, are able to fly.

2 Decide where to put *whole* in each sentence, and write *whole* and the following noun at the end.

a After fire destroyed their house, the family was put up in a hotel by the local authorities.
the whole family

b The forecast for the end of the week is for high winds and snow over the country.
....

c I certainly thought that the first two episodes were weak, but I could change my mind when I've seen the series.
....

d There is now a generation of teenagers who cannot live without texting and phoning.
....

e Late in the evening there was heavy rain, and now the area is under water.
....

f Mother Teresa, who died yesterday aged 87, spent her life caring for the poor.
....

quantity: none, all, each, every

3 Complete the text with *most of*, *all of* and *none of*.

However hard they try to solve the problem, a ....*all of*........ the world's large cities suffer from traffic problems. b .... them were not planned to cope with so many vehicles, so the streets are narrow, and there is not enough space for parking. A number of different solutions to this problem have been suggested, but c .... them has been completely successful. For example, many cities try to discourage the use of private cars in the centre, but even so it is impossible to keep d .... the traffic away. As e .... the larger shops, offices, hotels, railway stations etc are in the centre of the city, there will always be a need for buses and taxis and some private cars. An obvious answer is to move f .... the hotels, offices and large stations out of the city centre. It would be impossible to move g .... them, but it would still make the situation better. The new areas would have plenty of parking and public transport, so they would have h .... the problems of the old city centre.

GLOSSARY

4 Underline the correct option.

a It's difficult to describe a typical school system, as *all* / *each* / *every* countries are different.

b In some countries, *all* / *each* / *every* school chooses its own curriculum, or programme of study.

c In others, the government decides *all* / *each* / *every* detail of the educational programme.

d Class sizes vary as well, and in some places there are more than 40 pupils in *all* / *each* / *every* class.

e In other places, classes are small, and the teacher has more time to spend with *all* / *each* / *every* individual pupil.

f In some countries the government provides *all* / *each* / *every* textbooks completely free of charge.

g In other countries, however, *all* / *each* / *every* schoolbook for the different subjects has to be bought from the school, or from a bookshop.

h In some school systems *all* / *each* / *every* pupils eat their midday meal at school.

i In other places, however, *all* / *each* / *every* pupil makes his or her own arrangements, some going home and returning, and others bringing a packed lunch.

j *All* / *Each* / *Every* we can be certain about is that no two countries are exactly the same where education is concerned.

5 Complete the sentence with *both ... and* or *neither ... nor*. Check the factual answers on page 208.

a   ..Both.. Alexander ....and.... Napoleon were leaders who conquered a number of other countries.

b   .... Alexander .... Napoleon died in his own country.

c   .... Alexander .... Napoleon successfully handed on power to a son.

d   .... Alexander .... Napoleon managed to completely defeat all their enemies.

e   .... Alexander .... Napoleon successfully invaded Egypt.

f   .... Alexander .... Napoleon were excellent generals who won a large number of battles.

g   .... Alexander .... Napoleon led their armies to far distant countries.

h   .... Alexander .... Napoleon married more than once, and had a number of children.

i   .... Alexander .... Napoleon lived to an old age.

j   .... Alexander .... Napoleon were poisoned, according to some historians.

6 Choose the correct option, A, B or C, to complete the text.

Nowadays a ....B.... us spend a lot of time watching DVDs or going to the cinema, but so far there is b .... sign that we have stopped reading books. It sometimes seems that c .... child in the world has read a Harry Potter book, and d .... people on the beach, and not only older people, seem to be reading something. Obviously it is possible to enjoy e .... books and films, but books do seem to have a number of advantages. With new DVDs costing around €30 f .... , it is clearly cheaper to read. g .... you need to enjoy a book is a comfortable chair, after all. Films show you all the action in colour, but for many people h .... of the special effects in a film is as good as the pictures in their own imagination. And the i .... experience of reading a good book can be a lot more rewarding. Of course, films can be great too, but in the end, j .... of us has to decide how we would rather spend our time.

a **A** *every*	**B** *most of*	**C** *all*
b **A** *no*	**B** *none*	**C** *neither*
c **A** *whole*	**B** *every*	**C** *all*
d **A** *most of*	**B** *all*	**C** *most*
e **A** *both*	**B** *neither*	**C** *every*
f **A** *every*	**B** *all*	**C** *each*
g **A** *Either*	**B** *All*	**C** *None*
h **A** *all*	**B** *none*	**C** *every*
i **A** *whole*	**B** *most*	**C** *both*
j **A** *none*	**B** *all*	**C** *each*

GLOSSARY

EXTENSION ACTIVITY

1 Write eight true examples beginning:
All   Not all   Most   Every

2 Check that you have the correct answers to Exercise 6. Translate it into your own language.

social studies

quantity: *none, all, each, every*

34 pronouns

I, me, my etc

I is a subject pronoun, *me* an object pronoun and *my* a possessive adjective.

Subject pronoun	I	you	she	he	it	we	they
Object pronoun	me	you	her	him	it	us	them
Possessive adjective	my	your	her	his	its	our	their

mine etc

Mine is a possessive pronoun. *This bike is mine* means *This is my bike*. We cannot put a noun after a possessive pronoun.

> *Whose bike is this?*   *It's **mine**.*

Possessive pronoun	mine	yours	hers	his	–	ours	theirs

a (noun) of (possessive pronoun)

Use a possessive pronoun with a noun in this expression.

> *This is **an interest of his**.*   ***This** great **country of ours**.*

It is very common with *friend*. We can also use *friend of* + a name with a possessive apostrophe.

> *Is she **a friend of yours**?*   *No, she's **a friend of Martin's**.*

Use myself etc

● for emphasis, and with some verbs.

> *Can you make me some tea?*   *Why don't you make it **yourself**!*

● as an object with verbs that describe doing something to ourselves.

> *Look at **yourself** in the mirror, and ask **yourself** this question.*
> *Sally is too young to wash **herself** and put **herself** to bed.*
> Other verbs often used like this: *cut, enjoy, hurt, behave.*
> *Did he hurt **himself**?*   *Please **behave yourselves**!*
> *Enjoy **yourselves**!*   *I've cut **myself**.*
> *Cut, enjoy, hurt* can also have an object, but not *behave*.
> *Enjoy your meal!*   *Please behave!*

some-, any-, no-, every- pronouns

Use *someone, anyone, no-one, everyone*   (See also **Unit 31**)

● following the same rules as *some, any* and *no*.

Use *somebody, anybody, nobody, everybody* with the same meaning.

> *There's **someone** outside. (I don't know who it is).*
> *Is **anyone** there?*   *There isn't **anyone**.*   *There's **no-one**.*

Everyone means 'all the people', with a singular verb.

> ***Everyone** knows that Paris is the capital of France.*

Use *something, anything, nothing, everything*

● in the same way as *someone* etc.

> *Have you got **anything** for me?*   *There's **something** wrong.*
> *There's **nothing** here.*   ***Everything** is all right!*

somewhere, anywhere, nowhere, everywhere

These are adverbials, and are used in the same way as *someone* etc.

> *They **couldn't** find the cat **anywhere**.*
> *Insects can be found **everywhere** on Earth.*
> *There is **nowhere** for children to play in this area.*

Use else

● after *some-, any-, no-, every-* pronouns to mean 'other' or 'more'.

> *I didn't realize it was you. I thought it was **someone else**.*
> ***Nothing else** really matters.*

1 Complete the sentences about the pharaoh Tutankhamun with personal pronouns (*I, you, he* etc) and possessive adjectives (*my, your, his* etc).

a _He_ has been famous ever since _____ tomb was discovered in 1922.

b However, little is known about _____ for certain.

c _____ began _____ reign with the name of Tutankhaten at the age of nine.

d Because of his youth, it was probably _____ chief minister Ay who ruled instead of _____.

e While still a boy, _____ married Ankhesenpaaten.

f As a result of political changes, both _____ names were later changed.

g Tutankhamun's death took place when _____ was still a teenager.

h The ancient Egyptians buried _____ young pharaoh in a tomb full of beautiful objects.

i In modern times these objects have been seen by thousands of tourists and _____ have made Tutankhamun famous.

j If you want to see _____ death mask and other amazing objects, you will have to visit the Egyptian Museum in Cairo.

2 Complete the sentence with a possessive or an object pronoun.

a This CD belongs to me. This CD is _mine._

b This is his calculator. This calculator is _____

c That bike belongs to her. That bike's _____

d This ball is ours. This ball belongs to _____

e That is your desk. That desk is _____

f We own this house. This house is _____

g Those boots are theirs. Those boots belong to _____

h That's mine. It belongs to _____

i Those are their books. These books are _____

j Is this yours? Does this belong to _____?

3 Rewrite each sentence so that it contains the word in capitals.

a Harry is one of my friends. **MINE**
Harry is a friend of mine.

b That idea was theirs. **THEIR**

c This one belongs to us. **OURS**

d This is my pencil, but where's the one that belongs to you? **YOURS**

e Sue is talking to one of her friends. **HERS**

f This is his bike. **HIM**

g Do they own that house? **THEIRS**

h That cup is yours. **YOUR**

4 Complete the sentences giving advice to climbers with a reflexive pronoun (*myself* etc).

a If you are climbing alone, and have an accident, you have to try and keep calm. You have to ask ....*yourself*........ a number of questions.

b Have you hurt .... in any way?

c Sometimes when we have injured .... , we don't even realize that this has happened.

d Some people may not realize they have cut .... until they see the blood.

e It's important to think carefully: 'Can I look after .... in this situation?

f In some cases you may have to make a difficult decision to save ....

g In a famous case, climber Aron Ralston trapped his arm, and was forced to cut it off in order to free ....

h Very few people think that they .... could do that kind of thing.

i But most of us would have to consider doing it if we found .... in a similar situation.

history

5 Complete the sentence so that it contains a word beginning *some-*, *any-*, *no-*, *every-*.

a We have all heard of the Pyramid of Giza, one of the seven wonders of the ancient world.
   ....*Everyone has*........ heard of the Pyramid of Giza, one of the seven wonders of the ancient world.

b It is not known exactly how such a huge pyramid was built.
   .... exactly how such a huge pyramid was built.

c This huge project probably involved all the people who could work.
   This huge project probably involved .... who could work.

d We can also assume that it must have been designed and planned.
   We can also assume that .... must have designed and planned it.

e Most pyramids were tombs, but now they are empty inside.
   Most pyramids were tombs, but now .... inside.

f If you ask people whether there were pyramids in Greece, they would probably answer 'No'.
   If you ask .... whether there are pyramids in Greece, they would probably answer 'No'.

g People all suppose that the Egyptian pyramids are the oldest, but this may not be true.
   .... that the Egyptian pyramids are the oldest, but this may not be true.

h People don't visit the Greek pyramid of Hellenikon, but in fact it may be older than any of the Egyptian pyramids.
   .... the Greek pyramid of Hellenikon, but in fact it may be older than any of the Egyptian pyramids.

i People don't know exactly why it was built, but it is believed to be a monument over a tomb.
   .... exactly why it was built, but it is believed to be a monument over a tomb.

j It's not one of the seven wonders of the world, but it is an interesting thing.
   It's not one of the seven wonders of the world, but it is ....

GLOSSARY

6 Replace the underlined part of the sentence with a word beginning *some-*, *any-*, *no-*, *every-*, and *else*.

a There's <u>another thing</u> I want to ask.
......*something else*......

b I think I'd like advice from <u>another person</u>.
....

c <u>Another thing</u> is worrying me.
....

d We're alone. <u>All the other people</u> have left.
....

e Jim is mad about football. He thinks about <u>only that</u>. ....

f Is there <u>another person</u> waiting outside?
....

g Does <u>another person</u> want to use the computer?
....

h There isn't <u>another thing</u> in the box. It's empty.
....

i Mary has just told me that she loves <u>another person</u>! ....

j Please be quick. <u>Another person</u> wants the computer. ....

7 Complete the sentence with *somewhere*, *anywhere*, *nowhere*, or *everywhere*.

a Eighty per cent of the flora and fauna on the Galapagos Islands exists......*nowhere*......else.

b A mosquito will lay its eggs.............................. there is water.

c Every second, someone.............................. in Africa is infected with tuberculosis.

d Forests in general and rainforests in particular are in danger..............................

e Is there.............................. on Earth where life is impossible?

f All animals need.............................. to feed and sleep in safety.

g Tsunamis are most often caused by earthquakes.............................. in the Pacific.

h Is there.............................. in the universe without heat energy of some kind?

i Bacteria are micro-organisms that grow.............................. on Earth.

j .... on Earth are glaciers easier to study than in Iceland.

8 Complete the text with one suitable word in each space.

One of the adventures of Odysseus is the story of Polyphemus the Cyclops, a one-eyed giant. Odysseus arrived at an island with a......*his*......men, and took some of them to the cave where Polyphemus lived. There wasn't b.............................. else in the cave, only some sheep and goats. When the Cyclops arrived, he shut c.............................. in his cave by rolling a huge rock over the entrance and then killed some of the men. d.............................. else could move the rock, so Odysseus knew that it would be foolish to kill the Cyclops. He had to think of e.............................. else to do. He waited until the evening and made the Cyclops drunk. He told the Cyclops that his name was f.............................. . When the giant was asleep, Odysseus and his men pushed a huge piece of wood into his eye, so that he became blind. The Cyclops shouted with pain, and some other giants heard and asked him who had injured g.............................. . He told them Odysseus's name, and so they laughed, and supposed that he had just hurt h.............................. . Odysseus and his men escaped by hiding i.............................. under the sheep as they left the cave in the morning. Polyphemus couldn't see or feel j.............................. . The giant threw huge rocks at the Greeks' ship, but they managed to escape from the island.

GLOSSARY

EXTENSION ACTIVITY

Write ten sentences using *someone*, *no-one*, *everyone*, *somewhere* and *nowhere*.

35 adjectives

Adjectives describe things. They generally come in front of nouns. They have one form and do not change for singular and plural or before masculine and feminine nouns.

*This subject can be **interesting**.*   *Hilary Clinton is **famous**.*

They can appear on their own without a noun after some verbs: *be, look, seem, appear, become, get*.

*This **seems interesting**.*   *You're **becoming difficult**.*   *It's **getting hot**.*

Some adjectives eg *alive, alike, ashamed, alone, asleep, awake, afraid*, can only be used after *be, seem, appear to, look*.

*He's not **awake**.*   *He's **asleep**.*

*He **looks afraid**.*   *He **appears to be asleep**.*

order of adjectives

When we use more than one adjective, we use this general order. Note that a noun can do the work of an adjective.

opinion / quality	*famous, interesting*
size	*small, large*
age	*old*
shape	*round, square*
temperature	*hot, cold*
colour	*red, blue*
where it comes from	*Spanish, Italian*
what it is made of	*glass, metal*
what it is for	*football*

*a **famous old football** stadium*   *a **small round metal** object*

Avoid using more than three adjectives together.

gradable adjectives and intensifiers

Some adjectives, eg those that describe age, size, beauty, can be measured or graded, and are called gradable. We can use intensifiers eg *very, extremely* with them.

*This tree is **extremely old**.*   *It's a **very beautiful** painting.*

*This problem is **extremely difficult**.*   *I feel **very unhappy**.*

Other adjectives cannot be graded because the qualities they describe are either present or absent.

*This painting is **superb**.*   *This problem is **impossible**.*

We cannot say ~~This painting is very superb~~.

We cannot make comparative forms of non-gradable adjectives. For example, we cannot say ~~This problem is more impossible than that one~~.

We can use the intensifiers *really, absolutely* with non-gradable adjectives.

*This painting is **really superb**.*   *This problem is **absolutely impossible**.*

Typical non-gradable adjectives include: *microscopic, enormous, freezing, boiling, wonderful, terrible, excellent, perfect*.

adjectives ending in *-ed* and *-ing*

Some adjectives have two forms, one ending in *-ed* and one in *-ing*.

*Are you **interested** in painting?*

*Yes. I think Paula Rego's paintings are **interesting**.*

Something is:	*interesting, boring, frightening, surprising, confusing* etc
Someone feels:	*interested, bored, frightened, surprised, confused* etc

*You can see from the painting that the girl is really **frightened**.*

1 Complete each sentence about paintings in a gallery so that it contains a word from the list.

afraid   alike   alive   alone   ashamed   ~~asleep~~   awake   dead

a The boy in the painting doesn't seem to have woken up.
The boy in the painting _seems to be asleep._

b Both girls in this painting look the same.
The girls in this painting _____

c I'm not sure that the person in this painting is alive.
I think the person in this painting
_____

d He isn't asleep, but looks as if he is in a dream.
He _____ but looks as if he is in a dream.

e Does this painting frighten you?
_____ of this painting?

f It's a painting of a battle and most of the soldiers are dead.
It's a painting of a battle and very few soldiers are _____

2 Put the adjectives in brackets in the correct order to complete the sentence. Then decide which city in the box the speaker is talking about.

Cairo   Istanbul   ~~London~~   Tokyo   Moscow   Paris   Sydney   Venice

a The best way to get around in the city is to get on a _big, red_ bus. (red, big)   London

b The city is full of _____ palaces along the sides of the canals. (old, wonderful)

c Just outside the city you soon see the _____ shapes of the Pyramids. (stone, vast)

d From the top of the _____ tower you can look across the French capital. (graceful, iron)

e At the heart of the city is this _____ fortress which is still home to the president. (medieval, well-known)

f This is a _____ city, not a centre for historic buildings, but still a great place to visit. (busy, commercial)

g This spectacular city where Europe and Asia meet has _____ buildings, as well as ancient palaces. (modern, tall)

3 Write each possible intensifier at the end of the sentence. One, both or neither may be possible.

a This fish is (really, absolutely) fresh. _really, absolutely_
b Unfortunately the food in the hotel was (very, extremely) terrible. _____
c The mushroom soup was (very, absolutely) tasty. _____
d I find raw fish (absolutely, very) impossible to eat. _____
e This drink should be (very, completely) cold when it is served. _____
f The cheese was good and (extremely, very) cheap. _____
g I'm afraid the meat is (very, really) salty. _____

social studies

4 Underline the correct form.

There are some students who feel a depressed / depressing by studying, especially subjects which they find b confused / confusing. They often leave their work until the last minute, and then find the amount they have to do is simply c exhausted / exhausting, or they are d embarrassed / embarrassing to admit that they need help. They simply become more and more e worried / worrying, and then work even less than before. Or they blame the school system, because the subjects they are studying are just not f interested / interesting. However, you may be g surprised / surprising to know that very few students feel this way, according to recent research. In fact, most students don't find school work h annoying / annoyed at all. They are usually i excited / exciting by the subjects they are studying, and they feel j satisfied / satisfying when they do something well.

adjectives

36 adverbs

An adverb describes an action (a verb), saying how, when or where something happens.

*The girl was sitting **uncomfortably** on the floor.*

*I'll see you **tomorrow**. Wait **outside**.*

(FORM)

Some adverbs of manner (how) add *-ly* to the adjective. Adjectives ending *-e* drop *-e*. Adjectives ending in *-y* change *-y* to *-i*.

uncomfortable	uncomforta**bly**	careful	careful**ly**
happy	happ**ily**	real	real**ly**

irregular adverbs

Some adverbs have an irregular form, eg *good → well*.

adverbs with the same form as adjectives

early	*fast*	*hard*	*high*	*late*	*low*	*right*	*wrong*

Hard and *hardly* are often confused. *Hardly* means 'almost not'. *Hard* is an adverb form meaning 'using a lot of energy'.

*I can **hardly** hear you!*   *Are you working **hard**?*

adjectives that look like adverbs

Some adjectives ending *-ly* look like adverbs but are not, eg *friendly, lovely, lonely, likely, lively, silly*.

frequency adverbs

These describe how often something happens.

*People **often** think that bats are birds, but they are mammals.*

0%	10%	25%	75%	90%	100%
never	*rarely*	*sometimes*	*often*	*usually*	*always*

Put the frequency adverb between the subject and verb, but after *be*.

*A painting **often tells** a story.*   *What sort of films do you **usually go** and see?*

*Cartoon films **are usually** entertaining.*

intensifiers   (see **Unit 35** on gradable adjectives)

Adverbs like *very, really, extremely* are used to make adjectives or adverbs stronger.

*I think this film is **really** terrible.*   *Everyone has worked **extremely** carefully.*

too, very

Too means more than is necessary, *very* means a lot. Compare the meanings:

*I'm **too tired**, I can't work any more.*

*This is a **very interesting** painting.*

Too is often used with *to*-infinitive to explain why something is not possible.

*I'm **too tired to work**.*

well, ill, bad, badly

Well and *badly* are adverbs and describe how an action is performed.

*She writes **well**.*   *He plays tennis **badly**.*

Well and *ill* are adjectives describing health.

*I don't **feel well**.*   *You **look ill**.*

With verbs like *look, seem, feel* we do not use an adverb.

*This fish **smells bad**.*   *That **looks good**.*

1 Decide whether the words underlined are acting as adjectives or adverbs.

a Some people think modern paintings are 'difficult'.   ......adjective......

b They find them confusing because they are not 'pictures'   ....

c They say that a good photograph would be better.   ....

d At least, they say, a photo does show the real world.   ....

e It's also hard to persuade them that the artist worked hard.   ....

f Some modern painting could easily have been painted by a child.   ....

g Artists sometimes make the situation more difficult.   ....

h They write explanations of their work which can seem unnecessary.   ....

i They may not seem to have very much connection with the art.   ....

j Still, if the work seems interesting then it is worth looking at.   ....

2 Complete the sentence with an adverb formed from the adjective in brackets.

a The play begins rather (slow) ....slowly........ with a scene at a bus stop.

b Just as you think the main characters are going to live (happy) .... ever after, the film takes an unexpected twist.

c This book is (beautiful) .... written, but in the end the story is disappointing.

d Mark's guitar playing is pretty good, but he sings so (bad) .... that I just wanted him to stop.

e The whole show was (real) .... entertaining and the singers and dancers showed a lot of enthusiasm.

f This is a (true) .... great book. Go out and buy it today.

g This is an (incredible) .... good album, with a lot of fantastic tracks.

h Jim Carrey in the main role is (unbelievable) .... funny.

3 Put the frequency adverb in brackets into the most appropriate space in the sentence.
Decide whether the statement describes a good listener, or a bad listener.

a I .....often..... finish .... sentences for other people.   (often)
Good or bad listener? ....

b Other people .... seem to be comfortable .... when they talk to me.   (usually)
Good or bad listener? ....

c When .... people talk to me, I .... look at the floor.   (sometimes)
Good or bad listener? ....

d If I don't .... like a person's voice, I .... pay attention to them.   (never)
Good or bad listener? ....

e I .... try to be sympathetic when .... people talk about their problems.   (usually)
Good or bad listener? ....

f I .... try to give people my complete attention when they .... speak to me.   (always)
Good or bad listener? ....

g I .... interrupt people before they have .... finished what they are saying.   (rarely)
Good or bad listener? ....

h I .... laugh at what .... people say to me, and upset them.   (sometimes)
Good or bad listener? ....

adverbs

4 Make an adverb ending in -ly from the word in brackets, and use it to complete the sentence.

a Cholera is a disease spread by dirty water, either when people drink the water, or eat food which has been washed in the water, and not _properly_ cooked. (proper)

b ...., until the mid 19th century, people believed that the disease travelled through the air. (unfortunate)

c In the crowded cities of 19th-century Britain, cholera spread .... (easy)

d Most doctors .... believed that fresh air and a better diet would prevent the disease. (wrong)

e Huge fires were .... lit in the streets to drive away the infection, and the clothes of victims were also burned. (usual)

f The streets were also cleaned .... with powerful chemicals. (thorough)

g However, people continued to suffer .... (dreadful)

h In 1854, a doctor in London, John Snow, ... proved that cholera spread through infected drinking water. (definite)

i He did this by .... collecting statistics about the infection in one part of London. (careful)

Dr John Snow

j He managed to prove that in an area where deaths from cholera were highest, the water was .... responsible for cholera infection. (entire) Improvements made to sewers and supplies of drinking water later led to a decrease in deaths from cholera.

GLOSSARY

5 Use the prompts to make a question with the frequency adverb in brackets.

a you / take the lead in group discussions? (usually)

Do you usually take the lead in discussions ?

b you / feel / unable to say anything interesting? (sometimes)

.... ?

c you / change / your opinion after you hear what others say? (often)

.... ?

d you / listen carefully to what all the others are saying? (always)

.... ?

e you / feel that nobody is interested in what you say? (sometimes)

.... ?

f you / find ways of keeping other people's attention? (usually)

.... ?

g you / avoid saying what you really think? (often)

.... ?

h you / encourage other members of the group to speak? (always)

.... ?

6 <u>Underline</u> the correct word.

a I recommend this book. I think it's *too / <u>very</u>* interesting.

b This is a *too / very* unusual film, and probably won't appeal to everyone.

c This book has more than 700 pages, so it's *too / very* long to read in an afternoon!

d I liked this film because it is *too / very* funny, and it made me laugh a lot.

e What I like most about this book is that the characters are *too / very* true-to-life.

f This film is *too / very* romantic, and it really made me cry!

g I couldn't understand this book at all! The language is just *too / very* difficult.

h There are some *too / very* good scenes in this film, but on the whole I didn't like it.

7 Decide whether the word underlined is used as an adjective or adverb.

a We had a <u>lovely</u> time in the hotel.
........................*adjective*........................

b All the staff greeted us <u>warmly</u>.
....

c And they spoke to us very <u>politely</u>.
....

d Most people we met in the town were very <u>friendly</u>.
....

e You certainly never feel <u>lonely</u> in a place like this!
....

f The night life is also very <u>lively</u>.
....

g We are very <u>likely</u> to go back next year.
....

h We would certainly <u>thoroughly</u> recommend it.
....

8 Complete the sentence with *well, ill, bad, badly, hard,* or *hardly*.

a Last Thursday I woke up feeling ....*ill.*..........

b When I got up I realized I could .... walk.

c I had exercised .... in the gym the night before.

d My left ankle seemed to be .... swollen.

e I didn't feel at all .... but I had to go to the doctor's.

f I found it .... to walk there, but I managed it in the end.

g The .... news was that I needed an x-ray and had to go to the hospital.

h The doctor there told me there was nothing seriously wrong. I could .... believe it!

EXTENSION ACTIVITY

1 Write a sentence for each adverb.

carefully   slowly   happily   badly   hard

2 Check that your answers to Exercise 8 are correct. Translate your answers into your own language.

*Need more practice? Go to the **Review** on page 192.*

adverbs

37 making comparisons

Use comparative forms of adjectives

- to compare two things with *than*.
  *People are **bigger than** snakes.*

- to compare two things without *than*.
  *Which are **bigger**, people or snakes?   People are **bigger**.*

- to compare two things with *than*, repeating *be*, or the auxiliary from the verb.
  *I'm taller **than you are**. You look shorter **than I do**.*

- with a *than*-clause.
  *This book is more interesting **than I expected**.*

spelling rules

- one-syllable words add -*er*   *long – longer*
- one-syllable words ending vowel + consonant, double the consonant   *hot – hotter*
- words ending in -*y* change -*y* to -*i* and add -*er*
- two-syllable words ending -*y* change -*y* to -*i* and add -*er*
  angry – angrier   happy – happier   lucky – luckier
- some two-syllable adjectives use -*er* or *more*. Use *more* if you are in doubt.
  more common / commoner   more narrow / narrower
  more pleasant / pleasanter   more polite / politer   more simple / simpler
- most two- and three- syllable words put *more* in front
  more modern   more expensive   more comfortable
- irregular adjectives
  good – better   bad – worse   far – farther or further

Make comparisons with

- a comparative form + *than*.
  *The bite of an Egyptian Cobra is more poisonous **than** the bite of an Indian Cobra.*

- *less* + adjective + *than*, *not as* + *adjective* + *as*
  *The bite of an Indian Cobra is **less** poisonous **than** the bite of an Egyptian Cobra.*
  *The bite of an Indian Cobra is **not as** poisonous **as** the bite of an Egyptian Cobra.*

- *(just) as* + adjective + *as* when two things compare equally.
  *I don't care which one is more poisonous. I'm **(just) as scared** of them both.*

comparative adjective + comparative adjective

Use two comparative adjectives joined by *and* for a changing situation.
  *Learning gets **harder and harder** as people grow older.*
Use *the* + comparative, *the* + comparative for the same meaning.
  ***The older** people get, **the harder** learning is.*

intensifiers

Use intensifiers *much, a lot* etc

- to say how great the comparison is.
  *It's **a lot hotter** than yesterday.   This chair is **much more comfortable**.*

1 Write a comparative sentence using the information and an adjective from the list. Make any necessary changes, leaving out any unnecessary detail.

> deep   dry   high   large   ~~long~~   low   old   small

a The River Mackenzie, Canada: 4,240 km
   The River Niger, Africa: 4,170 km
   The River Mackenzie is longer than the River Niger.

b Lake Victoria, Africa: 69,484 km²
   Lake Michigan, North America: 57,757 km²

c The Marianas Trench, Pacific Ocean: 10,900 m
   The Japan Trench, Northern Pacific: 9,000 m

d Mont Blanc, France: 4,807 m
   Mount Elbrus, Russia: 5,642 m

e Arica, Chile: average rainfall 0.76 mm per year
   The Libyan Sahara Desert: average rainfall, less than 15 mm per year

f The oldest rocks in Scotland: 3 billion years old
   The oldest rocks in Canada: 4 billion years old

g The lowest recorded temperature in Finland: –57°C
   The lowest recorded temperature in Sweden: –52°C

h The island state of Nauru, South Pacific: 21 km²
   Monaco: 1.6 km²

2 Complete the second sentence so that it means the same as the first sentence, using the adjective in capitals.

a The first question in the test was easier than the second one.   DIFFICULT
   The second question in the test was ......*more difficult than the first one.*......

b I think my sweets taste better than yours.   TASTY
   I think my sweets ....

c Staying at home for a holiday is cheaper than travelling abroad.   EXPENSIVE
   Travelling abroad for a holiday ....

d The Royal Hotel is more old-fashioned than the Holton Hotel.   MODERN
   The Holton Hotel ....

e This chair isn't as comfortable as the sofa.   COMFORTABLE
   The sofa ....

f I think water refreshes me more than milk does.   REFRESHING
   I think water is ....

g Romantic films interest me more than war films.   INTERESTING
   I find ....

h Jim's suitcase was lighter than Jack's suitcase.   HEAVY
   Jim's suitcase ....

making comparisons

3 Complete the sentence with one word.

a I expected my exam results to be better.
   My exam results were _worse_ than I expected.

b Harry doesn't look so clever.
   Harry is _____ than he looks.

c The black coat is smaller than the brown one.
   The brown coat is _____ than the black one.

d Helen's brother is older than her.
   Helen is _____ than her brother.

e Jim Carrey's previous film wasn't as funny as his latest one.
   Jim Carrey's latest film is _____ than the previous one.

f I thought the station was nearer.
   The station was _____ than I thought.

g Maths lessons don't seem as short as English lessons.
   Maths lessons seem _____ than English lessons.

h I'm sure this year is colder than last year.
   I'm sure last year was _____ than this year.

i I'm not as happy as I used to be.
   I used to be _____ than I am now.

j The weather yesterday was worse.
   The weather today is _____ than it was yesterday.

4 Rewrite the first sentence so that it contains the word or words in capitals.

a This book isn't as interesting as that one.   LESS
   This book is less interesting than that one.

b A bike is less expensive than a scooter.   MORE
   _____

c You're taller than I am.   AS
   _____

d The first explanation is unlikely, and so is the second.   JUST
   _____

e Carol thought the accident was less serious than it was.   MORE
   _____

f My arm isn't as painful as it was.   THAN
   _____

5 Complete the text with an adjective from the list, using a comparative form where necessary.

cheap	clever	difficult	easy
fast	important	up-to-date	~~essential~~

Nowadays using computers is more and more a _essential_ . We can't do without them, and you don't have to be an expert to use one, as using a computer is b _____ and _____ all the time. You don't need to be rich either, as computers are also becoming c _____ and _____ as time goes on. Also, if you are studying, the Internet is becoming more and more d _____ as a place to find information. This used to take a long time, but the latest machines are a great improvement. The e _____ the computer, the _____ it works. However, protecting computers from viruses is becoming more and more f _____ as the people who invent viruses are becoming g _____ and _____ . The Internet has become a dangerous place, so it is more and more h _____ to be very careful when we use computers.

6 Choose the correct form, A, B or C, to complete the text.

When you look into the night sky, you may not be able to tell the difference between stars and planets, but planets are **a** ....A.... to Earth. However, they are still very far away, and a journey to Mars would be about nine months, **b** .... than a journey to the Moon (about three days). Even if your future space ship was **c** .... the simple space probes we have now, it would still take you a couple of years to get to Jupiter, which is **d** .... Earth – more than 1,300 times, in fact, and it's more than 300 times **e** .... Jupiter is a giant ball of gas and the atmospheric pressure is **f** .... it is on Earth. If you could land there, you would be **g** .... – more than twice as much. The whole planet is **h** .... Earth as well, and scientists think that the centre of the planet may be as hot as 10,000°C. Interestingly, the day on Jupiter is **i** .... , and only lasts about ten hours, but a year on Jupiter lasts for 11 Earth years. So when you came back, you would be **j** .... when you set out!

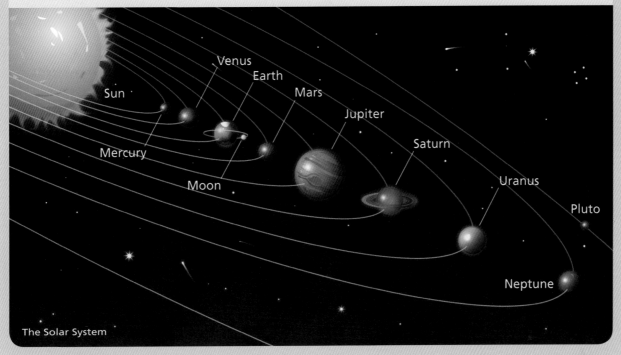

The Solar System

a **A** *a lot nearer*	**B** *nearer than*	**C** *less near than*
b **A** *more longer*	**B** *as long as*	**C** *much longer*
c **A** *more fast*	**B** *a lot faster than*	**C** *not as fast as*
d **A** *very much bigger than*	**B** *as big as*	**C** *less big than*
e **A** *as dense as*	**B** *more dense*	**C** *less dense than*
f **A** *a lot greater than*	**B** *just as great*	**C** *less great*
g **A** *more than heavy*	**B** *less heavy*	**C** *much heavier*
h **A** *as hot as*	**B** *a lot hotter than*	**C** *hotter*
i **A** *a lot shorter*	**B** *shorter than*	**C** *less short*
j **A** *more old*	**B** *older*	**C** *much older than*

EXTENSION ACTIVITY

1 Write six sentences comparing yourself now with yourself aged eight.
2 Write six sentences comparing cars and bikes.

GLOSSARY

making comparisons

38 superlatives and comparatives

forming superlatives

– the spelling rules are the same as for comparatives, but add -est

    long – **the longest**   hot – **the hottest**   happy – **the happiest**

– form the superlative of longer adjectives by putting *most* or *least* in front

    the most modern   **the least** expensive   **the most** comfortable

– irregular forms

    good – **the best**   bad – **the worst**

Use the superlative forms of adjectives

● to compare one thing with a lot of other things of the same kind. Put the superlative adjective between *the* and (noun).

*Most experts say that the Anaconda is **the biggest snake** in the world.*
***The largest one** ever captured was about 9 metres in length.*

● with *ever* and present perfect to talk about experiences.

*This is **the easiest language I've ever learned**.*

We use present perfect because we are talking about the speaker's lifetime experience, which is unfinished.

We can also use comparative adjectives when we talk about experiences.

***Have you ever seen a bigger snake** (than this one)?*

forming comparative adverbs

– adverbs ending -ly use *more*   slowly – **more** slowly

    *Jim runs **more slowly than** anyone I know!*

– adverbs with the same forms as adjectives without -ly add -er

    fast – fast**er**   hard – hard**er**

– irregular forms   well – **better**

Use comparative adverbs

● to compare two actions.

*Anna runs **faster than** the rest of the team.*

● without *than*.

*Who **runs faster**, Anna or Helen?*   *Anna **runs faster**.*

● with *than*, repeating the auxiliary from the verb.

*I run faster **than you do**.*

forming superlative adverbs

– adverbs ending -ly use *the most / least*   slowly – **the most** slowly

    *Jim runs the **most slowly** of anyone I know!*

– adverbs without -ly add -est   fast – **the fast**est

– irregular forms   well – **the best**

Use superlative adverbs

● to compare one action with a lot of other actions of the same kind, using *of*.

*Everyone worked hard, but Kate worked (the) **hardest**.*
*Kate worked **the hardest** of all the girls in her class.*

1 Complete the sentence with the superlative form of the adjective in capitals.

a The ___heaviest___ whale ever caught weighed more than 171,000 kg.   HEAVY

b The _____ whale recorded was over 33 m in length.   LONG

c A specimen of king's holly, a plant found in the rainforest of Tasmania,
is one of the _____ plants on Earth – over 43,000 years old.   OLD

d The cheetah is the _____ creature on Earth, and is capable of
running at over 110 kph.   FAST

e The _____ part of the ocean where a fish has been found was
8,372 m down in the Puerto Rican Trench.   DEEP

f The _____ fish in the sea is the sailfish, which can travel at 100 kph.   SPEEDY

g No prizes for guessing the world's _____ fish. It is the deadly
piranha fish.   FEROCIOUS

h The sea wasp, which lives off the north coast of Australia, is the
_____ creature in the sea. If it stings you, you have between
30 seconds and four minutes to live.   POISONOUS

i The _____ spider in the world is the goliath spider from
South America, which can be 28 cm across.   LARGE

j And the _____ mammal is probably Savi's pygmy shrew, a
mouse-like creature, which weighs between 1 and 3 grams.   SMALL

2 Complete the sentence so that it means the same as the first sentence, and includes a superlative adjective.

a I've never sat in a more comfortable classroom than this.
This is the ___most comfortable classroom I've ever___ sat in.

b I've never eaten a tastier school lunch than this.
This is the _____ eaten.

c I've never read a worse book than this.
This is the _____ read.

d We've never had a more useful English lesson than this.
This is the _____ had.

e I've never solved an easier problem than this.
This is the _____ solved.

f I've never taken a longer test than this.
This is the _____ taken.

g I've never written a more difficult test than this.
This is the _____ written.

h I've never seen a more entertaining school play than this.
This is the _____ seen.

i We've never used a more interesting textbook than this.
This is the _____ used.

j I've never had a better friend than you.
You are the _____ had.

3 Rewrite the underlined part of the sentence, using a comparative form of an adverb in the list

| easy | fast | ~~hard~~ | heavy | long | often | slow | well |

a When you tell a lie, your brain has to work <u>more</u>. *harder*

b If you cut your hair a lot it won't grow <u>at an increased speed</u>.

c Acts of forgetting occur <u>with increased frequency</u> as people get older.

d Some crystals grow <u>at a lower speed</u> in space.

e Goats' milk is digested <u>with less difficulty</u> than cows' milk.

f People may live <u>for a greater number of years</u> by eating less.

g People drive <u>with more skill</u> along tree-lined streets.

h As a low weather front approaches, it starts to drizzle and then rains <u>a lot</u> as a warm front approaches.

4 Complete each sentence with a suitable form of an adverb from the list. Then decide if each fact is true or false. Check the factual answers on page 208.

| carefully | clearly | early | ~~easily~~ | fast |
| heavily | loudly | quickly | quietly | slowly |

a Hot water can in fact freeze ......*more easily*...... than cold water.

b Bird flu spreads to humans .... than thought.

c Scientists believe that human beings speak .... now than 250 years ago.

d Brazil's Amazon rainforest is disappearing .... than scientists previously estimated.

e Students who use green pens write ....

f The Earth vibrates and makes a humming noise, and does this .... in the afternoon.

g Teenagers are drinking alcohol earlier and .... than ever before.

h Most younger people think .... in the afternoon.

i Eagles wake up .... than any other birds.

j Eating .... does not reduce your appetite.

A bald headed eagle

GLOSSARY

5 Choose the correct form, A, B, C or D, to complete the sentence.

a You left school ......A...... than I did.

b Mirror, mirror on the wall, who is .... of them all?

c What's .... book you've ever read?

d Helen's teacher congratulated her for working so .... before the exams.

e Our company can help you to manage your money ....

f You can type .... I can.

g I find French .... to speak than Italian.

h Which moves .... , a snail or a worm?

i Have you ever eaten .... meal than this?

j Picasso's paintings are among ....

a A *later*	B *more lately*	C *most lately*	D *more late*
b A *the more beautiful*	B *as beautiful*	C *the most beautiful*	D *more beautiful*
c A *more interesting*	B *the most interesting*	C *the more interesting*	D *more interesting than*
d A *hardly*	B *hardest*	C *hard*	D *harder*
e A *successful*	B *just as successful*	C *more successful than*	D *more successfully*
f A *much faster than*	B *more fast as*	C *just as fast than*	D *fastest than*
g A *difficult*	B *more difficult*	C *as difficult*	D *most difficult*
h A *quicker than*	B *as quick as*	C *more quickly*	D *as quickest*
i A *as good*	B *the best*	C *the good*	D *a better*
j A *the most expensive*	B *more expensive*	C *as expensive*	D *not as expensive*

geography

6 Complete the text with the most suitable form of the adjective in brackets.

London is one of **a** (large) ......the largest........ cities in the world. Its population is **b** (low) .... than Tokyo or Shanghai, but it is one of **c** (popular) .... tourist destinations of all. London is probably **d** (famous) .... for its museums, galleries, palaces and other sights, but it also includes a **e** (wide) .... range of peoples, cultures and religions than many other places. People used to say that it was **f** (dirty) .... city too, but it is now much **g** (clean) .... than it was. To the surprise of many people, it now has some of **h** (good) .... restaurants in Europe too. For some people, this makes London **i** (exciting) .... city in Europe. Unfortunately, London is definitely not **j** (expensive) .... city in Europe, though a holiday in London is good value for money, considering what there is to see and do there.

GLOSSARY

EXTENSION ACTIVITY

1 Make a list of facts about your country, using superlative adjectives.

2 Write a sentence for each adjective or adverb.
the most uncomfortable   the hardest
the least expensive   more quickly
more carefully   more quietly

superlatives and comparatives

39 place prepositions, prepositions in phrases, place adverbs

in, at, on

Use *in* for things enclosed in something else. We use *in* with towns and countries.

Sugar dissolves **in water**.   The cell is found **in the upper part of the leaf**.

in Ghana   **in Pisa**   **in the north of Italy**

Use *at* with a place.

Ask **at the cinema** for details.   **At the point** where the two lines meet …

Use *on* for things on the surface or side of something, and with islands.

Some lichens grow **on bare rock**.   There were no trees **on the island**.

We generally use *on* for trains, buses, ships and planes, and *in* for cars.

I met an old friend **on the train**.

into, out of

Into describes movement in and *out of* is the opposite. In everyday speech, *out* is used instead of *out of*.

Two men came **into the bank.**   Everyone ran **out of the burning building**.

Out of is also the opposite of *in*.

Mr Smith is **out of the building** at the moment.

inside, outside

Inside is used to describe something in a room etc, especially when the speaker is outside.

The police were watching what was happening **inside the bank**.

Can you stand **outside the door,** please.

to, from

Use *to* with verbs of movement, change etc, though not with *home*.

Not many children **go to school** in Burkina Faso.   I **went home** at 6.00.

Use *to* and *from* to describe the two points of a movement.

It changes **from a liquid to a solid**.

below, under, beneath

Below means 'at a lower level' and occurs in phrases such as *below zero; below average; see below for more information*.

Under can mean 'covered by', as in *under the bed* and *under a pile of books*.

We also use it in these phrases:

Look it up **under 'Mammals'**.   Children **under five** are admitted free.

Beneath means 'exactly under' and can be used in place of under.

We sat **beneath / under a tree**.   **Beneath / under a pile** of books …

above, over

Above means at a higher level than something, and not touching it.

Put your hands **above** your head.   There is a forest **above** the village.

Over is the opposite of *under*, and can mean 'touching or covering'.

They put a blanket **over** him to keep him warm.

Above and *over* can be used to mean the same thing, especially when something is at a higher level exactly vertically.

They lived in a flat **above / over** the bank.

preposition + noun + of

at the end of	at the side of	at the beginning of	at the end of
at the front of	at the back of	at the bottom of	at the top of
in front of	in the middle of		

*The cinema is **at the end of** the street.*
*Two very tall people were sitting **in front of** me.*

prepositions as adverbs

Many prepositions are used as adverbs.

*Is Susan **in**?* (at home)   *No, she's **out**.* (not at home)
*From the mountain, we could see a village far **below**.*

Other examples: *away* (on holiday); *indoors; inside; outside; underneath.*

*Peter is **away** at the moment. He's on a trip abroad. In France, actually.*
*Let's go **indoors** / **inside**. It's getting cold **outside**.*
*If you can't find it **on top**, look **underneath**.*

....

1 <u>Underline</u> the correct option.

a   More than a thousand people came *at* / *<u>to</u>* the match.

b   I'm sorry, but no children *beneath* / *under* twelve are allowed.

c   The noise was loud, so I put my hands *above* / *over* my ears.

d   Are you going *at* / *to* the cinema this evening?

e   There was a bird singing in the tree just *outside* / *out of* the window.

f   David didn't feel well while he was *in* / *on* the ship.

g   Get out *of* / *from* my house, or I'll call the police.

h   Her left leg had to be cut off *above* / *over* the knee.

i   David Bowie was born *at* / *in* London in 1947.

j   Maria was walking *in* / *into* the garden picking flowers.

2 Rewrite each sentence so that it contains the word in capitals.

a   Can you tell me whether Jim is at home?   IN
    Can you tell me whether Jim is in?

b   Mary has gone to live in a foreign country.   ABROAD

c   Shall we go into the house now?   INDOORS

d   This snake is red on the top but green on the bottom.   UNDERNEATH

e   Don't come in, please.   OUTSIDE

f   David has gone on a trip.   AWAY

g   Alan lives on the other side of the road.   OPPOSITE

h   Sorry, but Sue isn't here at the moment.   OUT

3 Complete the text with *in*, *at* and *on*.

Many archaeologists had searched for the tombs of Pharaohs **a** ....*in*.... the Valley of the Kings
b .... Egypt. Only Howard Carter believed he knew where the tomb might be. He had a map
of the valley, and **c** .... it he had marked all the excavations until he discovered a space. **d** ....
the ground there was a pile of stones and earth from earlier excavations. Some steps were uncovered,
and **e** .... the bottom of the steps was a door. **f** .... the door was the symbol of Tutankhamun.
Carter had to wait for Lord Carnarvon, who was **g** .... home **h** .... England, to arrive. Carnarvon
was paying for the work. When he arrived **i** .... the excavation, after digging some more, Carter and
his workers broke through a door and found themselves **j** .... the tomb. **k** .... this point they
thought they had failed, because the tomb was empty. Then they found another door, which led to an
undisturbed room. There were many beautiful things **l** .... this room, and wonderful paintings
m .... the walls. Most of the objects from the tomb are now displayed **n** .... a local museum.

GLOSSARY

4 Complete the sentence with *in*, *at*, *on* or *to*.

a Columbus and his three ships started on the voyage ....*to*.... America in August 1492.
b They stopped first .... one of the Canary Islands.
c On 12 October they came .... the coast of the Bahamas.
d From there they went .... Cuba, where one of the ships, the *Pinto*, left in search of gold ....
   an island called 'Babeque'.
e Columbus continued with the other two ships
   and they came .... Hispaniola on 5 December.
f Unfortunately, the flagship *Santa Maria* ran aground
   .... a reef on Christmas Eve, and sank the next day.
g Columbus built a fort .... the shore and left
   some of his men there, because there was not room
   for all the men .... the tiny *Niña*, the other ship.
h While he was on his way back .... Spain,
   Columbus found the *Pinto* again.
i The two ships left together, but were parted by
   a storm .... the North Atlantic.
j Both ships arrived .... Lisbon on 15 March
   within a few hours of each other.

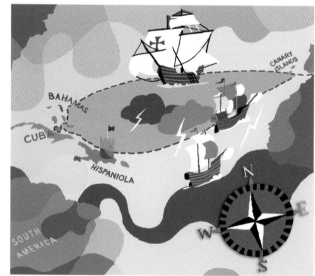

5 Complete the sentence with a suitable preposition.

a The uvula is a small piece of flesh that hangs down ....*at*.... the back of your throat.
b The island of Alcatraz is .... the middle of San Francisco Bay.
c Write your address .... the top of the letter on the right-hand side.
d It was hard to watch the match because there were several tall people standing .... front of me.
e .... the end of the play, the whole audience burst into applause.
f The man was completely bald .... the top of his head.
g Anna felt tired, so she stopped the car .... the side of the road and got out.
h Divers cannot work .... the bottom of the sea for very long.

6 Choose the correct option, A, B, C or D, to complete the text.

We know that the inside of the Earth has a metallic core (or central part), a rocky mantle (or outer part), and a thin crust or surface. As a result of high pressure **a** _____*B*_____ the core, it is hotter **b** _____ the centre of the Earth than it is **c** _____ the Sun. The mantle is a layer of dense rock that lies **d** _____ the surface and above the liquid core.

The crust is the thinnest layer, being only about 35 km deep **e** _____ continents, and **f** _____ the oceans it is even thinner – only 5 km. Because of the crust's low density the material floats **g** _____ the denser mantle. The crust is divided into sections called tectonic plates. The Earth as we now know it was formed in four different stages. First of all, the most dense material (eg iron) sank **h** _____ the centre of the planet. Lighter materials and gases stayed **i** _____ the surface and **j** _____ the atmosphere. The dense material formed the core of the Earth, and the lighter solids formed the crust. In the second stage, impacts from objects eg asteroids, comets, left the kind of crater marks we can still see **k** _____ the Moon.

During the third stage, lava came up **l** _____ the Earth's crust and rain began to fall **m** _____ the sky. The first heavy rains formed oceans and lakes.

The fourth stage is still going on now as the surface changes. Mountains are rising **n** _____ some areas. Large areas of solid material, tectonic plates, are moving just **o** _____ the surface.

Crust   Mantle

Inner core   Outer core

a	A *to*	B *at*	C *from*	D *outside*
b	A *to*	B *from*	C *under*	D *at*
c	A *on*	B *under*	C *to*	D *from*
d	A *into*	B *outside*	C *below*	D *on*
e	A *to*	B *at*	C *under*	D *in*
f	A *under*	B *in*	C *on*	D *outside*
g	A *on*	B *from*	C *under*	D *out of*
h	A *at*	B *in*	C *on*	D *to*

i	A *in*	B *to*	C *at*	D *from*
j	A *at*	B *on*	C *under*	D *in*
k	A *in*	B *on*	C *to*	D *from*
l	A *in*	B *from*	C *at*	D *outside*
m	A *from*	B *to*	C *under*	D *in*
n	A *at*	B *to*	C *in*	D *on*
o	A *to*	B *from*	C *below*	D *in*

GLOSSARY

place prepositions, prepositions in phrases, place adverbs

EXTENSION ACTIVITY

1 Check that you have the correct answers to Exercise 3. Translate the sentences into your own language.

2 Write a sentence with each phrase.
at the back of   at the end of   at the bottom of
in the middle of   in front of   into the room

40 time (1)

at, in, within, on

Use *at* with clock time and *midday*, *midnight* and *night*. Note: we cannot say ~~at last night~~ .

   at 5.12 am   **at midday**   **at midnight**   **at night**

Use *at* with *Christmas*, *Easter* and *New Year*.

   *What are you doing **at Christmas**?*

Use *at* with expressions showing definite times.

   *What are you doing **at the moment**?*   *I'll see you **at the end of** the week.*

   *Ms Graham is busy **at present**.*   *What were you doing **at the time of** the robbery?*

Use *in* with months, years, seasons, and *morning, afternoon, evening*.

   in April   **in 1906**   **in spring / summer / autumn / winter**

   in the morning   **in the afternoon**   **in the evening**

Use *in* with units of time (*week, hour, moment* etc) to refer to future points.

   *I'll be back **in a week**.*   *I'll see you **in a moment**.*

If we use *time*, we usually add an apostrophe.

   *I'll see you **in six months' time**.*

Within means inside or during a period of time.

   *The work must be completed **within a month**. Four other cases have been reported **within the past week**.*

Use *on* with dates, days of the week and expressions with *day*. Note: we don't say '~~on next Friday~~'.

   on April 18th   **on Tuesday**

   on the last day of August   *We're going out **on my birthday**.*

next, last

Use *next* for the future, and *last* for the past with *week, month, year, summer* etc.

   *I'll see you **next week**.*   ***Last summer** was the driest for twenty years.*

since, for, ago, ages

Use *since* with a point in time and *for* with a period of time.

   *I've been waiting **since six o'clock***   *I've been waiting **for two hours**.*

Use *ago* to measure time in the past.

   *The earthquake took place more than **100 years ago**.*

For ages means for a long time. It follows present perfect simple as it describes a period of time up to the present eg *I haven't seen you **for ages**.*

It's ages since ... is followed by a past simple verb, as *since* describes a point in time.

   ***It's ages since I last went** to the theatre.*

from, to, till, until / till

Use *from* and *to* for the start and finish of a period of time eg *I'll be there from 5.00 to 6.30.*

Until means up to a point in time, and then stopping. *Till* is an informal form of *until*.

   *I waited **until seven o' clock**, and then left.*

   *Some people were trapped under buildings **until the following day**.*

Use *not + until* to show when something finally happens.

   *Helen **didn't arrive** at the party **until** 11.30. It **wasn't until** much later that the truth finally came out.*

by, by the time

Use *by* to mean at some point in the period of time before.

   *The city was rebuilt **by the end of** the following year.*

Use *by the time* to describe events which will be, or were, too late.

   ***By the time we get** to the party, it will be over!*   (We'll be too late)

   ***By the time (that) we got** to the station, the train had left.*   (We were too late)

during

Use *during* to mean 'in a period of time', either at one point, or for the whole period.

   ***During the night**, people felt a sudden shock.*   (one point)

   ***During winter**, some animals in cold countries sleep for long periods.*   (whole period)

1 Complete each question with *at*, *in* or *on*. Check the factual answers on page 208.
What happened …

a ....*in*....1918 .... November 11th .... 5 am?

b .... 1937 .... the 26th of April .... the late afternoon?

c .... 1793 .... about 11 o'clock .... January 21st?

d .... 1865 .... about 10 o'clock .... the evening .... the 14th of April?

e .... 1928 .... November 18th?

f .... 1969 .... 20th July .... about 3.00 am GMT?

g .... 1903 .... Dec 17th .... about 10.30 .... the morning?

h .... July 16th .... the early morning .... 1945?

i .... the evening .... the 26th November .... 1962?

j .... 2004 .... about 1.00 am GMT .... the 26th December?

2 Complete the sentence with *at*, *in*, *on*, *next* or *last*.

a The ....*next*.... time you visit us, you must stay for dinner.

b Wait here, and I'll be back .... a few minutes.

c I haven't seen Helen since .... month.

d Are you having a party .... your birthday?

e Your salary will be paid .... the end of the month.

f We didn't take a trip abroad .... summer, but we're going to Crete this summer.

g Peter managed to break his leg .... the first day of his skiing holiday.

h Are you going to university .... year?

i Take some warm clothes, because the temperature drops .... night.

j .... two weeks' time, the school year will be over!

So how was the skiing holiday?

3 Complete the text with *next*, *last*, *since*, *for*, and *ago*.

Visitors from space

Scientists believe that the **a** ...last... time a large object from outer space hit the Earth was in 1908. Luckily it landed in a sparsely-populated area of Siberia, but people 60 km away from the crash site were thrown to the ground. When it happened, just over a hundred years **b** ...., scientists thought the explosion might have been caused by part of a comet. **c** .... then, research has shown that it was a stone meteorite which exploded in the atmosphere. Objects of this kind have been striking the Earth **d** .... millions of years, but serious explosions are rare. Astronomers are trying to predict when the **e** .... serious impact might be.

The Transit of Venus

A Transit of Venus is an astronomical event, when the planet Venus is exactly between the Earth and the Sun, so it is seen crossing the face of the Sun as a small black disc. The **f** .... Venus Transit took place in 2004 and the **g** .... one will occur in 2012. Nearly 400 years **h** .... , the astronomer Kepler predicted the event would take place in 1631, but did not realize it could not be seen in Europe. **i** .... then, there have been transits in 1639, 1761, 1769, 1974, 1882 and 2004. Obviously such events have been taking place **j** .... millions of years, but the event was not seen by astronomers until 1769, when two astronomers in England both observed it. If you missed it in 2004, and miss it in 2012, there will be another Venus Transit in 2117, but that is a long time to wait!

4 Complete the sentence with *from*, *to*, *until*, *by*, or *during*.

a Some animals cannot survive ...from... autumn .... spring because of the cold weather.

b They hibernate (which means they sleep through the winter) as a way of keeping themselves alive .... the spring.

c Another reason for hibernation is that it is hard to find food .... the winter.

d .... the time winter comes, they need to have enough body fat to keep them alive while they hibernate.

e .... autumn, hibernating animals collect food for storage, and eat more food than usual.

f If there is a shortage of food at that time, the animal might not live .... spring when it can find its food again.

g .... the end of hibernation, the animals live off their body fat.

h .... hibernation, they lower their metabolic rate – the rate at which they use energy.

i Animals may hibernate for several months, but they do not remain completely inactive .... this time.

j Some hibernate in a series of short periods lasting .... a few days .... a few weeks.

5 Rewrite the second sentence so that it means the same as the first sentence, and contains the word in capitals.

a   Paula only arrived at school at 12.30.   DIDN'T
    Paula didn't arrive at school until 12.30.

b   My library card runs out at the end of July.   ON

c   We arrived at the cinema, but the film had finished.   BY

d   What were you doing when the accident happened?   TIME

e   It's three o'clock now, and I've been waiting since two.   FOR

f   At some time in the night there was an earthquake.   DURING

g   I waited but I left at 4.30.   UNTIL

h   I'll have finished in a week's time.   WITHIN

i   I haven't seen George for ages.   SINCE

j   It's Monday today, so I'll see you next Monday.   IN

6 Complete the text with words from page 156.

Lenses have been used a _____for_____ hundreds of years to light fires. As long
b _____ as 424 BC, a burning-glass is mentioned in Aristophanes' play *The
Clouds*. c _____ that there are references to lenses in Roman writing, but
mainly to glass spheres filled with water. The Arabian mathematician Ibn Sahl who lived
d _____ about 940 e _____ 1000 AD wrote about lenses. Another
Arabian scholar, Alhazen (965-1038), who lived slightly f _____ than Ibn Sahl,
wrote the first description of how the lens in the human eye forms an image on the
retina. Recent excavations in Sweden have also shown that the Vikings used lenses
g _____ the 11th and 12th centuries. True glass lenses were not invented
h _____ the 13th century, probably in Italy. i _____ then, lenses
have been used in reading glasses and other optical instruments, such as telescopes and
microscopes. The telescope seems to have been invented by Dutch lens makers j _____
the 17th century. The microscope seems to have been invented k _____ about the same time.

GLOSSARY

EXTENSION ACTIVITY

1 Write a true statement about yourself with
each of these time words.
on   last   since   ago   till   during

2 Check that you have the correct answers to Exercise
5. Translate the sentences into your own language.

science

time (1)

41

time (2)

now

Now means 'at the present time'.
By now means 'at some time before now'.
From now on means 'from the present moment'.

Helen is **now** the new student representative.
We should have heard some news **by now**.
From now on, this class will meet in Room 2.

then

Then means 'at a particular time in the past'.

Einstein was **then** working in a government office in Zurich.

We could also say at the time / at that time. We can also use then with future reference.

'Let's meet outside the cinema at 8.00.' 'Ok, I'll see you **then**.'

Until then, by then, before then are also possible.

I'm leaving on Saturday morning. **Until then**, I'm staying in a hotel.
Phone Maria at 6.00. She should have finished work **by then**.
You can come on Thursday? Can't you come **before then**?

Then also introduces the next thing that happens.

First open the back of the radio. **Then** remove the batteries.

soon

Soon means 'in a short time from now'.

If it doesn't stop raining **soon**, we'll go home.
Soon after the match began, a fight started behind us.
Please call me back as **soon** as you can / as **soon** as possible.

once, at once, immediately

Once refers to a point in the past when something happened.

We **once** spent Christmas in Thailand.

Once also describes a situation in the past, usually before a change that has taken place.

Helen was **once** national judo champion.   (She isn't now)

At once and immediately mean 'without delay'.

Stop doing that **at once**!
When Jim saw the men go into the bank, he **immediately** called the police.

on time, in time

On time refers to a timetabled event which happened as planned.

The train arrived **on time**.   Dina handed in her project **on time**.

In time refers to an event which happens early enough. We can also say just in time, and in plenty of time.

We got home **just in time** to watch the TV news.
Our bus was delayed, and we didn't reach the airport **in time**.

at the end, in the end

At the end describes the final point of a period of time.

At the end of the film, everyone clapped.   I'll see you **at the end** of the week.

In the end means the same as finally, or 'after a period of time'.

I was thinking of buying a new bike, but **in the end** I decided I couldn't afford it.

later, after, afterwards, before

Later is an adverb and means 'at a later time'. We can also say later on.

I'll see you **later**.   Can you phone me **later on**?

After can be used as a preposition with an object, or as an adverb without. Afterwards is an adverb and can stand alone.

I'll see you **after** the lesson.   It's a long film. What are you doing **afterwards**?

Use before as an adverb or as a preposition.

I saw her **before** the lesson. (preposition)   I've seen this film **before**. (adverb)

just, yet, already, still

Use *just* for very recent events. *I've **just** had an idea!*

Use *yet* in negative sentences and questions for possible future actions.

*Have you finished **yet**?*   *Not **yet**!*   *I haven't started **yet**!*

Use *already* to describe actions before now. In questions, *already* expresses surprise that something has been done so quickly.

*I've **already** seen this film.*   (before now)

*Have you done your homework **already**?*   (this surprises me)

Use *still* when we describe actions that are continuing.

*I'm **still** reading your book. I haven't finished it.*

....

1 Choose the correct option, A, B, C or D, to complete the sentence.

a It seems that the Olympic Stadium will not be finished ......*B*...... for the Games.

b I haven't eaten .... , so I feel really hungry.

c I won't be long, I'll be back ....

d Could you let me have my book back .... ?

e I've .... had an idea. Why don't we go and see Kate?

f .... I wanted to be an engineer, but now I want to study computers.

g I thought I had caught a cold, but .... it was nothing.

h Maria promised to return my books .... she could.

a	A *immediately*	B *in time*	C *yet*	D *soon*
b	A *now*	B *soon*	C *at once*	D *yet*
c	A *already*	B *just*	C *once*	D *soon*
d	A *in the end*	B *after*	C *yet*	D *as soon as you can*
e	A *already*	B *soon*	C *just*	D *now*
f	A *by then*	B *later on*	C *once*	D *just*
g	A *in the end*	B *at once*	C *in time*	D *still*
h	A *as soon as*	B *before*	C *in time*	D *just*

2 <u>Underline</u> the correct option.

a You should have finished your project *soon* / <u>*by now*</u>.

b I nearly dropped the eggs, but managed to catch them just *in time* / *on time*.

c Let's meet *after* / *later* school and talk about it.

d From *now on* / *later on*, things are going to be different!

e The results come out next week, so *before* / *until* then, you'll have to wait.

f 'The meeting starts at 7.30.' 'Right, I'll see you *at once* / *then*.'

g Our teacher *once* / *at once* sang in a rock band.

h *At* / *In* the end of the match, the spectators ran onto the pitch.

i Mix the butter and sugar and *then* / *after* add the eggs.

j *Immediately* / *As soon as* she came into the room, I knew we were going to be friends.

社会科目

3 Choose the correct option, A, B or C, to complete the sentence.

a Alexander Fleming is usually described as the scientist who discovered penicillin in 1928, but in fact at least two other scientists had noticed its antibiotic effect __B__ he did.

b The antibiotic effects of penicillin had _____ been recorded in France by a Costa Rican scientist.

c Fleming conducted experiments with penicillin, but _____ decided that it would not work as an antibiotic in humans.

d Luckily, other scientists continued with the research and were _____ making progress when the Second World War began in 1939.

e However, at that point they had not _____ treated any patients.

f A few years _____, in 1942, Bumstead and Hess became the first doctors in the world to save a patient using penicillin.

g At this point, Dorothy Hodgkin had _____ described the chemical structure of penicillin, so it was now possible for penicillin to be produced in large quantities.

h Penicillin is _____ used to treat many infections.

i However, _____ in the 1940s, the first cases of resistance to the drug had been reported.

j Because bacteria can change, they grow resistant to antibiotics, and scientists have not _____ found a solution to this problem.

	A	B	C
a	after	before	already
b	already	later	still
c	after	later	just
d	after	afterwards	still
e	yet	just	still
f	after	later	yet
g	just	still	yet
h	still	yet	already
i	yet	still	already
j	later	yet	already

Dorothy Hodgkin

GLOSSARY

4 Rewrite each sentence so that it contains the word or words in capitals.

a They'll be back after twelve. — IN
  They'll be back in the afternoon.

b Can you do it now, please? — AT

c When the lesson finished, Helen asked the teacher a question. — AT

d My head hasn't stopped aching. — STILL

e Jan wasn't late for his music lesson. — TIME

f It's eight o'clock and I've been waiting for two hours. — SINCE

g The film began, and a few minutes later all the lights came on. — SOON AFTER

h Lunch isn't ready yet, so before that we'll sit in the garden — THEN

162

i I'm still doing my homework.   YET

....

j When I've finished watching TV I'll start my work.   AFTERWARDS

....

history

5 Complete the text with suitable time words.

The Rosetta Stone

a .....*Until*..... they were deciphered nearly
two hundred years **b** .... , Egyptian
hieroglyphics could not be understood by European
scholars. **c** .... hieroglyphics were
deciphered, people had to guess what this form of
writing could mean. It was originally used by the
ancient Egyptian priests, **d** .... about
3000 BC **e** .... the time of the Roman
Empire. One of the men who deciphered hieroglyphics
was Jean-François Champollion
(1790–1832), a self-taught linguist who had
f .... learned Latin and Greek
g .... the age of nine. When he entered the
School of Oriental Languages in Paris
h .... 1807, he had already suggested,

i .... the age of sixteen, that the ancient Egyptian language was Coptic. **j** .... the age
of nineteen Champollion became assistant professor of history in Grenoble. Here he continued his studies and
k .... this period he started to examine texts brought from Egypt. The French had sent an army
there **l** .... 1798, and a year **m** .... a group of soldiers had accidentally discovered the
Rosetta Stone, on which was written the same text in three languages – in hieroglyphics, in demotic Egyptian,
the everyday language, and in Ancient Greek. **n** .... 1801, however, the French army in Egypt
was defeated by the British, and soon **o** .... , the Rosetta stone was taken to London. There, by
comparing the different kinds of writing on the Stone, Thomas Young showed that some of the hieroglyphs on
the stone wrote the name Ptolemy. Luckily Champollion was able to study a copy of the text on the stone, and
p .... 1824 he published an explanation of the hieroglyphic system. **q** .... then,
archaeologists have been able to read thousands of inscriptions left behind by the ancient Egyptians. The Rosetta
Stone is **r** .... in the British Museum in London.

GLOSSARY

EXTENSION ACTIVITY

1 Write a true statement with each time word.
soon   on time   once   yet   still

2 Check that you have the correct answers to Exercise 2.
Translate the sentences into your own language.

time (2)

42 prepositions after verbs, adjectives, and before nouns

verb + preposition   (See also **Units 43** and **44**)

Many verbs are followed by a particular preposition, or by different prepositions for different meanings eg *laugh at / laugh with*. Always check in a dictionary for meaning and usage.

verb + preposition + noun

Everyone **laughed at** the cartoon.
I can't **deal with** this problem.
I **suffer from** panic attacks.
You can **depend on** us.
They were **protesting against** the war.
We **laughed about** the problem the next day.

I'll **pay for** your ticket.
I find it hard to **cope with** stress.
How do they **differ from** one another?
You can't **rely on** Tom to arrive on time.
They're **talking / arguing about** history.
What does the word 'input' **refer to**?

verb + preposition + noun / -ing

We **apologize for** the delay.
He can't **concentrate on** his work.
I'm not **used to studying** late at night.
They **succeeded in making** matters worse.

Dr Sims **specializes in** back problems.
Let me **congratulate you on** your success.
I **insist on seeing** the manager.

verb + noun + preposition + noun

I always **confuse 'lie' with 'lay'**.
I'll have to **discuss this with your parents**.

They **blamed everything on me**.
I **prefer tea to coffee**.

verb + person + preposition + noun / -ing

They **accused her of cheating**.
You **remind me of someone** I once knew.

Can you **provide us with a copy**?

adjective + preposition

An adjective can be followed by different prepositions for different meanings eg *be angry with someone / be angry about something*.

You're **right / wrong about** that.
I'm not **sure about** the answer.
I'm **sorry for** being late.
Are you **afraid of** spiders?
Are you **angry with** me?
I'm **bored with** the same old routine.
Kate isn't **keen on** animals.
We were **shocked / annoyed by** the news.

I'm **sorry / upset / angry about** that.
Our town is **famous for** its cakes.
Who is **responsible for** this mess?
Speech is **different from** writing.
I'm **annoyed with** you!
I wish I was **good at** maths.
Is your sister **married to** him?
Are you **interested in** jazz?

preposition + noun phrases

Is this boat **for sale**?
We found the answer **in the end**.
In practice it doesn't work.
Are we **in danger** (of + ing)?
It happens **on average** once a year.
They received the letter **by mistake**.
The bus was **out of control**.
Sorry, I'm **out of practice**.
Everything is **under control**.

Are you **on holiday** here?
That sounds good **in theory**.
My little brother is **in trouble**.
In fact, this is true.
I think he did it **on purpose**.
After running, I was **out of breath**.
Don't worry, he is **out of danger**.
I was **under the impression** you knew.
There's no school tomorrow **after all**.

1 Complete the sentence with a suitable preposition.

a Most people would expect a work environment
to differ ....*from*....... an educational
environment.

b When you start your first job, you may find that
you are not used .... the way that
your colleagues behave.

c You may not understand what people are talking
....

d You may have to ask a lot of questions, and worry
that other people can't rely .... you.

e Or you may find it difficult at first to cope
.... the demands your job places
on you.

f But there is no reason to suffer ....
feelings of anxiety.

g You have to concentrate .... learning
the job, and understanding the people around
you.

h Don't worry that people are laughing
.... you, or making fun of you because
you are new to the job.

i You'll soon learn to deal .... everyday
problems, and gain in confidence.

j Don't be afraid to ask for advice, and you'll
soon be congratulating yourself ....
your success.

2 Rewrite each sentence so that it begins as shown and contains an adjective and preposition.

a You really annoy me sometimes.
Sometimes I'm ....*really annoyed with you.*.......

b The things we saw on the news shocked us all.
We were all ....

c I'm sorry but I lost your magazine.
I'm sorry for ....

d Who caused the accident?
Who was ....

e I don't really like horror films.
I'm not ....

f Football and rugby are not the same.
Football is ....

g Are Madonna and Guy Ritchie married?
Is Madonna ....

h Does playing computer games interest you?
Are you ....

i I find doing the same things every day boring.
I'm ....

j Going to the top of high buildings makes some people afraid.
Some people are ....

3 Complete the text with the words from the list. Use each word once only.

| all | average | control | end | fact |
| impression | practice | purpose | ~~theory~~ | trouble |

In a _theory_ people are either morning people, who get up very early, or afternoon people, who don't, but things may not be quite as simple as this. People who sleep until late may not do this on b _____ . They may just be under the c _____ that they are afternoon people, so they simply couldn't get up early even if they tried. Or they think that they could get up early, but they are out of d _____ . It's just a question of getting used to it. Then one day they realize that morning people are more successful. They decide they have to change, but then their problems start. For example, you may really want to get up at 5.00 am, but when the alarm clock goes off, you decide that perhaps you are an afternoon person after e _____ . And so you fall asleep again. What can you do?

Some research suggests that people who want to get up early often go to bed too early, and this is what lands them in f _____ when the alarm clock rings. Their sleep patterns are out of g _____ , and either they can't get to sleep or they wake up too early, or they can't wake up until late. In h _____ , we may not need the same number of hours sleep every night. As long as we sleep roughly the same amount on i _____ over a period of time, we probably get enough sleep. So in the j _____ we may be better off going to sleep only when we really feel tired, provided we always get up at a fixed time each day.

GLOSSARY

4 Rewrite each sentence so it contains the word in capitals.

a In the end I managed to find the answer.   SUCCEEDED
   In the end I succeeded in finding the answer.

b Martin's teacher said that he had cheated.   ACCUSED

c We get a free lunch at school.   PROVIDES

d I must have my money back!   INSIST

e They said the fire was Anna's fault.   BLAMED

f When I see you, I think of my sister.   REMIND

g Getting up early in the morning is new to me.   USED

h Don't worry, you can trust Chris.   DEPEND

i What were you two discussing?   TALKING

j I like jazz better than rap.   PREFER

5 Complete the sentence with one suitable preposition.

a ......On...... average, a yawn lasts about six seconds.

b If you yawn .... purpose in front of other people, they will start yawning.

c You might be .... the impression that a yawn is a bad thing.

d People usually apologize .... yawning when they are in meetings or lessons.

e We often assume that we yawn because we are bored .... something.

f People often yawn, for example, when they can't concentrate .... their work.

g However, we are .... danger of simplifying the complex process of yawning.

h For example, athletes often yawn before races, and we can suppose that they are quite interested .... what they do.

i .... fact, scientists are not exactly sure why we yawn.

j Some believe that people yawn because they are suffering .... a shortage of oxygen.

k Others think that it is part of our animal past, and we are showing our teeth to other people to make them afraid .... us.

l Apparently, even if people read about the subject of yawning they start yawning .... the end.

m So if this article has succeeded .... making you yawn, don't worry about it.

n You are just being normal, ... all.

6 Complete the sentence so that it contains the words in capitals.

a Are you selling your bike?
Is ......*your bike for sale?*.....................................   SALE

b I haven't done this for a long time.
I'm ....   PRACTICE

c Eventually we stopped and turned back.
In ....   END

d Are you spending your holiday here?
Are ....   ON

e I thought it was Andy, but actually it was David.
I thought it was Andy, but ....   FACT

f I think you broke the window deliberately.
I think you broke the window ....   PURPOSE

g They told him that he could lose his life.
They told him that he was ....   DANGER

h The driver had no control over the train.
The train was ....   OUT

i I thought it was a holiday today.
I was ....   IMPRESSION

j We accidentally turned left instead of right.
We turned left ....   MISTAKE

EXTENSION ACTIVITY

1 Answer these questions about yourself.
What are you afraid of?
What interests you?
What are you good at?
What sort of things are you annoyed by?

2 What kind of things would you protest against?

prepositions after verbs, adjectives, and before nouns

167

43 phrasal verbs (1)

- We use phrasal verbs in everyday language rather than formal language.
- We cannot usually guess the meaning from the combination of words.
- Some of them have more than one meaning. Only a selection appears on this page.

two part verbs: unsplittable

verb + preposition

We cannot put the object between the verb and preposition. We can sometimes guess the meaning.

I **came across** this word in a magazine.	(find by chance)
What are you **getting at** exactly?	(suggest)
I won't **stand for** this behaviour any longer!	(tolerate)
It took me a long time to **get over** my illness.	(recover from)
The police are **looking into** the robbery.	(investigate)
Will you **look after** the baby?	(take care of)
Anna **takes after** her mother.	(look or behave like)
I **ran into** Tom the other day.	(meet by accident)
Tom is **heading for** trouble.	(go in the direction of)
When I laughed, everyone **joined in**.	(do the same activity)
Let's **run through** the details.	(explain)

two part verbs: splittable

verb + adverb particle

We can put the object between the verb and particle, or after the particle. If the object is a large number of words we put it after the particle. If the object is a pronoun eg *me, it, him*, we put it between the verb and the particle. We can sometimes guess the meaning.

Try to **carry out** a 'task analysis'.	(do a piece of work)
Can you **give in** your homework now.	(give it to the teacher)
Can you **fill in** this form?	(write information on it)
You can **leave out / miss out** the next exercise.	(don't do it)
We're trying to **sort out** the problem.	(deal with)
You can **work out** the answer for homework.	(find the solution)
Don't forget to **turn off** the lights.	(stop using)
We have **put off** the match until next week.	(postponed)
The bus **dropped off** the students outside the school.	(take to a place)
Out teacher **told us off** because we were noisy.	(criticize angrily)
Don't **let down** the team, will you!	(disappoint by not doing what was promised)
We'll come and **pick up** the others at 6.00.	(collect in a car)
Susan **brought up** three orphan children.	(look after a child until it becomes an adult)
People say it's hard to **give up** smoking.	(stop doing something)
You have to **look up** these words.	(find in a dictionary)

Note: always check in a dictionary for meaning and usage.

1 Use a phrasal verb from the list to replace the words <u>underlined</u>.

| came across | getting at | getting over | heading for | joined in |
| looked after | ~~looked into~~ | running into | running through | took after |

a A special committee <u>investigated</u> _looked into_ the government's actions, but found nothing wrong.

b Everyone said that Richard <u>was just like</u> .... his father.

c If things go on like this, the company is <u>going in the direction of</u> .... disaster!

d Our neighbour <u>took care of</u> .... our cats while we were away.

e When a man at the front started shouting, everyone else <u>did the same</u> ....

f I <u>found</u> .... this article while I was doing my project.

g Listen carefully, the teacher is <u>explaining</u> .... the details again.

h Maria is slowly <u>recovering from</u> .... her illness.

i I don't understand what she is <u>trying to say</u> ....

j I keep <u>meeting</u> .... Harry in the library.

2 Complete the sentence with a word from the list. Two words are used twice.

| come | get | head | join | look | run | stand | take |

a We couldn't find anyone to ...._look_........
after our three pet fish while we were away.

b Tony is disappointed to have lost the match,
but he'll .... over it in time.

c I don't see much of David, but I occasionally
.... into him in the library.

d Do you .... after your father, or
your mother?

e Our teacher told us she wasn't going to
.... for any more bad behaviour.

f Could you .... through the
programme again? I'm sure there's an
error somewhere.

g We made a complaint to the airline about our
missing luggage, and they said they would
.... into the matter.

h Anna knew a lot about tropical fish, but she
had never .... across one like this
one before.

i When the other children play together, Peter
seems too shy to .... in.

j When the alarm bell rang, everyone started
to .... for the exit.

3 Rewrite the sentence so the word <u>underlined</u> is in a different place.

a Don't forget to give your homework <u>in</u> at the end of the lesson.
  Don't forget to give in your homework at the end of the lesson.

b The maths teacher has put <u>off</u> the test until Friday.

c I'll come round and pick <u>up</u> the letter tomorrow.

d Make sure you look every new word <u>up</u>.

e Remember to turn <u>off</u> the TV when you go to bed.

f Don't worry, we'll sort the travel arrangements <u>out</u> next week.

g Please fill <u>in</u> the form as carefully as you can.

h The bus drops <u>off</u> passengers right outside the hotel.

i You have let <u>down</u> the whole class, and I'm very disappointed.

j An elderly couple brought the children <u>up</u> after their parents died.

the arts

4 Complete the text with the appropriate phrasal verbs from page 168.

A Japanese Folktale

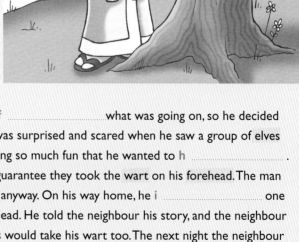

Once upon a time, a man had to a <u>carry out</u> some work in another village. The work was difficult and there were many problems to b .... He was tired and was c .... a cold, so he decided to d .... finishing the work until the next day. It was late by the time he left and he had to walk home over the mountains. Soon it started to get dark but luckily he e .... a tree where he could sleep. He was woken up in the middle of the night by strange noises. He couldn't f .... what was going on, so he decided to get up and g .... the situation. He was surprised and scared when he saw a group of elves singing and dancing around his tree, but they were having so much fun that he wanted to h .... The elves liked him and asked him to return, and as a guarantee they took the wart on his forehead. The man left feeling very happy because he didn't want his wart anyway. On his way home, he i .... one of his neighbours, who also had a big wart on his forehead. He told the neighbour his story, and the neighbour decided he would go that night, and hopefully the elves would take his wart too. The next night the neighbour went to the tree and found the elves. They thought he was the man from the night before and gave him back his wart! Now he had two warts instead of one, and went home feeling very j ....

GLOSSARY

170

5 Rewrite the sentence using the word in capitals.

a The trip to the National Gallery has been postponed until next Friday.   PUT
   The trip to the National Gallery has been put off until next Friday.

b Make sure you check the meaning of these words in a dictionary.   LOOK

c You don't have to do Exercise 9.   MISS

d A special team is trying to find out the cause of the accident.   LOOK

e I will not tolerate such bad language in the classroom!   STAND

f Don't leave the computer on when you leave.   TURN

g A taxi will come and collect you at 7.30.   PICK

h I wish I could stop eating chocolates.   GIVE

i Please complete the application form.   FILL

j Tina hasn't recovered from her illness yet.   GOT

6 Rewrite the sentence using a phrasal verb instead of the words underlined.

a Have you ever <u>found</u> this word before?
   Have you ever come across this word before?

b I'm <u>taking care</u> of the children until their mother comes home.

c Dina <u>is like</u> her mother's side of the family.

d The basketball match has been <u>moved</u> to next Wednesday.

e Make sure you <u>don't leave</u> the lights <u>on</u>.

f The police are <u>investigating</u> a fight outside the cinema.

g Let me <u>explain</u> the details of the plan just once more.

h Jane found it hard to <u>recover from</u> the death of her pet dog.

i Mr Sims had to <u>stop</u> driving when he reached the age of 85.

j Peter promised to come and sing in the concert, but he <u>disappointed</u> us.

EXTENSION ACTIVITY

1 Write a true sentence about yourself with each phrasal verb.
get over   look after
take after   give up
look up

2 Check that you have the correct answers to Exercise 6. Translate the sentences into your own language.

*Need more practice? Go to the **Review** on page 192.*

phrasal verbs (1)

171

44 phrasal verbs (2)

two-part verbs: no object

verb + adverb particle
These verbs do not have an object (intransitive).

The traffic **builds up** here every day.	(increase)
My car has **broken down** again.	(stop working)
It's important to **speak out**.	(be frank, give an opinion)
What exactly is **going on**?	(happen)
The feeling of shock gradually **wore off**.	(go away)
Stop **showing off**!	(behave to attract attention)
Jim always **turns up** late.	(arrive, often unexpectedly)
Everything **turned out** all right in the end.	(have a particular result)

three-part verbs: unsplittable

verb + adverb particle + preposition
The object always comes after the preposition.

Have you **come up with** any ideas yet?	(think of)
When are you going to **get round to** your work?	(finally do something)
We've **come up against** a problem.	(met a difficulty)
She didn't **get away with** cheating in the exam.	(escape capture or detection)
Maria has **gone down with** a bad cold.	(become ill with a disease etc)
I can't **put up with** Alan! He annoys me!	(accept something / someone unpleasant)
We want to **do away with** school uniform.	(abolish)
I'm really **looking forward to** seeing you.	(think with pleasure about the future)

verb + adverb particle + preposition + object or *verb + particle* (no *object*)

We've **run out of** milk again.	(have none left)
The milk has **run out**.	
I'll **catch up with** you later.	(go faster to reach someone)
Anna can't **catch up**.	
Do you **get on with** / **along with** David?	(have a good relationship with)
Do you two **get along**?	
I can't **keep up with** the class.	(go at the same speed as)
I'm finding it hard to **keep up**.	

Note: always check in a dictionary for meaning and usage.

1 Underline the correct option, A, B, C or D, to complete each sentence.

a Misunderstandings are common in relationships, simply because communication _breaks down_

b Even when two people .... extremely well, they still have to talk to one another.

c It's not unusual for people to .... because of some annoying habit.

d For example, if someone often .... late, this can be very annoying.

e It can also be very annoying if your partner .... in front of others.

f Many people just accept these problems, and ignore what is ....

g However, a sense of resentment often .... between two people if issues are left unresolved.

h Good communication usually .... to be the only way to deal with the situation.

a A _breaks down_   B _goes on_   C _turns up_   D _shows off_

b A _turn up_   B _go on_   C _build up_   D _get along_

c A _show off_   B _fall out_   C _get along_   D _turn up_

d A _builds up_   B _falls out_   C _breaks down_   D _turns up_

e A _turns up_   B _gets along_   C _shows off_   D _goes on_

f A _going on_   B _turning out_   C _getting along_   D _turning up_

g A _breaks down_   B _shows off_   C _turns out_   D _builds up_

h A _turns out_   B _gets along_   C _shows off_   D _goes on_

2 Rewrite the sentence so that it contains a phrasal verb from the list instead of the words underlined. Change the tense etc if necessary.

come up against	come up with	do away with	get away with	get along with
~~get round to~~	go down with	keep up with	put up with	run out of

a I'm finding it difficult to <u>find time for</u> my geography project.
   I'm finding it difficult to get round to my geography project.

b I'm afraid we've <u>found ourselves facing</u> a rather serious problem.

c Tim thought he had <u>escaped unpunished</u> after cheating in the exam.

d Have you <u>thought of</u> any good ideas yet?

e The school <u>got rid of</u> end-of-year tests.

f Unfortunately Helen <u>fell ill with</u> flu on the first day of her holiday.

g I <u>worked at the same speed as</u> the rest of the class.

h I'm sorry, but I really can't <u>tolerate</u> this terrible noise.

i Tom <u>used all his</u> money three days before the end of the holiday.

j Kate seems to <u>be very friendly with</u> her new teacher.

3 Complete each sentence with a word from the list. You can use a word more than once.

down   off   on   out   up

a I was really tired, and I couldn't keep
......*up*...... with the others.

b Steve is one of those people who shows
.... all the time.

c I've worked with Paula for two years, but we don't
really get ....

d By the time we left, the traffic had begun to build
.... and we had to keep stopping.

e After a few days, the pain in my wrist began to
wear ....

f Maria won't be coming with us, as she has
gone .... with flu.

g Jack turned .... halfway through the
lesson, and looked very embarrassed.

h I can't write any more. I've simply run
.... of ideas.

i Dina has come .... with a good idea
for using less electricity.

j Halfway up the mountain, the bus broke
.... and all the passengers had to
get out.

4 Complete the sentence with a phrasal verb from the list. Change the tense if necessary.

come up with   drop (someone) off   fill in   get away with   get over
give up   ~~leave out~~   look into   put off   work out

a Basic tomato and basil sauce – you can ......*leave out*...... the basil if you don't have
any available, or use half a teaspoon of dried basil instead.

b Learn how to .... your feelings of shyness quickly and permanently!

c Scientists .... ways of treating cancer by strengthening the immune
system.

d .... the details at parts 3 and 4 of this form, and return it to us at the
address shown above.

e Wallace and Gromit's Children's Foundation is challenging pupils in schools
throughout the UK to .... ideas for new inventions in 'Wallace's
Inventing Competition'.

f We'll give you some ideas of how you might build it. You can .... the
details and change the plan as you see fit.

g When Alan's mother .... at school the next morning, he felt
confident and happy again.

h The wedding of Prince Charles and Camilla Parker Bowles .... until
Saturday to allow the prince to attend the funeral of Pope John Paul II.

i I have decided to .... eating meat. What are some of the difficulties
of becoming a vegetarian?

j She might well have .... the crime had she not been arrested for
robbery while carrying documents relating to two of her false identities.

5 Rewrite each sentence so that it contains the words in capitals as part of a phrasal verb.

a Most students searching for information try to find the details on the Internet. LOOK
 Most students searching for information look up the details on the Internet.

b Doctors say that the unpleasant effects of the new malaria pill soon go away. WEAR

c The battery loses power completely after about three months. RUN

d The three astronauts said they were feeling happy about coming back down to Earth. LOOK

e Continue to learn about the latest science news with *Science Magazine*. KEEP

f There is a great deal of confusion and the authorities are still trying to deal with the situation. SORT

g The launch of the next Mars mission has been postponed until next April. PUT

social studies

6 Complete the text with the appropriate phrasal verbs from page 172.

The world of work

It's official: people are more stressed now than they were in the past. Although our quality of life is better, we seem to have more to worry about than previous generations. Here are some stressful situations you may

a *come up against* at work, and ways to solve them.

Your boss is scary, and you don't want to b ....

You are asked for your opinion, but don't want to say what you really think because you don't want to annoy your boss. c .... your boss is very important, so try to give your opinion politely.

You d .... **a great idea, and someone else steals it.**

You work hard, but a colleague gets all the credit. The best thing to do is make a note of all your ideas, and send them to your boss. Then if someone else says they thought of it first, your boss will know what's really

e ....

Your colleague always f .... **late, and you have to do their work.**

Some people never do their share of their work, and when they finally g .... doing something, it's usually not very good. Try not to let your anger with them h .... , and tell them calmly that you refuse to do any more of their work.

Your computer / telephone / photocopier i ....

You can't finish your work because a vital piece of equipment isn't working. Take a deep breath, make yourself a cup of coffee and relax. You can j .... the work later.

phrasal verbs (2)

GLOSSARY

EXTENSION ACTIVITY

1 Write a true sentence about yourself with each phrasal verb.

break down   get away with   look forward to   run out of   get along with

45 conjunctions, adverbs and prepositions as connectors

because, so, as, since

Use *because, so, as* and *since* to link an action with its purpose.

> *We went home early,* **because** / **as** / **since** *we felt tired.*
> *We felt tired,* **so** *we went home early.*

for example, such as

Use *for example* and *such as* to give examples. We usually put a comma after *for example*.

> *Eat lots of green vegetables,* **such as** *cabbage and spinach.*
> *Try taking more excercise.* **For example,** *you could walk to work.*

instead (of)

Use *instead* when we say that one thing replaces another. We can put it at the end or beginning of a clause or sentence.

> *He was too tired to go out so* **(instead)** *he watched television* **(instead)**.
> *We could watch television* **instead of** *going out.*

according to

Use *according to* when we say where an idea or statement has come from.

> **According to** *Freud, we learn through fairy tales, myths, jokes, and folklore.*

however, yet, although / though, even though, while

Make contrasts with *however, although, even though,* and *while*.

However comments on what has come before. Use it to begin and end sentences, or put it inside a sentence to separate parts of the sentence. Note that *however* always has punctuation before and after it.

> *Crude oil itself is not very useful.* **However,** *its compounds have many uses.*
> *Its compounds (,* **however,**) *have many uses (,* **however**.)

Yet has a similar meaning to *although*, or *but*. It cannot come at the beginning of a sentence.

> *Crude oil itself is not very useful,* **yet** *its compounds have many uses.*

Although is followed by two contrasting ideas. The *although*-clause starts or finishes the sentence. *Though* is another form of *although*.

> **Although** *crude oil itself is not very useful, its compounds have many uses.*
> *The compounds of crude oil have many uses,* **although** *crude oil itself is not very useful.*

Use *while* in the same way. It does not have a time meaning in this use.

> **While** *crude oil is not very useful, its compounds have many uses.*

Use *even though* to make a surprising contrast. It has the same positions as *although*.

> *We continue using oil-based products,* **even though** *many pollute the environment.*

as well, too, also

As well and *too* go at the end of a clause or sentence. *Also* goes in the middle of a clause, before a verb, or after an auxiliary or modal.

> *The roots of acacia trees grow deep in the soil, but spread outwards* **too**.
> *The roots of acacia trees grow deep in the soil, but spread outwards* **as well**.
> *The roots of acacia trees grow deep in the soil, but* **also** *spread / can* **also** *spread outwards.*

1 Rewrite each sentence so that it contains *according to*.

a Experts say that school science textbooks are not good at teaching science.
 According to experts, school science textbooks are not good at teaching science.

b Their reports say that most books cover too many topics.

....

c These experts believe that the classroom activities in the books don't help students learn basic
 scientific ideas.

....

d One scientist said the books are 'full of unconnected facts'.

....

e Some educational experts say that students learn science more effectively when they try to
 answer an everyday question.

....

f These experts say that a question such as 'Why is the sky blue?' is the kind of science question
 students like answering.

....

g This theory suggests that students learn better if they carry out project work based on this
 kind of question.

....

h However, many science teachers believe that the school syllabus does not allow enough time
 for this kind of exploration.

....

2 Rewrite each set of sentences as <u>one</u> sentence so that it contains *instead*. Add *or*, *and*, *but*
 and *so* where necessary.

a You don't have to use butter. You can use olive oil.
 You don't have to use butter, you can use olive oil instead.

b Cooking spoils the flavour of carrots. Eat them raw.

....

c This is usually made with apples. Or you could try pears.

....

d Fresh fish is best for this recipe. You can use frozen fish.

....

e Try leaving out salt. Use other spices.

....

f Sweets are fattening. Eat fresh fruit.

....

g You don't have to use cream. You can use yoghurt.

....

h In some versions of this dish beef is not used. Lamb is used.

....

conjunctions, adverbs and prepositions as connectors

3 Use the words to make <u>one</u> sentence containing the words in brackets. You may have to change the order.

Managing your revision

a Work out how long you've got to prepare and then divide the time into short manageable sections. You need a schedule. (so)

<u>You need a schedule, so work out how long you've got to prepare and then divide the time into short manageable sections</u>

b You risk losing motivation if you fail to reach them. Don't set unrealistic goals. (as)

c Make sure your goals follow the SMART system. These are the best types of goals. (since)

d S = Specific Try to be very precise about what you want to achieve. This will give you a definite target, eg I will read three pages of history before 6.00. (because)

e M = Measurable You can measure what you have achieved. Ask someone to test you on what you have studied. (so)

f A = Achievable If you set yourself too much, you won't be able to do it. You have to be honest with yourself about what you can achieve. (because)

g R = Rewards Give yourself a reward when you achieve your target. This will make you feel good! (as)

h T = Time Give yourself a deadline. You need to feel some pressure if you want to work well. (since)

4 Complete the sentence with *however, even though, although,* or *while*. More than one answer may be possible.

a Oil is an important part of the global economy. ......How.ever,..... it is becoming more expensive all the time.

b Some large industrial countries, such as the USA and Russia, produce their own oil, ... most European countries have to import their oil.

c And .... in 2001 the USA, for example, produced 181 million barrels of oil, it still imported 273 million barrels from other countries.

d .... many countries produce large amounts of oil, exploration must continue to find new oil fields.

e New fields have been found under the sea, ... it is harder to extract the oil in these places.

f ...., new technology may solve this problem.

g .... the demand for oil is rising all over the world, oil is a non-renewable resource, so supplies will eventually run out.

h .... this is an obvious fact, there is still disagreement as to how long oil supplies will last.

5 Rewrite each set of sentences as ONE sentence containing the word in capitals. Make any other necessary changes.

a Every living organism needs energy to maintain its body. It needs energy to grow.　　ALSO
　Every living organism needs energy to maintain its body and also grow.

b Omnivores are animals that eat plants. They eat other animals.　　TOO

．．

c Decomposers are organisms that eat dead animals and dead plants. They enable other plants to feed off the dead material.　　AS WELL

．．

d Producers are plants that use photosynthesis to turn the energy of the Sun into food. They are the lowest layer of the food web.　　ALSO

．．

e Primary consumers are the animals that eat the producer layer. They are called *herbivores* too.　　ALSO

．．

f Secondary consumers eat the primary consumers and are carnivores. Some of them eat plants.　　AS WELL

．．

geography

6 Complete the text with one suitable word or phrase from page 176 in each space.

Wind power is another way of producing electricity. a ___Although___ wind power produces just 0.4% of the world's electricity, many countries are building wind farms, b .... this has many advantages over other methods. Compared to a power station using oil or coal, c .... , a wind farm produces no air pollution and wind itself will never run out. d .... , a wind farm only works well when it is built in the right place. Wind plants generate electricity only when the wind blows, e .... if there is no wind, there is no electricity. On the other hand, f .... there are many advantages, there are g .... some problems, h .... noise and the way the turbines spoil the look of the countryside. i .... wind farms are often built on mountains or near the sea, the people who visit these places often feel that they have been spoilt by the wind turbines. One solution to this problem may be to avoid building the farms on land, and where possible to build them on man-made islands out at sea j .... k .... this is a solution for countries with long coastlines, it is obviously not the answer everywhere. l .... visitors to areas with wind farms usually complain about the noise and the spoilt view, people who live nearby often get used to wind farms. There may m .... be problems with wildlife. Birds, n .... , are often killed by the turbines. o .... there are problems with wind farms, they are clearly better for the environment than most other forms of power station.

GLOSSARY

EXTENSION ACTIVITY

1 Write one or two sentences with each word or phrase as they are used on page 176.
　　so　　for example　　according to　　although　　too

2 Copy out five of the examples from page 176, and translate each one into your own language.
　　*Need more practice? Go to the **Review** on page 192.*

conjunctions, adverbs and prepositions as connectors

46 relative clauses

These come after relative pronouns *who / whom* for people, *which / that* for things, *whose* for possession. Relative clauses can refer to the subject of the sentence or the object. They behave in different ways. In object clauses, it is possible to leave out the relative pronoun *which / that*.

> *Glaciers are rivers of ice **which** form in cold climates on mountains. The amount of fresh water **(that)** glaciers contain is greater than all other lakes and rivers on Earth.*

Subject: *which form in cold climates*   This refers to ***glaciers***, the subject of ***form***.
Object: *that glaciers contain*   This refers to ***water***, the object of ***contain***.

Note that in a subject clause there is never a subject pronoun after the relative pronoun.

> *Glaciers are rivers of ice. **They** form in cold climates on mountains.*
> *Glaciers are rivers of ice **which** ~~they~~ form in cold climates on mountains.*

subject: *who* or *that*

Use *who / that* to refer to people in subject relative clauses. When we refer to a named person we generally use *who*, and *that* in informal speech and writing.

> *Charles Dickens was the novelist **who** wrote David Copperfield.*
> *Louis Agassiz was the first scientist **who** argued that there had been an Ice Age in the past.*

subject: *which* or *that*

Use *which / that* to refer to things in subject relative clauses.

> *Last week I bought a new computer **which** is much faster than the old one.*
> *In 1840 Agassiz published Etudes sur les glaciers **which** was the first book to describe the movements of glaciers and the way they changed the landscape.*

subject: *whose*

Use *whose* to refer to things belonging to people.

> *That was the man **whose** car was stolen.*
> *Louis Agassiz had a son, Alexander, **whose** main interest was mining.*

omitting the relative pronoun

When you omit the relative pronoun in an object clause, you might also need to omit the verb after it.

> *The photos **(which were)** used on the web site are fascinating.*
> *The glaciers **(which were)** described in the book are in danger of melting.*

object: *who, that, whom* or zero

Use *who / whom / that* in an object relative clause when we refer to people.
Whom is used in formal language, or after a preposition.

> *He is one of the scientists **who** / **whom** / **that** I admire most.*

It is possible to leave out the relative pronoun in this kind of sentence.

> *He is one of the scientists I admire most.*

object: *which, that* or zero

Use *which / that* in an object relative clause when we refer to people.

> *This is Pickwick Papers, one of the first books **which** / **that** Dickens wrote.*

It is possible to leave out the relative pronoun in this kind of sentence.

> *This is Pickwick Papers, one of the first books Dickens wrote.*

object: *of which*

Use *of which* in an object relative clause when we refer to one thing belonging to another. It is used in formal language.

> *This is his third book, the publication **of which** made such an impression.*

It is possible to use *whose* in informal language. It is also possible to avoid this kind of construction.

> *This is his third book, **whose** publication made such an impression.*
> *This is his third book, **the one that** made such an impression when it was published.*

1 Tick the sentence if the words <u>underlined</u> can be left out, or write 'no' if it cannot.

a Charles Dickens was one of the first authors <u>whose</u> books reached a wide public. No

b This was partly because, with the first book <u>that</u> he wrote, he introduced a range of mainly London characters which people found interesting and amusing. ✓

c He invented people <u>whose</u> names often suggested what they were like.

d For example, David Copperfield has an unfeeling stepfather <u>who is</u> called Mr Murdstone.

e It was also a result of changes in publishing <u>which were</u> introduced at around the time he began writing.

f Books became cheaper because of new methods of printing <u>which</u> used steam-powered machinery.

g His novels were published as serials, and people waited impatiently to read the next part <u>that</u> he produced.

h He was one of the first novelists <u>who</u> also worked as a magazine editor, journalist and social campaigner.

i The magazine <u>that</u> he edited, *Household Words*, was mainly his own writing.

j Dickens was also famous for the dramatic readings <u>that</u> he gave from his own novels.

2 Match the famous people **a** to **h** with information **1** to **8**. Then complete sentences about them, including the relative pronoun *who*.

a Linnaeus _was a botanist who worked out a method of naming plants and animals_

b Marie Curie

c Aristotle

d Mary Shelley

e André-Marie Ampère

f Sonja Henie

g Maria Montessori

h Marco Polo

1 He was a physicist and made an instrument for measuring current and voltage.

2 She was a physicist and the first woman to receive a Nobel Prize.

3 She was a writer and wrote the novel *Frankenstein*.

4 ~~He was a botanist and worked out a method of naming plants and animals.~~

5 She was an ice-skater and took part in the Olympic Games at the age of 11.

6 He was a merchant and visited China in the 13th century.

7 He was a philosopher and taught Alexander the Great.

8 She was a doctor and invented a new method of teaching young children.

3 Rewrite each pair of sentences as one sentence, using *whose*. Make any necessary changes.

a J S Bach had two sons. Their music was better known than his for many years.
J S Bach had two sons whose music was better known than his for many years.

b John F Kennedy had a brother Robert. His death was also a political assassination.

c Lord Byron the poet had a daughter, Ada Lovelace. Her work in mathematics led to the development of the first computer.

d Pablo Picasso had a daughter, Paloma. Her fashion designs have become famous worldwide.

e John Lennon had a son, Julian. His music career has not been as successful as his father's.

relative clauses

181

f The astronomer William Herschel had a sister, Caroline. Her research contributed to his discoveries.

g Paul McCartney has a daughter, Stella. Her career in fashion design has been very successful.

4 Rewrite each pair of sentences as one sentence, using *which*. Make any necessary changes.

a The word *cell* comes from the Latin *cella*. This means *a small room*.
The word cell comes from the Latin cella which means a small room.

b All cells have a membrane or skin. It covers the cell.

c Inside the cell is a substance called the *cytoplasm*. It contains a number of chemicals.

d All cells contain DNA. This holds genetic information.

e They also contain RNA. It includes the information the cells need to build proteins.

f All cells contain a nucleus. This controls the actions of the cell.

g Bacteria consist of only one cell. This can divide and make other new bacteria.

h One of the most complex structures is the human body. It contains over 100,000 billion cells.

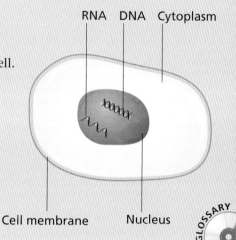

RNA DNA Cytoplasm

Cell membrane   Nucleus   GLOSSARY

5 Rewrite each pair of sentences as one sentence, containing the relative pronoun in capitals, or zero pronoun.

a Einstein is a scientist. I admire him. WHO
    Einstein is a scientist who I admire.

b Shakespeare is a writer. I don't understand him. ZERO

c Marie Curie is a scientist. We are studying her. WHOM

d Newton is a physicist. We often discuss him. ZERO

e Homer is an ancient Greek writer. We study him in translation. WHO

f Leonardo is an artist. Everybody knows him. THAT

g Jane Austen is an author. Most people enjoy her. ZERO

h Beethoven is a composer. I like him. THAT

6 Rewrite the sentence, beginning as shown. Do not use a relative pronoun.

a I made this lamp in a craft lesson.
This is   *the lamp I made in a craft lesson.*

b We lost this ball in the park last week.
This is

c I wrote this poem in my first year.
This is

d She painted this portrait as part of her project.
This is

e We used this computer to get the results.
This is

f We found this dog in the playground.
This is

g I borrowed this book from the library.
This is

h Mr Smith took this photo of the basketball team.
This is

geography

7 Complete the text with a suitable relative pronoun in each space (including *of which*).
Leave the space blank if this is possible.

Antarctica is mainly known for the penguins and seals a   *that*   live there, but recently scientists have discovered the remains of two dinosaurs b _____ lived there millions of years ago. These are not the first dinosaur fossils c _____ have been discovered in Antarctica, and bring the total to eight. The first new discovery was a plant-eating dinosaur d _____ was found by a mountain climber. Scientists e _____ examined the fossils say it is a plant-eating dinosaur f _____ is nearly 200 million years old. The parts of the animal g _____ they examined suggest that it was nine metres long and two metres tall. Dinosaurs h _____ have been found in other parts of the world are as long as 30 metres, however. So this specimen, the discovery i _____ has excited researchers, is rather small. On the other side of Antarctica, dinosaur bones j _____ were discovered by accident have also proved interesting. This second dinosaur was a meat-eater k _____ stood about two metres tall. Scientists l _____ were sheltering from bad weather found the bones near the sea. The dinosaur they discovered, m _____ bones were next to fossils of sea life, probably died and was washed out to sea after its death. Dinosaurs are creatures n _____ could not survive in cold conditions, but in their time, Antarctica was different. It didn't have the cold climate o _____ it has today, but was warm and wet.

GLOSSARY

EXTENSION ACTIVITY

1 Copy out five of the examples from page 180, and translate each one into your own language.

2 Check that you have the correct answers to Exercise 6. Translate the sentences into your own language.

*Need more practice? Go to the **Review** on page 192.*

relative clauses

47 defining and non-defining relative clauses

In written language, defining clauses give important information about the subject or object, and are not separated by commas.

*Friction is the force **that resists** the movement of one object against another.*

In written language non-defining clauses give extra information, which we could leave out, and are separated by commas. We cannot use *that* as a relative pronoun.

*Wrapping an object in aluminium foil, **which reduces energy loss**, keeps food hot.*

object clauses with prepositions: *whom, who*

In object clauses when we refer to people and use a preposition, we use *whom* in formal language.

*Enter the address of the person **to whom** you want to forward the message.*

It is more usual informally to use *who* and put the preposition at the end.

*Enter the address of the person **(who)** you want to forward the message **to**.*

object clauses with prepositions: preposition + *which, whose*

Formal
*This is the spacecraft **in which** the astronauts visited the Moon.*
*The tree **from which** this drug is obtained only grows in the rainforest.*
*The instrument **with which** we measure air pressure is called a barometer.*
*Dr Gibson, the scientist **on whose** research the article is based, agreed.*

Informal
(more usual)
*This is the spacecraft **(which)** the astronauts visited the Moon **in**.*
*The tree **(which)** this drug is obtained **from** only grows in the rainforest.*
*The instrument **(which)** we measure air pressure **with** is called a barometer.*
*Dr Gibson, the scientist **whose** research the article is based **on**, agreed.*

reason: *why*

Clauses of reason use *why* or *the reason why*.

*I've just passed my driving test, and that's **why** I'm so happy.*
*When water finds a natural opening in the ground that is lower than the water table, a spring comes into existence. This is **the reason why** most springs are found in low places or valleys.*

time: *when*

Clauses of time use *when* or *the time / year* etc *when*. We can also use *the* + time word + *in which* in more formal language.

***1969 was when** the first men went to the Moon.*
*It was also **the year in which** the Venera 5 space probe landed on Venus.*

place: *where*

Clauses of place use *where* or *the place where*.

*A habitat is **the place where** an animal or plant species lives.*

sentence relative: *which*

Use *which* to refer to the sentence or clause that comes before it, not just the word before it. There must be a comma before *which*.

*Tina got very good marks in the exam, **which** pleased all her teachers.*

1 Make a non-defining relative clause from the two sentences. Make any necessary changes.

a The polar bear is a large bear that lives in the Arctic. It is also known as the white bear.
  The polar bear, which is also known as the white bear, is a large bear that lives in the Arctic.

b The polar bear is found all across the Arctic. It has a population of about 20,000.

c About 60% of the bears are found in Canada. They hunt well on land and in water.

d The polar bear may become extinct by the end of the century. It is threatened by global warming.

e The sea ice in the Arctic is beginning to melt. Bears use this as a platform when they hunt seals.

f The polar bear is the largest land predator. It is twice the weight of a lion or tiger.

g The males weigh between 400 kg and 600 kg. They are twice the size of the females.

h The bear cubs remain with their mothers for ten months. They are born helpless and blind.

i Adult bears live for as long as 30 years. They do not hibernate.

j Polar bears can often be seen in open water kilometres from land. They are excellent swimmers.

2 Rewrite the formal sentence as an informal sentence ending with a preposition. Leave out the relative pronoun.

a Alan Graham is the teacher from whom I've learnt most.
  Alan Graham is the teacher I've learnt most from.

b He is someone for whom I have the greatest respect.

c We all admire people to whom we owe a lot.

d Especially if it is a person with whom we enjoy working.

e There are some people with whom you can easily form a relationship.

f But you don't always work with people for whom you feel admiration.

g And now here is the person for whom we have all been waiting.

h He is the man to whom I am pleased to present the Teacher of the Year Award.

defining and non-defining relative clauses

3 Rewrite each pair of sentences as one new sentence, using the preposition underlined followed by *which*.

a There are a number of trees and plants. Rubber is taken <u>from</u> them.

There are a number of trees and plants from which rubber is taken.

b The Para rubber tree is the major commercial source. Rubber is extracted <u>from</u> it.

....

c Brazil is the country. Rubber originates <u>from</u> there.

....

d Ancient Central American cultures collected rubber. They made balls <u>from</u> it.

....

e The Mayas made temporary shoes by using a rubber mixture. They dipped their feet <u>into</u> it.

....

f The people in Brazil used a mixture of rubber. They made waterproof clothes <u>from</u> it.

....

g In England people noticed it was a substance. You could rub out marks <u>with</u> it.

....

h This was the origin of the name. English people called it <u>by</u> this name.

....

4 <u>Underline</u> the correct option.

Easter Island, **a** <u>which is</u> / *which it is* in the Pacific Ocean more than 3,000 km from the coast of South America, has a terrible lesson to teach the modern world. When the first Europeans visited it in 1722, they found an island short of food on **b** *which* / *which are* about 3,000 people were living in a state of constant war. The Europeans were surprised to find a large number of huge statues, **c** *which* / *which they* had been moved over great distances, and **d** *to which* / *which* clearly belonged to a great civilization. The people **e** *whose* / *–* they found on the island, however, were poor and backward. The Europeans supposed that these people could not have built such large statues, **f** *which* / *which it* meant that some other mysterious people must have done so. However, modern research has shown that the inhabitants of Easter Island were responsible for the terrible condition **g** *in which* / *–* the Europeans had found them in. The inhabitants were divided into many family groups, **h** *which* / *which they* competed with each other. Their religion involved building huge statues, **i** *which* / *whose* consumed time and resources. Their home was a volcanic island on **j** *where* / *which* few trees grew, and **k** *which* / *which it* produced little food. To make matters worse, to build statues they cut down trees, **l** *which* / *which it* caused soil erosion. By the middle of the 16th century, the population had reached about 7,000, **m** *which* / *which was* too great for the island to support. By this time there were no more trees, **n** *which* / *which they* the islanders needed to build boats. There was not enough food **o** *which* / *with which* to feed such a large population, and they were unable to leave, so the population fell. By the end of the 19th century, there were only a hundred or so inhabitants remaining.

GLOSSARY

5 Complete the sentence using *why*, *when* or *where*.

a Most of us at some time have wanted to know ...*why*... leaves change colour and fall in autumn.

b It is difficult to predict exactly .... this will happen, as it depends on the autumn weather.

c It also depends on .... exactly the tree is growing, since some trees may receive more light than others.

d The leaves start to change colour .... the tree stops making chlorophyll, the substance which gives them a green colour.

e The trees stop making chlorophyll .... there is not enough light for the process of photosynthesis to work.

f Other colours in the leaf are hidden by the chlorophyll, and this is .... we only see these colours when the tree stops making chlorophyll.

g Red colours in the leaves are made by food trapped in the leaves .... the tree stops making food.

h Deciduous trees have adapted to survive the winter without leaves, which is one reason .... their leaves fall off in autumn.

i They are less likely to be damaged .... strong winds blow.

j Many deciduous trees also produce flowers .... they have no leaves, as this makes it easier for them to pollinate.

6 Complete the text with a relative pronoun in each space, or leave it blank if this is possible.

John Lennon, a ...*who*... was born in 1940, was a member of the Beatles, the British rock group. He grew up in Liverpool, b .... he performed in a number of groups, and met the other members of the Beatles. After studying at art college, c .... he disliked as much as he had disliked school, Lennon spent his time learning to be a musician. In 1962, the Beatles had their first hit record, d .... was soon followed by success in the USA. Lennon and Paul McCartney, another young musician e .... he had met in 1957, wrote most of the group's songs. The success of the Beatles, f .... was worldwide, created problems for Lennon, g .... often said exactly what he thought to the press and TV, and got into trouble. By the time the Beatles stopped working together, h .... came about during the late 1960s, Lennon's songs had become both political and highly personal. His personal life, i .... was made more difficult by his problems with drugs and alcohol, was also often in the news. He and his wife Cynthia were divorced, and he married Yoko Ono, with j .... he carried out political protests. They also made records together, and went to live in the USA, k .... Lennon continued his solo career. In the mid 70s he took a break from music l .... lasted for five years. In 1980 he started to record a new album, m .... was still unfinished n .... he was shot dead by Mark Chapman, a fan o .... wanted to become famous, on 8 December 1980.

GLOSSARY

the arts

defining and non-defining relative clauses

EXTENSION ACTIVITY

Copy out five of the examples from page 184, and translate each one into your own language.

*Need more practice? Go to the **Review** on page 192.*

48 purpose and result

purpose infinitive

Use the *to*-infinitive for describing the purpose of an action, when the subject of the action and the purpose are the same.

> *We used the information in the table **to complete** the graph.*
> (*we use / we completed* = same subject)

need and purpose infinitive

We often use the purpose infinitive with *need*, often with an object after *need*.

> *Wait a minute, we **need to discuss** this.*   *You **need a special key** to open it.*

explaining purpose

Use *so (that) + can / could* to explain the purpose of an action, especially when there is a lot of detail.

> *We measured the amount of water in the jar every day, **so we could** work out the average daily rainfall.*

Use *so (that) + can / could* when we describe the purpose of an action, but the subject of the action and the purpose are different.

> *We displayed the information in the classroom **so the rest of the class could** read it.*
> (*we displayed / they read* = **different subjects**)

Use *so that + didn't / wouldn't* to describe an action the purpose of which is to stop something happening.

> *We used an umbrella **so we didn't / wouldn't** get wet.*

for

Use *for* to describe the purpose of a thing using *for + noun /- ing*.

> *Soap is good **for washing** things because of the shape of its molecules.*

too + adjective + *to*-infinitive

Use *too* + adjective + *to*-infinitive when we describe a situation and its result. The result involves something negative, eg you can't do it, something bad might happen etc.

> *These molecules **are too small** (for us) **to see** with the naked eye.*

adjective + *enough* + *to*-infinitive

Use adjective + *enough* + *to*-infinitive in the same way, when the result has a positive meaning.

> *This comet is **bright enough to see** with binoculars.*

It is possible to add a negative, eg *not large enough* means the same as *too small*.

> *These molecules are **not large enough to see** with the naked eye.*

explaining a result

Use *so* + adjective + *(that)* to explain a result.

> *Some comets are **so bright that** people think they are planets or stars.*

We often use *so* + adjective + *(that)* with *can / could*.

> *These molecules are **so small (that) we can't** see them with the naked eye.*

Use *such a* in front of an adjective used with a singular noun.

> *It is **such a bright comet that** you can see it with binoculars.*

Use *such* in front of an adjective used with plural nouns.

> *Molecules are **such small parts** of matter **that** we can't see them with the naked eye.*

Use *so* with an adverb + *(that)* to explain a result.

> *They searched the sky **so carefully that** they found three new comets.*

because of, as a result of

Use the preposition phrase *because of* + noun or *as a result of* + noun to describe a result. Put the *because of / as a result of* clause at the beginning or end of the sentence.

> ***Because of** the great distances involved, it is hard to see any details.*
> *Pollution has been increasing **as a result of** air traffic.*

1 Use the information to complete a new sentence so that it contains the word or words in capitals. Make any necessary changes.

a Rich Romans wanted a comfortable life. Roman slaves worked hard. SO THAT
Roman slaves *worked hard so that rich Romans could have a comfortable life*

b When enemies shot arrows at Roman soldiers, they put their shields over their heads. They did this as a way of protecting themselves. TO
When enemies shot arrows at Roman soldiers, they _____

c The Romans built a road system all over Europe. This helped their armies move quickly from one place to another. SO THAT
The Romans built a road system all over Europe _____

d When the Romans wanted to catch mice, they used other animals so they could catch them. TO
When the Romans wanted to catch mice, they _____

e The Romans used a pointed metal stylus when they wrote on pieces of wood covered in wax. TO
The Romans used a pointed metal stylus _____

f The Romans buried their dead beside the road outside their town. They didn't want the ghosts to return to their old homes. SO THAT
The Romans buried their dead beside the road outside their town _____

2 Complete the sentences **a** to **h** with information from **1** to **8**, and *for*.

> 1 do maths problems   2 heat things in a lab   3 look at things that are too small to see
> 4 make someone's voice louder   5 ~~measure air pressure~~   6 measure humidity
> 7 measure and move liquid   8 measure temperature

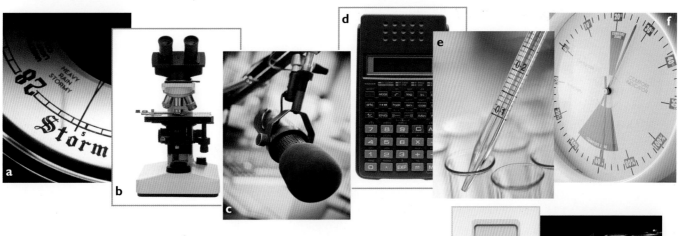

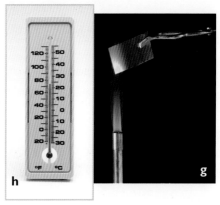

a A barometer is used *for measuring air pressure.*
b A microscope _____
c A microphone _____
d A calculator _____
e A pipette _____
f A hygrometer _____
g A Bunsen burner _____
h A thermometer _____

purpose and result

189

3 Rewrite the sentence so that it contains *too* + adjective + *to*-infinitive. Do not include *for us*.

a   Some parts of the universe are very distant so we can't visit them.
Some parts of the universe are too distant to visit.

b   The atmosphere of Mars is very thin and we can't breathe it.

c   Venus is very hot and we couldn't land on it.

d   For most people, a journey into space is very expensive and they can't take it.

e   Trips to most other planets are very dangerous so we don't consider them.

f   The universe is very large, and we can't explore it completely.

g   Perhaps its meaning is difficult and so we can't grasp it.

4 Rewrite the sentence so it contains the word *enough*.

a   If all the blood vessels in the body formed one line, it would be very long and would reach more than twice round the Earth.
If all the blood vessels in the body formed one line, it would be long enough to reach more than twice round the Earth.

b   Some metals, eg sodium, are light and they float.

c   A week after it is born, a baby gazelle is strong and can run with adults.

d   The planet Pluto is very small and can't have a proper atmosphere.

e   The dinosaurs were not adaptable and didn't survive climate change.

f   If a spider's web had threads as thick as a pencil, it would be so strong that it could catch a Boeing 707 jet!

5 Rewrite the sentence so it contains *so* or *such*.

a   Tropical rain is sometimes heavy enough to damage the leaves of trees.
Tropical rain is sometimes so heavy that it can damage the leaves of trees.

b   The bee hummingbird is small (6.2 cm long) and people often think it is an insect.

c   Jupiter's moon Europa is cold and the ice on the surface is probably as hard as rock.

d   A Camel Spider is a greedy eater and will eat until it cannot move.

e   The Sun is hot and the chemical elements found on Earth exist on the Sun as gases.

f   The African Elephant is heavy and it's only able to move at the speed of a fast walk.

6 Rewrite the sentence so that it begins as shown, making any necessary changes.

a More than half a million people visit the famous caves in Han-sur-Leses every year.
Because of _its caves, more than half a million people visit Han-sur-Leses every year._

b Most of the caves are too dangerous for visitors to enter as there are falling rocks.
As a result ....

c The river's disappearance beneath a hill led ancient people to throw objects into the water.
Because of ....

d The beauty of its unexplored cave system made it a challenge to cavers for many years.
Because of ....

e Its disappearance under the rocks made the course of the river through the cave unknown.
As a result of ....

f The ice-cold water meant that many explorers of the cave system lost their lives.
As a result ....

g The importance of the caves, however, means that they are open to scientific researchers.
However, because of ....

h And the course of the river has now been traced thanks to recent explorations.
And as a result of ....

7 Complete the text with one suitable word in each space.

Most people now have a home computer, a ...So........... they can
shop online or download music or send and receive e-mails. Many
others, who find commuting to work so stressful b .... they
can't stand it, use a computer to work from home. A computer is
also useful c .... playing music, or storing photos, and a
hundred and one other things. d .... of its usefulness, the
computer has changed our lives. In fact, it's e .... useful that many of us wonder how on earth
we managed before it was invented. It is f .... an essential part of everyday life, that we run
the risk of forgetting the disadvantages of the electronic lifestyle. It's g .... easy for us to send
an e-mail instead of a letter. Shopping online is h .... convenient i .... we can forget
the thousands of delivery vans which have to bring the things we buy to our homes. Soon the roads
will be j .... crowded with delivery vans, that we won't be able to travel anywhere! And aren't
shops good places for buying things? Perhaps we need time k .... get away from the computer
and realize that it might be better to read a book or go for a walk. This is l .... an obvious fact
that I can't understand why I didn't think of it before, but I have been looking at a great web site which
explains everything!

GLOSSARY

EXTENSION ACTIVITY

1 Write examples for each of these words and phrases.
to go shopping   so that   for   too big   so heavy

2 Check that you have the correct answers to Exercise 7. Translate the text into your own language.

*Need more practice? Go to the **Review** on page 192.*

Review

How to use this section

a As extra practice if you have finished the rest of the unit and the Extension Activities.

b To test yourself. Do the exercise, check your answers, then decide if you need to have a look at the presentation page again.

c If you need extra practice, read the presentation page(s) again, then try to do the extra exercise(s).

Unit 2 present continuous

<u>Underline</u> the correct form.

Hello again from the rainforest. You won't believe this, but I **a** *sit* / <u>*am sitting*</u> in a small boat on a river in South America. I **b** *don't know* / *am not knowing* the name of the river in English, but now we **c** *travel* / *are travelling* through the rainforest. It's really hot, and water **d** *drips* / *is dripping* from my face, so I **e** *apologize* / *am apologizing* for my bad handwriting. The batteries of my camera **f** *run out* / *are running out* too, so don't expect many photos. The other problem here is the rain. It **g** *rains* / *is raining* nearly every day, which is why they **h** *call* / *are calling* it a rainforest I **i** *suppose* / *am supposing*! Luckily **j** *it doesn't rain* / *it isn't raining* at the moment, but I'll have to be quick. In general, I **k** *have* / *am having* a really good time, and I **l** *find out* / *am finding out* a lot about the flora and fauna in the rainforest. The trees here **m** *grow* / *are growing* to 60 metres, which **n** *makes* / *is making* it very dark all the time in the forest. There aren't really any paths, and people **o** *travel* / *are travelling* everywhere by water, or by plane. Of course we ecotourists **p** *take* / *are taking* this trip for fun, because we **q** *want* / *are wanting* to. What else can I tell you? Well, everything **r** *smells* / *is smelling* really bad here. And it's very noisy, because the birds and animals **s** *seem* / *are seeming* to stay awake all night. Ugh, sorry, a horrible spider **t** *crawls* / *is crawling* along my leg. That's all for now!

Score: _____ / 20

Unit 3 past simple

Write the past simple form of the following words.

a be	*was/were*	f buy		k make		p tell	
b go		g study		l win		q read	
c have		h pay		m write		r pick	
d eat		i bring		n drink		s sing	
e wait		j cook		o swim		t run	

Score: _____ / 20

Unit 5 present perfect simple

Write the past participle of the following verbs.

a be	*been*	f buy		k make		p tell	
b go		g study		l win		q read	
c have		h pay		m write		r pick	
d eat		i bring		n drink		s sing	
e wait		j cook		o swim		t run	

Score: _____ / 20

Unit 6 present perfect continuous

Choose the correct form, A or B, to complete the sentence.

a	_B_ _War and Peace_. It's really long, and I'm only halfway.	**a A** _I've read_	**B** _I've been reading_
b	_____ Maria all day, but there's never a reply.	**b A** _I've phoned_	**B** _I've been phoning_
c	_____ to the library and back, so I feel a bit tired.	**c A** _I've walked_	**B** _I've been walking_
d	_____ French for three years, but I still can't say a thing!	**d A** _I've learned_	**B** _I've been learning_
e	_____ the work I had to do, so now we can go out.	**e A** _I've done_	**B** _I've been doing_
f	_____ the vegetables, so you can start cooking them.	**f A** _I've washed_	**B** _I've been washing_
g	_____ all the ice-cream, and now I feel sick!	**g A** _I've been eating_	**B** _I've eaten_
h	_____ three letters so far, but I still have to write two more.	**h A** _I've written_	**B** _I've been writing_

Score: _____ / 8

Unit 7 past perfect

Underline the correct form.

1 Gottfried Liebnitz and Isaac Newton developed the mathematics we call calculus at about the same time in the 17th century, although their versions **a** _were_ / _had been_ slightly different. However, Newton was sure that he was first and that Leibnitz **b** _copied_ / _had copied_ him.

2 The Wright brothers made the first powered flight in 1903, but only four men and a boy **c** _saw_ / _had seen_ their plane fly. Until Wilbur Wright flew in front of a large crowd in France in 1908, most people refused to believe that their earlier flight **d** _succeeded_ / _had succeeded_.

3 Shakespeare **e** _used_ / _had used_ familiar stories and events from history in a lot of his plays, so the audience **f** _heard_ / _had heard_ the plots before. However, that didn't stop him being very successful.

4 Aristotle **g** _was_ / _had been_ a philosopher and teacher in ancient Greece. By the time he died in 322 BC, he **h** _had written_ / _wrote_ some of the most famous philosophical texts of all time, and had tutored Alexander the Great.

Score: _____ / 8

Unit 8 tense contrasts

Complete the text with the most suitable form of the verbs in brackets.

Bob Dylan **a** (become) _has become_ one of the most famous singer / song-writers of all time. At the age of 65 in 2006, he **b** (reach) _____ the top of the US album charts with _Modern Times_, the oldest living singer to do so. He **c** (record) _____ many other hit albums since he **d** (make) _____ his first album at the age of 21 while he **e** (perform) _____ as a folk singer in New York clubs. Although he first **f** (find) _____ fame as a folk singer, he **g** (try) _____ originally to be a rock and roll singer, but without success. In the mid-60s, Dylan **h** (start) _____ to perform rock songs with a group, instead of the solo folk songs which **i** (make) _____ him famous. At the time, many of his fans **j** (feel) _____ angry because they **k** (think) _____ that he **l** (do) _____ this simply for money. Many folk music fans still **m** (believe) _____ that he was wrong. In fact, Dylan's songs **n** (change) _____ in the time up to this point. As far as he was concerned, he **o** (do) _____ everything that he could with folk music already, and he **p** (need) _____ a different musical style to express his changing feelings. Dylan's career **q** (be) _____ a long one, and there is no sign that he **r** (think) _____ of retirement. He **s** (perform) _____ since the late 1950s and **t** (appear) _____ in several films too.

Score: _____ / 20

Unit 10 future time

Complete the dialogue with *will*, *be going to*, *shall*.

a 'What ____are____ you __going to__ do this evening?'

b 'I'm not sure. My brother _____ go to a basketball match. He bought the tickets yesterday. But I don't like basketball very much. What about you?'

c 'I don't have any plans. My parents _____ go to the theatre, but I think that's really boring. _____ we do something together?'

d 'That's a good idea. Do you like action films? I _____ borrow a DVD from my brother if you want to watch one.'

e 'No thanks, I saw a film yesterday. I know! Marie _____ go ice skating. _____ I phone her and ask if we can go?'

f 'Great. I _____ get my skates.'

Score: ____ / 6

Unit 13 tag questions

Complete the questions with a positive or negative past simple tag.

a Before the French Revolution, the king did whatever he wanted to do, __didn't he__ ?

b All the people paid high taxes, so they weren't very happy, _____ ?

c The people didn't have enough to eat, _____ ?

d The government tried to introduce new taxes, _____ ?

e The people formed a National Assembly, _____ ?

f The Assembly took power from the king, _____ ?

g The king tried to leave France, _____ ?

h The government executed thousands of aristocrats, _____ ?

i It also killed the king and the queen, _____ ?

j Napoleon Bonaparte took over the government and later became Emperor, _____ ?

Score: ____ / 10

Unit 15 *-ing* form

Complete the text with the *to*-infinitive or *-ing* form of the verbs in the box.

eat	lose	have	cook	go	prepare	eat	eat
do	cook	find	exercise	cook	wash up	cook	shop

Scientists have given us some very good advice about a ____eating____ healthily, but how many of us do what they say? We are used to b _____ fast food and chocolate, and don't have the time to spend c _____ , d _____ and e _____ all the time. If you want f _____ weight there are lots of diets you can try, and you should also try g _____ as much as possible. Healthy food means h _____ lots of fresh fruit and vegetables, and if you are interested in i _____ , a day of j _____ new recipes. However, if you are bored by k _____ , and dislike l _____ to the supermarket, it's going to be difficult m _____ healthily. You might be lucky and have someone who doesn't mind n _____ food for you. If this is true, then you should offer o _____ the washing up, or they may stop p _____ for you!

Score: ____ / 16

Unit 18 conditionals: true, real and unreal

1 Use the information to complete a real conditional sentence about the consequences of global warming.

a *weather patterns change → droughts and floods are more frequent*
If _weather patterns change, droughts and floods will be more frequent._

b *water becomes warmer in the gulf of Mexico → the strength of hurricanes increases*
If ....

c *rain falls at the wrong time → farmers are unable to grow their crops*
If ....

d *rainfall increases → there is more soil erosion, and deserts spread*
If ....

e *glaciers vanish → local areas become short of water*
If ....

f *permafrost melts in polar regions → the landscape changes*
If ....

g *polar ice melts → sea levels rise*
If ....

h *ecosystems change → some plants and animals change their habitat*
If ....

i *the Gulf Stream grows weak → northern Europe becomes colder*
If ....

j *temperatures rise → forest fires become more frequent*
If ....

Score: ____ / 10

2 Use the prompts to make an unreal conditional *if*-sentence.

a you melt a medium-sized iceberg / you have enough water to supply a big city for several weeks
If _you melted a medium-sized iceberg, you would have enough water to supply a big city for several weeks._

b Amazonia is a country / it is the ninth largest in the world
If ....

c you put all the cells from your brain in a straight line / they reach for 1,000 km
If ....

d you are a sloth / you spend 18 hours a day sleeping
If ....

e you have a piece of the Sun 2.5 cm square / it shines brighter than a thousand 60 watt light bulbs
If ....

f you have a piece of the Sun / it burns you to nothing!
If ....

g you fly a plane to Neptune / it takes nearly 290 years to get there
If ....

h all the matter in a baby becomes energy / it runs a power station for a year
If ....

Score: ____ / 8

Review

Unit 20 the passive and its uses

Complete the text with the passive form of the verbs in brackets.

Hundreds of movies **a** (produce) *are produced* all over the world every year. The most successful ones **b** (make) _____ in America, because they **c** (direct) _____ by famous people and lots of money **d** (spend) _____ on advertizing them. Hollywood films **e** (watch) _____ all over the world, but many countries have their own directors and stars. Bollywood films, which **f** (make) _____ in India, are becoming very popular in other countries. Beautiful costumes, music, singing and dancing **g** (love) _____ by moviegoers everywhere, and that's why so many Bollywood films **h** (show) _____ all over the world. According to many film critics, the best film ever made is *Citizen Kane*, which **i** (direct) _____ by Orson Welles in 1941. The story **j** (base) _____ on the life of a very powerful business man, and the studio that made the film **k** (threaten) _____ by legal action. Luckily, the film **l** (release) _____ and **m** (enjoy) _____ by audiences ever since.

Score: _____ / 13

Unit 23 modals: ability, obligation, criticism (past)

Rewrite each sentence so that it contains the word or words in capitals. Leave out any unnecessary words.

a It was impossible for ancient sailors to travel far because they usually followed the coastline.

COULDN'T

Ancient sailors couldn't travel far because they usually followed the coastline.

b Early ships were very small, but they were forced to carry a lot of fresh food and water.   HAD

c Small sailing ships found it impossible to survive heavy storms and very bad weather.   WERE

d There was no radio, so it was only possible for them to send messages home if they met other ships.

COULD

e They didn't have accurate maps, so it was necessary for them to guess their exact position.

HAD

f They didn't have radar, so it was necessary for them to keep a close look-out for dangerous rocks.

NEEDED

g It was necessary for them to see the Sun or the stars in order to navigate.   HAD

h There were no rescue organizations, so if they got into trouble, it was necessary for them to look after themselves.

HAD

Score: _____ / 8

Unit 24 modals: possibility, uncertainty, certainty (present, future)

Rewrite the sentence so that it contains *might*.

a   Perhaps a lot of terrible things will happen to the Earth.
    A lot of terrible things might happen to the Earth.

b   There is always the chance that an object from space will hit it.

....

c   Or it's possible that a huge volcanic eruption will change the climate.

....

d   Maybe hurricanes and tornadoes will spread across the world.

....

e   Or there's a chance that climate change will lead to a sudden Ice Age.

....

f   Of course it's possible that before that, a nuclear accident will destroy life on Earth.

....

g   There's also a chance that a new disease could kill nearly everyone.

....

h   Maybe aliens will invade the Earth and do the same thing.

....

i   On the other hand, it's possible that things will continue as they are!

....

j   So perhaps it's better not to worry so much.

....

Score: _____ / 10

Unit 27 countable and uncountable

Read the following text. Decide if the words and phrases underlined are countable (C) or uncountable (UC).

How to make vegetarian Spaghetti Bolognese

First of all you need an **a** <u>onion</u>, a few **b** <u>carrots</u> and some **c** <u>garlic</u>. Chop them up, then put some **d** <u>olive oil</u> in a saucepan and fry them for about five minutes. Add some chopped **e** <u>peppers</u> (green is best), a chopped **f** <u>courgette</u> and a few chopped **g** <u>mushrooms</u>. Fry for a further five minutes. Then add some **h** <u>red lentils</u>, **i** <u>a cup of water</u> and **j** <u>a tin of chopped tomatoes</u>. Bring to the boil and simmer for 15 to 20 **k** <u>minutes</u>. In a separate pan, add some **l** <u>pasta</u> to boiling **m** <u>water</u> and cook for about 10 minutes. When cooked, pour the water away and put the pasta on a plate. Serve the vegetarian Spaghetti Bolognese with **n** <u>salad</u> and **o** <u>Parmesan cheese</u>.

---

a   ...C..........................   i   ....

b   ....   j   ....

c   ....   k   ....

d   l   ....

e   ....   m   ....

f   ....   n   ....

g   ....   o   ....

h   ....

Score: _____ / 15

Unit 30 articles (2)

Complete the following text with *a / an*, *the* or leave blank for zero article.

Cairo is **a** _the_ capital city of **b** _____ Egypt. It has **c** _____
long and interesting history, and is still one of **d** _____ most
exciting **e** _____ places to visit. The ancient Egyptians are most
famous for building the pyramids, but their civilization achieved
many other great things. They had **f** _____ writing in the form of
hieroglyphics, which decorate **g** _____ tombs and monuments
of their pharaohs, and they produced beautiful stone and metal
objects which can be seen in **h** _____ Egyptian Museum. Pictures
in the tombs at Giza and Saqqara show how the ancient Egyptians
lived, the clothes they wore, and **i** _____ gods they worshipped.
j _____ visit to Cairo isn't complete without **k** _____ trip to
l _____ big bazaar Khan Al Khalili, where you can buy everything
from **m** _____ belly dancing costumes to dates, beautiful silver and
gold jewellery and papyrus pictures of camels and pyramids. You can
even have your name written in **n** _____ hieroglyphics!

Score: _____ / 14

Unit 35 adjectives

1 Put the adjectives in brackets in the correct order.

a In the vase is a bunch of _beautiful, small white_ _____ roses.
   (white, beautiful, small)

b It's a _____ painting.
   (medieval, round, large)

c This is a / an _____ gallery.
   (German, interesting, new)

d This was painted by a _____ artist.
   (renaissance, French, famous)

e The painting consists of rows of _____ stars.
   (green, plastic, tiny)

f We bought a / an _____ plate.
   (glass, Italian, small)

g At the end of the room was a / an _____ painting.
   (old, Spanish, large)

h Hanging from the arms were a number of _____ objects.
   (metal, shiny, circular)

i The painting is protected by a _____ screen.
   (transparent, large, plastic)

j The sculpture was bought by a / an _____ collector.
   (American, young, wealthy)

Score: _____ / 10

2 <u>Underline</u> the correct form.

Many students report that they often feel **a** <u>bored</u> / boring by studying. This is not **b** surprised / surprising when you consider how some students study. A recent report, which many teachers find **c** worried / worrying, suggests that a majority of students listen to music at the same time as studying.

However, what experts say about this issue is rather **d** confused / confusing. Some people study more effectively when they are **e** relaxed / relaxing, and listening to music may help. Students who are **f** worried / worrying by the pressure of school may find that they are in a better mood if their music is playing. When they become more **g** interested / interesting in what they are studying, they do not in fact 'listen' to the music at all. It just becomes background noise. On the other hand, there are certainly students who find the music more **h** entertained / entertaining than their school work, and never really concentrate on their work at all. So perhaps we shouldn't be **i** surprised / surprising to discover that listening to music helps some but not all, though this can also depend on the type of music. And it also depends on what students are supposed to be studying. Anyone who listens to music while trying to read and remember details will almost certainly be **j** distracted / distracting by the music. So in the end, perhaps it's a matter of 'what works for you'.

Score: _____ / 10

Unit 36 adverbs

Complete the sentence with *too*, *very* or *enough*.

a Nobody finds studying ....*very*........ easy at the best of times.

b If you are really .... tired to study, it can be a real effort to force yourself.

c Many students, however, are .... disorganized to study effectively.

d If you are .... busy, then you have to make good use of your time.

e It's not good .... to just sit down at the last minute and study for a long period.

f Using this method most people become .... exhausted to concentrate well.

g It's .... easy to spend hours with books open on the desk, but to achieve little.

h But if you stay up too late studying, you won't be alert .... the following day, which can add to your problems.

i You have to be .... careful to organize learning over a long period.

j Studying has to be done regularly, and divided into sections so that it is not .... tiring.

Score: _____ / 10

Unit 43 phrasal verbs

Choose the correct option, A, B, C or D, to complete the sentence.

a   It's not a difficult problem. I'm sure you can .... c ....
b   I had flu really badly, and I haven't .... it yet.
c   If you like, I can .... at the end of this street.
d   She was .... something, but I couldn't understand what it was.
e   Kate had to .... ballet lessons because she had too many other things to do.
f   We'll .... the case, and we'll let you know what we find out.
g   Could you come round and .... the baby on Saturday evening?
h   Pat kept talking on his mobile phone in class, until the teacher ....
i   The next exercise isn't very important, so we'll ....
j   I'll come round and .... at 7.00, so make sure you're ready!

a A *fill it in*	B *let it down*	C *work it out*	D *look it up*
b A *got over*	B *looked after*	C *run through*	D *come across*
c A *leave you out*	B *turn you off*	C *bring you up*	D *drop you off*
d A *standing for*	B *heading for*	C *getting at*	D *joining in*
e A *let down*	B *work out*	C *drop off*	D *give up*
f A *join in*	B *get over*	C *look into*	D *come across*
g A *look after*	B *fill in*	C *work out*	D *bring up*
h A *picked him up*	B *told him off*	C *let him down*	D *dropped him off*
i A *look it up*	B *sort it out*	C *miss it out*	D *put it off*
j A *leave you out*	B *drop you off*	C *tell you off*	D *pick you up*

Score: _____ / 10

Unit 45 conjunctions, adverbs and prepositions as connectors

Match the examples 1 to 6 on page 201 to the statements a to f, then connect the two using the words in brackets.

a   (For example) Human activities can upset the balance of nature.
Human activities can upset the balance of nature. For example, when humans burn wood, coal or petrol, sulphur and nitrogen compounds are added to the air, and these fall in rain and cause changes to the water of lakes and rivers so that fish die.

b   (such as) These games help younger children understand basic number concepts. Adding, subtracting, and getting to know numbers are explained in cartoons of everyday activities.

c   (for example) Some energy sources are called 'non-renewable' because in the end they will run out.

d   (For example) A risk factor is anything that increases a person's chance of getting a disease.

e (such as) The Wild Information page tells you what you want to know about wild animals. It includes information about dangerous predators.

....

....

....

f (such as) *Science Now* is great magazine which explores the science behind the news.

....

....

....

1 ~~When humans burn wood, coal or petrol, sulphur and nitrogen compounds are added to the air, and these fall in rain and cause changes to the water of lakes and rivers so that fish die.~~

2 Sunbathing too much is a risk factor for skin cancer, and smoking is a risk factor for lung cancer.

3 We cannot make oil, which was formed millions of years ago from the remains of ancient sea plants and animals.

4 ... why planes crash, and why athletes shouldn't use drugs.

5 ... playing football, getting on a bus, or going to the beach.

6 ... tigers, cheetahs and great white sharks.

Score: _____ / 6

Unit 46 relative clauses

Complete the sentence with *which* or *who*, or leave the space blank if this is possible.

a Scientists ....*who*........ study rocks are known as geologists.

b The genetic information .... you get from your parents makes you the person you are.

c The light .... leaves the Sun takes eight and a half minutes to reach the Earth.

d Louis Pasteur was a French scientist .... studied microbes.

e Cold-blooded animals are animals .... rely on heat from the Sun for their body temperature.

f Hydrogen is a fuel .... space rockets use.

g Breathing is a mechanical process .... fills the lungs with air.

h Acid is a substance .... we find in lemons, for example.

i Something .... poses a risk to people is known as an environmental hazard.

j The metal .... the manufacturers choose depends on their reason for using it.

Score: _____ / 10

Unit 47 defining and non-defining relative clauses

Make one sentence from the pair of sentences, using *which*.

a In the 14th century, Ibn Battuta, the Moroccan explorer, travelled more than 120,000 km on his journeys. This would be difficult even for a modern traveller.
   In the 14th century, Ibn Battuta, the Moroccan explorer, travelled more than 120,000 km on his journeys, which would be difficult even for a modern traveler.

b In the early years of the 15th century, European sailors usually refused to sail further south than the Canary Islands. This was understandable, as they believed that it was too dangerous to go further.

....

....

c In 1487, Bartolemeu Dias and his ships reached the Indian Ocean. This was a great achievement for the time.

d In 150 AD, the Greek geographer Ptolemy made a map of the world showing two lakes in Africa as the sources of the Nile. This was remarkable, considering that modern European explorers did not discover these lakes until the 1860s.

e Nobody thought that Marco Polo's book about China was true. This was not surprising because some parts of his story were so unbelievable.

f Archaeologists have found the remains of a Viking settlement in North America. This proves that the Vikings were the first Europeans to reach America.

Score: _____ / 6

Unit 48 purpose and result

Read the following information about tennis, then write similar sentences for the other sports.

> You need a racket, a ball and a net for playing tennis.
> To play tennis, you need a racket, a ball and a net.
> You need a racket, a ball and net so that you can play tennis.

a football: ball, two teams, goal posts _You need a ball, two teams and goal posts for playing football. To play football, you need a ball, two teams and goal posts. You need a ball, two teams and goal posts so that you can play football._

b baseball: bats, hard ball, two teams

c ping pong: ball, table, small bats

d ice hockey: puck, ice rink, ice skates

e polo: ball, horses, mallets

Score: _____ / 5

Wordlist

Red words based on Macmillan English Dictionary

*** most common and basic words
** very common words
* fairly common words

Unit 1

acid (n) **
antibiotic (n)
antibody (n) *
bacteria (n) **
breathe (vb) **
breed (vb) **
chick (n)
common (adj) ***
enzyme (n) *
harm (n) **
hatch (vb)
immunize (n)
infection (n) **
inject (vb) *
institution (n) ***
invader (n)
lay (an egg) (vb) ***
mask (n) **
mate (n) **
matter (n) ***
microorganism (n)
mucus (n)
patient (n) ***
plot (n) **
propose (vb) **
represent (vb) ***
saliva (n)
swallow (vb) **
train (vb) ***
vaccinate (n)
virus (n) ***
vote (vb) ***

Unit 2

crater (n)
deforestation (n)
developing (adj) **
equipment (n) ***
erosion (n) **
gas (n) ***
giant (adj) **
ground (n) ***
head (vb) ***
mission (n) **
patient (adj) **
population (n) ***
pressure (n) ***
rate (n) ***
rescue (vb) **
respond (vb) ***
rise (vb) ***
shake (vb) **
sharply (adv) **
smoke (vb) **
solar (adj) **
spacecraft (n)
species (n) ***

vanish (vb) **
volcano (n) *

Unit 3

conquer (vb) ***
construct (vb) ***
factory (n) ***
improve (vb) ***
invade (vb) *
march (vb) **
microscope (n) *
mine (n) *
poison (n) *
prove (vb) ***
soap (n) **
steam (n) **
stress (n) ***
sugar beet (n)
textile (n) **
transport (vb) **
vaccine (n)

Unit 4

active (volcano) (n) ***
army (n) ***
attack (vb) ***
banquet (n)
buoyancy (n)
cave (n) **
climate (n) **
coast (n) ***
complex (adj) ***
continent (n) **
density (n) **
dig (vb) **
Equator (n)
fall (vb) ***
free (adj) ***
gravity (n) *
insect (n) **
interrupt (vb) **
knot (n) **
land mass (n)
legend (n) **
local (adj) ***
nobleman (n)
observe (vb) ***
obviously (adv) ***
quarrel (n) *
rebellion (n)
record (n) ***
remains (n) **
settlement (n) **
soundproof (adj)
trade (vb) ***
wound (n) **

Unit 5

advance (n) **
atmosphere (n) **
climate change (n)
coal (n) ***
contribute (vb) ***
descend (vb) **
emission (n) **
expedition (n) **
experience (n) ***
force (n) ***

fossil (n) **
fossil fuel (n)
global warming (n) *
greenhouse effect (n)
greenhouse gas (n)
investigate (vb) ***
litter (n) *
oil (n) ***
origin (n) ***
overfishing (n)
polar (adj)
reduce (n) ***
remains (n) **
reproduce (vb) **
stable (adj) **
transplant (vb)

Unit 6

coral reef (n)
excavate (vb)
identify (vb) ***
image (n) ***
major (adj) ***
reef (n) *
satellite (n) **
service (vb) ***
shut down (phr vb)
site (n) **
source (n) ***
species (n) ***
spot (vb) **
telescope (n) *
tide (n) **

Unit 7

alliance (n) **
aristocratic (adj)
award (n) ***
blank (n)
bravery (n)
calculate (vb) **
civil war (n) *
craftsman (n)
damp (adj) **
density (n) **
deteriorate (vb) *
dishonest (adj) *
download (vb)
earthquake (n) *
exhausted (adj) *
expert (n) ***
governor (n) **
key (n) ***
mass (n) ***
pure (adj) ***
route (n) ***
scream (vb) **
screen (n) ***
shore (n) **
South Pole (n)
spill (vb) **
survive (vb) ***
tsunami (n)
volume (n) ***

Unit 8

authority (n) ***
compose (vb) **

composer (n) **
night shift (n)
opera (n) **
operation (n) ***
out of breath

Unit 9

conjunction (n)
erupt (vb)
geologist (n)
goggles (n)
local (adj) ***
lorry (n) **
organic (adj) *
solution (n) **
spectator (n)
traffic (n) ***
threat (n) ***
waste (n) ***
worldwide (adj) *

Unit 10

absorb (vb) **
artificial (n) **
atom (n) **
cancer (n) ***
collide (vb) *
core (n) **
cure (n) **
dense (adj) *
dwarf (n)
expand (vb) ***
expire (vb) *
fusion (n) *
giant (n) **
nuclear (adj) ***
phase (n) ***
poverty (n) **
retire (vb) **
schedule (n) **
solution (n) ***

Unit 11

annual (adj) ***
block (vb) ***
deciduous (adj)
dormant (adj)
drop (n) **
Equator (n)
fertilize (vb)
layer (n) ***
mate (vb) *
matter (vb) ***
poor (adj) ***
predator (n) **
reproduce (vb) **
rich (adj) ***
shallow (adj) **
slope (n) **
soil (n) ***
sonar (adj)
steep (adj) **
symbol (n) **
tadpole (n)
take a risk
temperate (adj)
tropical (adj) **

Unit 12
coal (n) ***
crust (n) *
erupt (vb)
lava (n)
layer (n) ***
melt (vb) **
migrate (vb) *
plate (n) ***
pressure (n) ***
remain (vb) ***
Richter scale (n)
severe (adj) ***
shake (vb) ***
stress (n) ***
tectonic (adj)

Unit 13
cable (n) **
portable (adj) *

Unit 14
conduct (vb) ***
conquer (vb) *
force (vb) ***
javelin (n)
laboratory (n) **
notice (n) ***
obey (vb) **
permit (vb) ***
practical (adj) ***
pretend (vb) **
tough (adj) ***
notice (n) ***
weightless (adj)

Unit 15
authority (n) ***
consider (vb) ***
effort (n) ***
expedition (n) **
hammer (n) *
hobby (n) *
muddle (n)
rate (n) ***
sunspot (n)
surrender (vb) *
unacceptable (adj) **
voluntary (adj) **
wage (n) ***
weight (n) ***

Unit 16
archaeologist (n) *
citizen (n) ***
devote (vb) **
evidence (n) ***
excavate (vb)
excavation (n)
fascinating (adj) **
inaccurate (adj)
jewellery (n) **
publicity (n) **
reject (vb) ***
spectacular (adj) **
thesis (n) **
wealth (n) **

Unit 17
goal (n) ***
motivate (vb) **
photosynthesis (n)

rainbow (n) *

Unit 18
alien (n) **
contract (vb) **
develop (vb) ***
kit (n) **
pole (n) **
regularly (adv) ***
spin (vb) **

Unit 19
algae (n)
battle (n) ***
border (n) ***
civil war (n) *
coast (n) ***
evolve (vb) **
extinct (adj) *
gate (n) ***
kingdom (n) ***
leader (n) ***
march (vb) **
opponent (n) **
powerful (adj) ***
predator (n) **
rightful (n)
sail (vb) **
sloth (n)
twig (n)
upside down (adv) *
voyage (n) *

Unit 20
arena (n) *
assembly (n) ***
coastline (n)
continuous (adj)
counteract (vb)
criticise (vb) **
derelict (adj)
diesel (n) *
dock (n) **
ecotourism (n)
employ (vb) ***
facility (n) ***
float (vb) **
global (adj) ***
habitat (n) *
hectare (n)
IT (n) *
lease (n) **
licence plate (n)
media (n) ***
murderer (n) *
obvious (adj) ***
on board
pack (vb) ***
post (n) ***
prototype (n) *
reality (n) ***
redevelop (vb)
resident (n) ***
retailer (n) *
store (n) ***
unit (n) ***
urban (adj) ***
venue (n) **
wrap (vb) **

Unit 21
alter (vb) **

blemish (n)
central heating (n)
cosmetic (adj)
fit (vb) ***
helmet (n) *
lift (vb) ***
mobile (phone) (n) **
plastic surgery (n)
reshape (n)
scar (n) *
spirits (n) ***
surgeon (n) **
thicken (vb)

Unit 22
calm (adj) **
division (n) ***
economically (adv) **
economy (n) ***
equation (n) **
family planning (n)
llama (n)
measure (n) ***
multiplication (n)
policy (n) ***
rapid (adj) ***
seaweed (n)
step (n) ***
swear (vb) **
victim (n) ***
vital (adj) ***

Unit 23
apprentice (n)
ban (vb) **
coal mine (n)
compete (vb) ***
compound (n) **
employ (vb) ***
employer (n) ***
execute (vb) **
fine (n) ***
freezing (adj) *
iceberg (n)
limit (vb) ***
master (n) ***
pyrites (n)
radioactive (adj) *
rust (vb)
shelter (n) **
tonne (n) **
trade (n) ***
wage (n) ***
wreck (n) *

Unit 24
advance (vb) **
benefits (n) ***
detect (vb) **
frequent (adj) **
growth hormone (n)
immune system (n)
opportunity (n) ***
repair (vb) **
sway (vb) *
tremor (n)
universal indicator (n)
unmanned (adj)

Unit 25
abandon (vb) **
drought (n)

epidemic (n)
goal (n) ***
medieval (adj) **
prosperous (adj)
put forward (phr vb)
ruling (adj) **
support (vb) ***
trace (n) **

Unit 26
enemy (n) ***

Unit 27
absorb (vb) **
coal (n) ***
convection (n)
current (n) *
extract (vb) **
ground (n) ***
liquid (n) **
outdoors (n)
source (n) ***
spread (vb) ***
surrounding (adj) **
upset (adj) **

Unit 28
attract (vb) ***
clerk (n) *
collide (vb) *
crop (n) **
crystal (n)
display (vb) ***
droplet (n)
freezing (n)
generation (n) ***
increase (vb) ***
investment (n) ***
lawyer (n) ***
nurse (n) ***
parliament (n) ***
remarry (vb)
report (n) ***
respect (n) ***
snowflake (n)
stretch (vb) ***
super- (prefix) (cooled)
treat (vb) ***

Unit 29
alpine (adj)
ensure (vb) ***
flow (vb) **
glacier (n)
ice sheet (n)
infrared (adj)
layer (n) ***
mass (n) ***
matter (n) ***
melt (vb) **
microwave (n) *
polar (adj)
seismic (adj)
snowfall (n)
surface (n) ***
transfer (vb) ***
turn (n) ***
typically (adv) **
vibrate (vb)
vibration (n) *

Unit 30
appear (vb) ***
assemble (vb) **
brochure (n) *
depression (n) **
lose (interest in) (vb) ***
meteorology (n)
motivation (n) **
National Curriculum (n)
permanent (adj) ***
psychologist (n) **
push (vb) ***
severe (adj) ***
shiver (n)
spreadsheet (n) *
surface (n) ***
thunderstorm (n)
treatment (n) ***
unrivalled (adj)

Unit 31
ape (n)
beak (n) *
cone (n) *
evaporate (vb)
extinct (adj) *
habitat (n) *
member (n) ***
parachute (n)
preserve (vb) ***
species (n) ***
spread (vb) ***
tide (n) **
webbed (feet) (adj)

Unit 32
assume (vb) ***
bare (adj) **
consist (of) (vb) ***
diet (n) ***
dune (n)
extreme (adj) **
fatty (adj)
fried (adj) **
generate (vb) ***
indication (n) **
lose (weight) (vb) ***
moisture (n)
nutritional (adj)
proof (n) **
reptile (n) *
rocky (adj) *
sandy (adj) *
scorpion (n)
shade (n) **
shortage (n) *
soft drink (n) *
store (vb) ***

Unit 33
action (n) ***
calcium carbonate (n)
cope (vb) ***
defeat (vb) **
discourage (vb) *
episode (n) **
forecast (n) **
individual (adj) ***
narrow (adj) ***
number (of) (n) ***

rewarding (adj)
roughly (adv) **
sign (n) ***
special effect (n)

Unit 34
assume (vb) ***
blind (adj) **
cave (n) **
design (vb) ***
drunk (adj) **
empty (adj) ***
escape (vb) ***
giant (n) **
hide (vb) ***
monument (n) **
orchid (n)
pain (n) ***
roll (vb) ***
tomb (n) *
tuberculosis (n)
wonder (n) ***

Unit 35
admit (vb) ***
according to (prep) ***
amount (n) ***
blame (vb) ***
commercial (adj) ***
fortress (n)
get around (phr vb)
graceful (adj) *
vast (adj) **

Unit 36
album (n) **
appeal (vb) ***
chemical (n) ***
crowded (adj) *
decrease (n) *
diet (n) ***
enthusiasm (n) **
infection (n) **
prevent (vb) ***
sewer (n)
responsible (adj) ***
statistics (n)
suffer (vb) ***
swollen (adj) *
sympathetic (adj) **
track (n) ***
true to life
twist (vb) **
upset (vb) **
victim (n) ***

Unit 37
atmospheric pressure (n)
dense (adj) *
planet (n) **
star (n) ***

Unit 38
considering (prep) **
culture (n) ***
destination (n) **
digest (vb) *
estimate (vb)
freeze (vb) **
gallery (n) **

hum (vb)
palace (n) **
previously (adv) ***
vibrate (vb)

Unit 39
applause (n)
crater (n)
crust (n) *
flagship (n)
float (vb) **
impact (n) ***
lava (n)
mark (n) ***
part (vb) *
pile (n) **
possession (n) **
run aground (adv)
space (n) ***
undisturbed (adj)

Unit 40
astronomical (adj)
comet (n)
crash (n) **
excavation (n)
hibernate (vb)
lens (n) *
optical (adj) *
reference (n) ***
retina (n)
sparse (adj)
sphere (n) **
strike (vb) ***

Unit 41
conducted (vb) ***
decipher (vb)
demotic (adj)
express (vb) ***
hieroglyphics (n)
inscription (n)
originally (adv) ***
patient (n) ***
pitch (n) **
publish (vb) ***
resistance (n) ***
resistant (adj)
treat (vb) ***
self-taught (adj)
(chemical) structure (n) ***

Unit 42
roughly (adv) **
fixed (adj) **
gain (vb) ***
land someone in (phr vb)
yawn (vb) *

Unit 43
elf (n)
forehead (n) **
Once upon a time
wart (n)

Unit 44
attend (vb) ***
boost (vb) **
colleague (n) ***
generation (n) ***

issue (n) ***
photocopier (n)
pitfall (n)
politely (adv) *
previous (adj) ***
resentment (n)
scam (n)
side effect (n) *
stress (n) ***
unresolved (adj)

Unit 45
achieve (vb) ***
barrel (n) **
carnivore (n)
coastline (n)
deadline (n) *
divide (vb) ***
effectively (adv) ***
fattening (adj)
food chain (n)
generate (vb) ***
goal (n) ***
herbivore (n)
honest (adj) **
maintain (vb) ***
oilfield (n)
power station (n)
renewable (adj)
reward (n) **
spoil (vb)
target (n) ***
turbine (n)
unconnected (adj)

Unit 46
DNA (n) *
election (n) ***
genetic (adj) **
membrane (n) *
novel (n) ***
novelist (n) *
protein (n) **
remains (n) **
seal (n) **
serial (n) *
shelter (vb) *
survive (vb) ***
unfeeling (adj)

Unit 47
backward (adj) *
compete (vb) ***
constant (adj) ***
dip (vb) **
erosion (n) **
flourish (vb) *
mysterious (adj) **
originate (vb) **
pollinate (vb)
protest (n) ***
resource (n) ***
state (n) ***

Unit 48
arrow (n) **
convenient (adj) **
grasp (vb) **
shield (n) **
stylus (n)

List of irregular verb forms

Infinitive	Past simple	Past participle
be	was / were	been
beat	beat	beaten
become	became	become
begin	began	begun
bend	bent	bent
bite	bit	bitten
blow	blew	blown
break	broke	broken
bring	brought	brought
build	built	built
burn	burned / burnt	burned / burnt
burst	burst	burst
buy	bought	bought
catch	caught	caught
choose	chose	chosen
come	came	come
cost	cost	cost
cut	cut	cut
deal	dealt	dealt
dig	dug	dug
do	did	done
draw	drew	drawn
drink	drank	drunk
drive	drove	driven
eat	ate	eaten
fall	fell	fallen
feed	fed	fed
feel	felt	felt
fight	fought	fought
find	found	found
fly	flew	flown
forgive	forgave	forgiven
freeze	froze	frozen
get	got	got
give	gave	given
go	went	gone
grow	grew	grown
hang	hung	hung
hear	heard	heard
hide	hid	hidden
hit	hit	hit
hold	held	held
hurt	hurt	hurt
keep	kept	kept

Infinitive	Past simple	Past participle
know	knew	known
lay	laid	laid
lead	led	led
learnt	learnt / learned	learnt / learned
leave	left	left
lend	lent	lent
let	let	let
lose	lost	lost
make	made	made
meet	met	met
pay	paid	paid
put	put	put
read	read	read
ride	rode	ridden
ring	rang	rung
rise	rose	risen
run	ran	run
say	said	said
see	saw	seen
sell	sold	sold
send	sent	sent
shake	shook	shaken
shine	shone	shone
shoot	shot	shot
sing	sang	sung
sink	sank	sunk
sit	sat	sat
sleep	slept	slept
speak	spoke	spoken
spend	spent	spent
stand	stood	stood
steal	stole	stolen
stick	stuck	stuck
swim	swam	swum
take	took	taken
teach	taught	taught
tear	tore	torn
tell	told	told
think	thought	thought
throw	threw	thrown
understand	understood	understood
wake	woke	woken
wear	wore	worn
win	won	won
write	wrote	written

Grammar index

Factual answers

Unit 1

Ex 6

a yes b about 80% c yes, tiny hairs called microvilli d about 2 m²
e yes f about a minute g pull – they can't push h vitamin A
i about 25,000.

Unit 3

Ex 2

All true except: d the army went as far as India;
f Caligula meant 'Little Boot'; h girls married at 14.

Ex 3

True: b and h.

Unit 5

Ex 6

a no b 438 days continuously in 1995 c no d no, only in films e
Yes, the first heart transplant took place in 1967 f No – they can't
even agree about where it was g No – though some have taught
animals to communicate using signs etc.

Unit 12

Ex 4

a B b A c A d B e C f C g C h A i B j B

Ex 5

LLANFAIRPWLLGWYNGYLLGOGERYCHWYRNDR
OBWLLLLANTYSILIOGOGOGOH is according to one source the
longest place name in the world, with 58 letters. It is a town in
North Wales meaning 'St Mary's Church in the hollow of the white
hazel near to the rapid whirlpool of Llantysilio of the red cave'
or 'St Mary's (Church) by the white aspen over the whirlpool,
and St Tysilio's (Church) by the red cave' in Welsh. Local people
apparently invented the name for the railway station in order to
encourage tourism.
TAUMATAWHAKATANGIHANGAKOAUAUOTAMAT
EATURIPUKAKAPIKIMAUNGAHORONUKUPOKAI
WHENUAKITANATAHU is the name of a hill in Southern Hawke's Bay
in New Zealand. Taumata was a Maori chief, and the word apparently
means 'The summit of the hill, where Taumata, who is known as the
land eater, slid down, climbed up and swallowed mountains, and
played on his nose flute to his loved one.'

Unit 18

Ex 3

Probable answers: a B b C c A d C e A f B

Unit 22

Ex 5

Things you should do: a, b, c, d, f. You shouldn't do e or g – they
are dangerous. You shouldn't do h – they might need medical
treatment.

Unit 31

Ex 1

a very little b no! c yes, the duck-billed platypus d yes, although
the atmosphere may not be the same as that on Earth e yes, the
walking catfish, though it really wriggles its way on land f about
40 species, penguins for example g no h no, though some apes
can be taught to communicate using sign language i no – this
would mean that there had once been sea-creatures living in
oceans, and forests j this wouldn't be impossible, but they haven't
yet been found.

Ex 2

a False – there are cars that use various kinds of gas, or alcohol
– but not water. b False – a group of animals in the Pacific region

called Monotremata lay eggs, and feed their young like mammals.
They are the duck-billed platypus and the echidna. c True – they
only live in the Arctic. d Nobody really knows, but they haven't
got in touch with us yet. e No active ones, but plenty of extinct
ones. f False – it rains occasionally.

Unit 32

Ex 1

a about 1,500 b nearly 21% of the air is made up of oxygen c over
15,000 species, and rising d over 500 million cubic kilometres, by
some estimates e ten main types, and up to 25 or more in all
f normally 32 g approximately 6,000,000,000,000,000,000,000,000
kg h about 80 million barrels by some estimates.

Unit 33

Ex 1

a All birds have feathers. b Most animals eat plants. c No
mammals have green or blue hair. d All reptiles are cold-blooded.
e Most mammals give birth to live young. f No mammals can
really fly, except for bats. g Most animals are colour-blind. h All
birds lay eggs. i There are no reptiles in the Arctic or Antarctic.
j Most birds are able to fly.

Ex 5

a Alexander conquered most of the Middle East and parts of Asia,
Napoleon conquered most of western and central Europe.
b Alexander died in Babylon, Napoleon on the island of St Helena.
c Alexander's generals took over his empire, Napoleon lost power
completely, and the French monarchy returned. d Alexander
couldn't conquer all of India, and Napoleon was forced to leave
Russia. e Alexander in 331 BC, Napoleon in 1798. f Alexander is
supposed to have won all his battles, Napoleon lost the Battle of
Waterloo. g Alexander to India, Napoleon to Russia. h Alexander
three or more times, Napoleon twice, each had several children.
i Alexander died aged about 33, Napoleon about 52. j Alexander
by his generals, Napoleon by the British, but both are doubtful.
Alexander probably died from malaria or an infected wound, and
Napoleon from stomach cancer.

Unit 38

Ex 4

a more easily b more quickly c more quietly d faster
e more carefully f more loudly g more heavily h more clearly
i earlier j more slowly
False: c, e and i. The others, believe it or not, are all true.

Unit 40

Ex 1

a French, British and German forces and their allies signed an
agreement to stop fighting. b Nazi planes bombed the Spanish
town of Guernica in the first terror air raid against civilians. Over
1,600 were killed, and the event inspired Picasso's painting. c The
execution by guillotine of the French king Louis XVI. d President
Lincoln of the USA was shot at Ford's Theatre. He died the next
day. e Mickey Mouse appeared in his first cartoon, *Steamboat
Willie*. f Neil Armstrong became the first human being to step
onto the Moon. g Orville Wright flew a powered aeroplane for
12 seconds – usually recognized as the first flight. h The first
atomic bomb was exploded in New Mexico, USA. i The Beatles
recorded *Please Please Me*, their first Number One hit single. j The
earthquake that caused the Asian tsunami took place in the Indian
Ocean. About 300,000 people would die as a result.

Answer key

Unit 1

Ex 1

a drive, cycles b rises, sets c travels d costs
e meets f reads g understand h starts i give j like

Ex 2

a don't do b doesn't play, doesn't like c don't think
d don't work e doesn't agree f don't want
g doesn't drive h aren't i don't stay j doesn't sing

Ex 3

a leaves, isn't b loves, don't interest c don't study, is
d don't dance, look e doesn't go, goes f does, doesn't
crash g doesn't have, has h needs, doesn't burn
i doesn't own, are j live, don't eat

Ex 4

a live b provides c dive d hold e stand f keeps
g breeds h lays i return j stands k keep l sleeps
m eats n hatches o comes p finds q feed
r spends s returns t look after

Ex 5

a don't get on b doesn't love c doesn't know
d doesn't allow e doesn't agree f doesn't forgive
g don't understand h doesn't care i doesn't see
j don't realize

Ex 6

a Do, stop b does, contain c Do, have
d does, cover e Does, grow f does, take
g Do, pull h does, produce i do, breathe

Ex 7

a does, do b prevents c doesn't allow d catch
e push f destroy g Do, help h use i don't work
j don't give k does, work l starts m doesn't get
n come o destroy

Unit 2

Ex 1

a are leaving b is rising, are using c is studying, is
studying d are standing e are staying f am going
g is chasing h is becoming i are training
j is listening

Ex 2

a do not understand b is it getting c don't agree
d reaches e lasts f are still searching g Are they
looking h doesn't seem i consists j has

Ex 3

a am speaking b is visiting c am standing
d looking e are climbing f are wearing g is standing
by h is rising i are setting j are trying k is going on
l is happening m is shaking n are climbing
o are shouting

Ex 4

a isn't going b isn't heading for c isn't sending
d isn't working e aren't receiving f aren't pointing
g aren't producing h isn't responding i aren't having
j aren't giving up

Ex 5

a Is the weather in your country changing? b Is it
growing warmer or colder? c Are storms happening
more often? d Is less snow falling in winter?
e Is summer getting hotter? f Are the changes
becoming a problem? g Are people worrying about
this? h Are they doing anything to help?

Ex 6

a means b doesn't stay c is growing d believe
e is falling f is happening g is rising h have
i die j look after

Ex 7

a knows, are disappearing b cover, contain c remove,
produce d are they vanishing e agree f is changing
g are cutting down, causing h is happening i are
burning, using j understand, are beginning

Unit 3

Ex 1

a developed b left c believed, wanted d arrived
e built f planted, worked, improved g arrived,
thought h saw, decided i killed, defeated, destroyed

Ex 2

a wore b took c drank d went e made f meant
g had h got i paid j knew

Ex 3

a Alexander the Great didn't marry Cleopatra.
b Nelson Mandela didn't become President of South
Africa in 1994. c Leonardo da Vinci didn't invent the
Internet. d Confucius the Chinese philosopher didn't
die in 1900. e Marco Polo didn't stay in China for five
years. f The ancient Romans didn't use steam engines
in their battles. g Genghis Khan didn't invade Italy
and capture Rome. h Christopher Columbus didn't

reach America by accident.   i William Shakespeare didn't write *Don Quixote*.

Ex 4

a When did the Industrial Revolution happen in Britain?   b How did work change?   c What did the first factories produce?   d What did new technology encourage?   e What power did factories use? f What did these factories require?   g Where did manufacturers construct their factories?   h Why did they decide to do this?   i What did factories also need?   j Where did industry in the UK develop?

Ex 5

a Did he come from a rich family?   b Did he grow up in London?   c Did he go to school?   d Did he know Latin?   e Did he get married?   f Did they have children?   g Did he begin writing plays in Stratford?   h Did he write 37 plays all by himself? i Did he make up all the characters and plots of his plays?   j Did he become rich and famous?

Ex 6

a studied   b became   c received   d owned e made   f had   g did the alcohol turn to acid h happened   i couldn't   j threw   k asked l didn't know   m examined   n found   o believed p caused   q Did milk, wine and vinegar behave in the same way   r disagreed   s made   t continued u invented   v proved   w worked   x developed

Unit 4

Ex 1

a was taking, discovered   b was working, dropped, invented   c arrived, was trying   d discovered, was looking   e was climbing, discovered   f was sitting, fell, understood   g was trying, made, stuck   h was observing, realized

Ex 2A

a Where was Edouard Benedictus working when he invented safety glass?   b Where was Columbus trying to go when he reached America?   c Where was Isaac Newton sitting according to the story about gravity?   d What was Dr Harry Coover hoping to invent?   e What was Galileo looking at through his telescope?

Ex 2B

f wasn't trying   g wasn't hoping   h wasn't looking for   i wasn't sitting   j wasn't conducting

Ex 3

a was growing up, became   b was attending, murdered   c was fighting, started, destroyed d led, was staying, undid   e was marching, defeated f founded, was visiting   g was travelling, gave h killed, were having   i was attacking, received, j was attending, fell, died

Ex 4

a used to write   b used to act   c used to do, used to set   d used to help   e used to teach, used to tell f used to work   g used to hold   h used to spend

Ex 5

a used to be   b used to form   c didn't use to be d used to exist   e used to be   f didn't use to live g did they use to eat, used to eat   h didn't use to stay, used to travel

Ex 6

a were looking for   b reached   c were living d tried   e fought   f drove   g gave up   h were working   i discovered   j proved   k sailed   l were arguing   m wanted   n took   o found   p were looking for   q was travelling   r learned   s arrived t received

Unit 5
Ex 1

a have sent   b have put up   c have collected d have planted   e have replaced   f have recycled g have shown   h have painted   i have installed j have organized

Ex 2

a has always come   b has fallen   c have caused d have not / haven't done   e have grown   f have not / haven't reproduced   g has reached   h have reduced   i have lost   j has become, have stopped

Ex 3

a Have you ever seen a humming bird?   b Have you ever read *War and Peace*?   c Have you ever visited San Marino?   d Have you ever swum in the Pacific Ocean?   e Have you ever taken a trip to the Sahara Desert?

Ex 4

a yet b since c yet d already e for, yet f since
g already h yet i already, yet

Ex 5

a have gone b have gone c have been d have gone
e have not been f have been g has gone h has not
been i have been j has gone

Ex 6

a Have scientists discovered a cure for the common
cold? b Have people lived for long periods in space
(yet)? c Have human beings landed on Mars (yet)?
d Have scientists invented time travel (yet)? e Have
doctors managed to transplant human hearts (yet)?
f Have archaeologists found the lost city of Atlantis
(yet)? g Have scientists ever taught an animal to talk?

Ex 7

a B b B c A d A e A f B g A h B i B j B
k B l B m A n A o A p B

Unit 6

Ex 1

a haven't been waiting b have been looking for
c have been studying d has been going e has been
having f have you been doing g have been working
h have been painting

Ex 2

a have recently identified b have been searching
c have found d has been exploring e have found
f have been looking g spotted h has been working
i has produced j have discovered k have managed

Ex 3

a How long have astronomers been looking for Pluto's
moons? b How long have archaeologists been hoping
to find Atlantis? c How long have scientists been using
satellites to discover new reefs? d How long have
physicists been investigating the origin of the universe?
e How long have scientists been observing Vesuvius?
f How long have biologists been trying to find new
species of mammal? g How long have archaeologists
been excavating the palace in Guatemala? h How long
have doctors been searching for a cure for HIV?

Unit 7
Ex 1

a finally reached b had actually arrived c found
d had got e had used f restored

Ex 2

a tried, had run b turned, had not saved c had not
paid, stopped d received, had sent e checked, had
done f had received, ran g downloaded, had made
h had gone, looked i had pressed, happened
j went, had happened

Ex 3

a came b died, served c returned, had won
d became e had risen, had formed f fought g had
died h ordered, had become i defeated j murdered,
had been

Ex 4

a C b C c A d C e C f C g A h A i B j A
k B l B m B n A o A p A q A r A s A t A

Ex 5

a wanted b gave c produced d had not used
e mixed f had done g asked h knew
i was thinking j was climbing k noticed l had
spilled m realized n had solved o had spilled
p jumped q ran r admitted s had cheated
t had discovered

Ex 6

a had been climbing b had been snowing, had hurt
c had been looking d had already phoned e had
also left f had prepared g had been heading h had
brought

Unit 8
Ex 1

a stopped, had robbed b turned on, was climbing
c arrived, had missed d tried, died e had made, had
gone f had just finished, hadn't had g didn't answer,
was painting h wasn't working, was i woke up, had
been snowing j landed, had been waiting

Ex 2

a left b completed c hasn't arrived d haven't played
e liked f did you go g hasn't taken h Have you seen
i did you realise j 've had

Ex 3

a gave up b had learned c were travelling d had
composed e was visiting f listened g had kept
h had published i managed j had listened k had
become l had m wrote n was working o fell

Ex 4

a A b B c C d A e D f B g A h A i D j B

Ex 5

a are you getting on b I haven't written
c I've been training d played e came f enjoyed
g I haven't done h arrived i went j was raining
k arrived l was crossing m splashed n changed
o is expecting p told q hasn't arrived r has
discovered s died t bought u was working
v recognized w painted x paid y say

Unit 9

Ex 1

a will be, will continue, will claim b will cause, will
probably destroy c will never want, will reach
d will crash, will cause e will come, will have to

Ex 2

a will hold b will take place c will provide
d will carry e will sell f will cost g will use

Ex 3

a 6 b 8 c 9 d 10 e 2 f 7 g 1 h 4 i 5 j 3

Ex 4

Suggested answers: a I'm not going to waste paper.
b I'm going to recycle paper and cardboard as much
as I can. c I'm going to recycle bottles, cans and
organic waste. d I'm not going to take plastic bags
from the supermarket. e I'm not going to make
unnecessary car journeys. f I'm going to walk or
use a bike. g I'm going to buy local produce. h
I'm going to take a shower not a bath. i I'm going
to change to low-energy light bulbs. j I'm going to
turn off unnecessary lights.

Ex 5

a The volcano is going to erupt. b The water is
going to disappear. c The river is going to flood
the houses. d The ship is going to hit the iceberg.
e It's going to snow (again). f The trees are going
to blow down. / The wind is going to blow down the
trees.

Ex 6

Suggested answers: a I'm going to do biology.
b I'll be back at two o'clock. c It isn't going to
work. d Shall I turn the lights on? e I'll sit with
Helen. f I'm going to study engineering.

Unit 10

Ex 1

a retires 7 b takes off 3 c continues 8 d starts 9
e takes place 4 f rises 10 g expires 6 h closes 2
i leaves 5 j open 1

Ex 2

a are holding b is coming c is giving d is
showing e are serving f is arriving g Is, meeting
h are picking, up, taking i is leaving

Ex 3

a will break b is going to come out c is going to
start d I won't drop it. e We're playing f I'll take
g I'm going to study h I'll see you

Ex 4

a I'll be lying b I'll be waiting c I'll be working
d I'll be starting e I'll be going f I'll be watching
g I'll be living h I'll be catching

Ex 5

a will have started b will / won't have invented
c will / won't have found d will / won't have
discovered e will / won't have moved f will /
won't have used g will / won't have become
h will / won't have made

Ex 6

a will continue b enters c will grow d finishes
e occurs f will become g collide h will form
i begins j will produce k will grow l increases
m will be n stops o expands p will absorb
q uses r will become s won't make t will be

Ex 7

a A b C c C d B e C f C g B h C i B j C

Unit 11

Ex 1

a There b there c There d there e There
f They g there h there i They j They k there
l There m They n This o There

Ex 2

a is a match on Tuesday. b are three ways you can
do this. c was a lot of snow yesterday. d isn't any
milk. e seems to be a strange man outside. f were
a lot of people at the rock concert. g were crowds
of people on the train. h is an interesting television
programme on at 8.00.

Ex 3

a their b They're c There d There e Their
f They're g Their h They're i They're j their

Ex 4

a It's b it's c its d its e It's f it's g its h It's

Ex 5

a There b there c It d It e There f It g It
h there i It j There

Ex 6

a it b There c It d there e There f There g it
h There i There j It k there l It m there n There
o it p it q there r There s it t there

Ex 7

a C b A c C d B e B f C g A h B i A j C
k B l A m C n A o C

Unit 12

Ex 1

a Is the Nile the longest river? b Have earthquakes
occurred in this country? c Had the volcano erupted
before? d Was there only one continent 200 million
years ago? e Were people expecting a tsunami in 2004?
f Will our climate be different in 50 years' time? g Has
the capital city continued to grow? h Are the Arabian
Desert and the Gobi Desert similar in size? i Has the
ice at the Poles started to melt? j Were many people
injured in the earthquake?

Ex 2

a they don't b it is c it can't d it does e they have
f they don't g we are h it is i they can j they
didn't

Ex 3

a 5 b 8 c 2 d 10 e 4 f 6 g 1 h 9 i 3 j 7
a Where does the name volcano come from? b How
many volcanoes are there on Earth? c Where does the
hot lava come from? d Why does the lava come out
of the volcano? e What does *dormant* mean? f How
long do most volcanoes remain active? g How do
scientists predict that a volcano will erupt? h What do
they measure the movements with? i What is a sign
that volcanoes are going to erupt? j What did people
once think caused volcanic eruptions?

Ex 4

a Do you know what the capital of Argentina is? b
Do you know how long the River Nile is? c Do you
know where Lake Titicaca is? d Do you know what
colour the flag of Mali is? e Do you know how many
states there are in Australia? f Do you know how high
Mount Everest is? g Do you know what the capital of
the Republic of Gambia is? h Do you know how many
official languages Switzerland has got? i Do you know
what the Finnish name for Finland is? j Do you know
what the population of the Republic of San Marino is?

Ex 5

a Do you know where Llanfairpwllgwyng..... is?
b Do you have any idea if / whether it is the name of
a real place? c Can you tell me if / whether it was
an invented name? d I wonder why they decided to
make up a name. e Could you tell me what the local
people say? f Do you have any idea where the name
Taumata..... comes from? g Do you know how you
pronounce it? h Do you understand what it means?
i Can you tell me which language this word is from? j
Could you tell me what the longest place name in your
country is?

Ex 6

a What moves when an earthquake occurs? b What
creates this stress? c How many earthquakes happen
every day? d What does a large earthquake do?
e When did a powerful earthquake hit the city of
Lisbon? f How many people died? g In which distant
country was the shock felt? h What do geologists now
believe?

Unit 13

Ex 1

a is it? b have they? c will it? d did they?
e can they? f is it?

Ex 2

a weren't you? b isn't it? c haven't you? d don't
they? e isn't she? f didn't it?

Ex 3

a A b B c A d B e B f A g A h B

Ex 4

a Most portable radios need batteries for power. So do
most CD players. b Airships don't need a runway to
land. Neither do helicopters. c Diesel engines produce
exhaust fumes. So do petrol engines. d Wind power
doesn't cause air pollution. Neither does wave power.
e Computers use electronic microchips. So do
calculators. f A wireless keyboard doesn't require a
connecting cable. Neither does a wireless mouse.
g Some cookers can use solar power. So can some
lighting systems.

Unit 14

Ex 1

In India all children <u>are supposed to go</u> to school between the ages of six and 14. In fact in the countryside it is very <u>difficult</u> for young children <u>to get</u> an education because the government has <u>failed to build</u> enough schools, and also because transport is difficult, and children <u>need to take</u> the bus to get to school. There are few buses so most children go on foot. On top of all these problems, many parents never went to school themselves, so they don't <u>expect</u> their children <u>to go</u>. Many parents are also so poor that they don't <u>let</u> their children <u>go</u> to school, but <u>prefer to send</u> them to work instead, because they need the money. Children from richer families, on the other hand, often live near good schools, and their parents <u>encourage</u> them <u>to pass</u> their exams so that they can get good jobs.

Ex 2

Suggested answers: a hope to   b manage to   c decide to   d learn how to   e prefer to   f long to   g need to   h aim to   i fail to   j try to

Ex 3

a The ancient Spartans made girls practise running, wrestling and throwing javelins.   b The ancient Spartans did not let a baby live if it was not fit and strong.   c The ancient Spartans made young children fight each other to make them tough.   d The ancient Spartans didn't let people take a lot of baths.   e The ancient Spartans made the children sleep on rushes, a kind of grass.   f The ancient Spartans didn't let people eat a lot of food.   g The ancient Spartans made all the boys join the army.   h The ancient Spartans didn't let boys cry when they fought.

Ex 4

a Francisco Pizarro decided to return to South America in 1532.   b He hoped to conquer the Incas.   c He also expected to become rich.   d When he reached the Inca city of Cajamarca, he pretended to be a friend.   e He threatened to kill his prisoner, the Emperor Atahualpa, unless the people brought him their gold and silver.   f But he did not intend to let the Emperor go free.   g He aimed to make sure that the Incas had no leader.   h He promised to set the Emperor free, but killed him.   i Pizarro also killed his friend Almagro, who refused to obey his orders.   j Almagro's friends managed to kill Pizarro three years later.

Ex 5

a It's difficult to learn how to live in space.   b It isn't easy to eat in weightless conditions.   c It's difficult to take enough exercise.   d It's very important for astronauts to be in good health.   e It's difficult to imagine what astronauts have to do.   f It's impossible to live a completely normal life in space.   g It's never boring going into space.   h Most astronauts feel happy to return to Earth.

Ex 6

Suggested answers: a sorry   b decided   c encouraged   d let   e allow   f managed   g supposed   h careful   i failed   j learned   k trying   l refused   m prepared   n threatened   o forced

Unit 15

Ex 1

a can't help   b avoid   c enjoy   d involves   e keep   f suggest   g means   h feel like   i go   j consider

Ex 2

a 6   b 2   c 8   d 4   e 3   f 1   g 5   h 7

Ex 3

a to do   b getting   c to take   d shopping   e to think   f to remember   g writing   h paying

Ex 4

a in   b by   c on   d of   e for   f at   g of   h in   i of   j between

Ex 5

a Are you interested in fossil-collecting?   b Does it involve walking long distances?   c I keep finding rocks that aren't really fossils.   d When you look for fossils on a cliff, you risk falling.   e I can't help thinking this is the wrong place to look for fossils.   f Going on the club trip means getting up early.   g I didn't remember to bring my hammer.   h I feel like sitting down and having a rest!   i I am good at finding fossils.   j It's not worth taking up a hobby unless you're serious about it.

Ex 6

a Collecting fossils can be very relaxing.   b Giving up smoking can be very difficult.   c Doing an exam without revising isn't a good idea.   d Learning a new sport is fun.   e Learning a foreign language takes lots of hard work.   f Seeing my favourite band play live was very exciting.   g Living on Mars will never be possible.   h Writing the report took a long time.   i Walking up this mountain is so tiring!   j Driving without a licence is illegal.

Ex 7

a to cross b to win c travelling d riding
e to find f discovering g to reach h to complete
i to arrive j crossing

Unit 16
Ex 1

a She said (that) she got up every day at 6.30. b He said (that) he had forgotten to phone the doctor.
c He said (that) everybody liked comedy films.
d He said (that) he was thinking about it. e She said (that) she had been reading the paper. f She said (that) scientists didn't understand everything.
g He said (that) he had decided to look for a new job.
h He said (that) he could swim 5,000 metres. i She said (that) she was going to have a baby. j He said (that) he would phone on Friday.

Ex 2

a her b her c him d his e she f him g they
h him i his j there k their l him m the
n his o theirs

Ex 3

a said b told c said d said e told f told g told
h said i told

Ex 4

a He told journalists (that) he had always been interested in the story of Troy. b He said (that) his father had read the stories to him when he was a child.
c He said (that) he had always believed that Troy was a real place. d He said (that) at an early age he had decided to discover the site of the city. e He said (that) for many years he had worked as a merchant in the USA and Russia. f He said (that) he was a wealthy man and he had retired from business. g He said (that) he had first been / gone to the site at Hissarlik in 1868.
h He said (that) since then he had spent a lot of his own money on the excavation. i He said (that) he was working with a British archaeologist. j He said (that) they were hoping to prove that Hissarlik was the site of ancient Troy.

Ex 5

a She told the journalists (that) she was the director of the dig. b She said (that) she wanted to explain how they had found the site, and what they had been doing there. c She told them (that) she was sure (that) they had read the publicity handout, and (that) they knew something about it. d She said (that) it was important to give them the latest information. e She told them (that) she was going to give a description of some of the interesting discoveries they had made there. f She said (that) she would give them a general account of

the project. g She told them (that) she would show some slides of the site. h She said (that) there would be a chance for all of them to look at some fascinating objects. i She told them (that) they had brought some of the more spectacular finds. j She said (that) they were waiting for them in the room next door. k She told them (that) they would be able to take photographs.
l She said (that) they had been very patient.

Unit 17
Ex 1A

a The teacher asked me if / whether I had done my homework. b I asked the teacher if / whether we were starting a new lesson. c The teacher asked me if / whether I was paying attention. d I asked the teacher if / whether I had to write it down. e The teacher asked me if / whether I was feeling all right.

Ex 1B

f 'Do you have / Have you got a spare pen?' g 'Are you going to start?' h 'Is it all right to use a pencil?' i 'Do you know the answer?' j 'Is it the end of the lesson?'

Ex 2A

a The teacher asked us how many colours there are in a rainbow. b The teacher asked us what a tadpole turns into. c The teacher asked us how fish take oxygen from the water. d The teacher asked us how many stomachs a cow has. e The teacher asked us what scientists mean by gravity.

Ex 2B

f The teacher asked us when the Second World War had begun. g The teacher asked us why Romeo had drunk the poison. h The teacher asked us what Edison had done in 1877. i The teacher asked us what Gregor Mendel had been famous for. j The teacher asked us what Marie Curie had discovered.

Ex 3A

a I asked him if / whether he lived there. b He asked me what my name was. c I asked her what time it was. / what the time was. d She asked me if / whether I was sitting there. e I asked her if / whether she wanted some coffee.

Ex 3B

f 'When does the next train leave?' g 'Where is the bus station?' h 'Do you have / Have you got any change?'
i 'What are you staring at?' j 'Are you waiting for us?'

Ex 4

a The teacher told John to the fill the jar with water. b The teacher asked Angela to help him. c The teacher told Michael not to spill the water. d The teacher asked Alison if she would pour / to pour a little water into the test tube. e The teacher told Steve to light the gas. f The teacher told Alan not to touch it with his finger. g The teacher told Sarah to heat the water gently until it boiled. h The teacher asked all of them to watch the water carefully.

Ex 5

a 1 b 8 c 7 d 6 e 2 f 4 g 3 h 5

Ex 6

Suggested answers: a said his advice was b told, to choose a workout c told /advised them / the audience to avoid activities that were d suggested doing it a bit differently each time e explained that making sure you have f warned that overtraining can g reminded them / the audience to eat h said they / the audience shouldn't use

Unit 18

Ex 1

a If you heat water to 100°C, it boils. b If you boil water, it turns into steam. c If you cool the steam, it turns back into water d If you heat a piece of metal, it expands. e If you freeze a piece of metal, it contracts. f If you freeze water, it expands.

Ex 2

a If everyone recycles paper, companies won't cut down so many trees. b If everyone recycles metal and glass, we won't waste valuable resources. c If everyone recycles paper, metal and glass, we won't produce so much rubbish. d If everyone turns off unwanted lights, we will save a lot of electricity. e If everyone walks or cycles, we won't waste so much oil and petrol. f If everyone insulates their houses, we won't waste so much energy for heating. g If countries use more wind and water power, they won't depend so much on power stations. h If countries use power stations less, they will cause less air pollution.

Ex 3

a What would happen if you travelled through the Earth to the other side? b What would happen if the Earth suddenly stopped going round? c What would happen if we didn't have a Moon? d What would happen if all the ice at the poles melted? e What would happen if there was no more electricity? f What would happen if aliens received messages from the Earth and decided to visit us?

Ex 4A

a You won't succeed in sport unless you train hard. b You can improve your performance as long as you train regularly. c It doesn't really matter whether you succeed or not, as long as you enjoy your sport. d You won't develop as an athlete unless you eat and sleep properly.

Ex 4B

e Take a spare pair of running shoes in case you need them. f Take a waterproof coat with you in case it rains. g Take a warm jumper in case you get cold when you stop. h Take a first-aid kit in case someone gets injured.

Ex 5

a used, would be able b were, would see c turn off, won't be able d didn't, would weigh e don't have, will let f looked, would be, would be g smoke, take place h removed, would be able

Unit 19

Ex 1

a had marched, would have conquered b had gone, would have succeeded c had built, would have crossed, (would have) landed d had not hit, would not have arrived e had continued, would have sailed f had not read, would not have tried g had sailed, would have reached h had not thought, would not have conquered i had not found, would not have made j had not taken, would not have written

Ex 2

Suggested answers: a If I hadn't brought a map with me, we would be lost. b If I hadn't explained my new ideas to the Church, I wouldn't be in trouble. c If I hadn't exaggerated some of the descriptions in my book, perhaps more people would believe me. d If we hadn't gone to the theatre last night, he would be alive today. e If I had spent more time on my paintings, more of them would be finished. f If I hadn't invaded Russia, perhaps I would still be Emperor of France.

Ex 3

Suggested answers: a If the Trojans hadn't taken the wooden horse into Troy, the Greeks would not have captured the city.   **b** If the Greeks hadn't won the battle of Marathon, Darius and his army wouldn't have gone home.   **c** If Julius Caesar hadn't made the decision to cross the River Rubicon, he wouldn't have become leader of the Roman state.   **d** If Isabella hadn't married Ferdinand, Spain wouldn't have become one of the most powerful countries in Europe.   **e** If Harold's army hadn't been tired, William wouldn't have become king of England.

Ex 4

a I wish I knew the answer to this problem.   **b** I wish I had a calculator.   **c** I wish I understood the problem.   **d** I wish my teacher explained things to me.   **e** I wish I was / were in a different class.   **f** I wish I did French instead.   **g** I wish I lived in France.   **h** I wish I didn't have to do my homework.

Ex 5

a I wish I hadn't met him.   **b** I wish I'd stayed at home.   **c** I wish I hadn't decided to go to a wizard school.   **d** I wish I had stayed in China.   **e** I wish I hadn't sat under an apple tree.   **f** I wish I hadn't run away with him.   **g** I wish I hadn't made him.   **h** I wish I had put some clothes on.

Ex 6

a I wish you'd hand your work in on time!   **b** I wish you wouldn't make so many mistakes!   **c** I wish you wouldn't drop litter on the floor!   **d** I wish you would pay attention!   **e** I wish you wouldn't talk during the test!   **f** I wish you would listen to what I'm saying!   **g** I wish you wouldn't interrupt people!   **h** I wish you wouldn't throw things across the room!   **i** I wish you would behave!   **j** I wish you would make less noise / wouldn't make so much noise!

Ex 7

a were   **b** would spend   **c** stays   **d** do not realize   **e** go   **f** swim   **g** remained   **h** would die   **i** had been   **j** would have seen   **k** continue   **l** will become

Unit 20

Ex 1

a were lit   **b** was invented   **c** were shown   **d** were used   **e** was designed   **f** was made   **g** were sold   **h** were replaced   **i** was written   **j** were introduced

Ex 2

a As a first step, a computer is used to plan the exact shape of the car.   **b** Then this computer programme is fed into a machine and a plastic prototype is produced.   **c** The actual toy cars are produced in a factory abroad.   **d** The bodies are made from plastic.   **e** Small electric motors are added to the cars, and they are painted. Licence plates are also attached.   **f** At the next stage, the cars are inspected, then they are wrapped and packed into cardboard boxes.   **g** Finally, the cars are shipped to Britain.

Ex 3

a have been made   **b** has been advertised   **c** will be constructed   **d** will be taken   **e** will be powered   **f** will be carried   **g** will be provided   **h** will be used   **i** has not been built   **j** has been criticized

Ex 4

a The global expansion in tourism has been made possible by cheaper air travel.   **b** A growth in tourism has been experienced by countries all over the world.   **c** The popular Mediterranean resorts have been visited by millions of tourists since the 1970s.   **d** Recently more distant locations in Africa, Asia and South America have been chosen by tourists.   **e** Some countries have been badly affected by mass tourism.   **f** Large hotels have been built on unspoilt coastline by international companies.   **g** Local wildlife has been disturbed by these developments.   **h** Coral reefs and other habitats have been damaged by tourists.   **i** Local people have also been displaced by such developments.   **j** The idea of ecotourism has been developed by some governments to counteract some of these problems.

Ex 5

a have been redeveloped   **b** has / have been transformed   **c** had been built   **d** had been lost   **e** had been closed   **f** has been spent   **g** have been improved   **h** have been built   **i** have been created   **j** have been constructed   **k** have been planted   **l** have been created   **m** have been opened   **n** have been done   **o** has been given

Ex 6A

a Ships with sails were built more than 5,000 years ago.   **b** A hot-air balloon was constructed in 1783.   **c** The steam ship was developed in the 19th century.   **d** The first successful passenger railway was opened in 1830.   **e** The first passenger airlines were started after the First World War.

Ex 6B

f The first books were probably printed by the Chinese more than a thousand years ago.   g The first modern typewriters were sold by the Remington company in the 1870s.   h The first words were recorded on a gramophone record by Edison in 1877.   i The first modern cinema was created by the Lumière brothers in France in 1895.   j The tape recorder was invented by Valdemar Poulsen in 1899.

Unit 21

Ex 1

a I am having my photograph taken.   b is having her hair cut.   c is having a tooth taken out. d are having our kitchen painted.   e am having it (my car) serviced.   f are having their new central heating fitted.

Ex 2

a Tim had his nose broken while he was playing football.   b Maria had her bike stolen last week. c Mr Grover had his car damaged last week. d Anna had her mobile taken.   e Our garden wall had paint sprayed on it.   f We had our house broken into.   g One policeman had his helmet knocked off.   h We had our windows smashed with a brick.

Ex 3

a People have scars and blemishes removed.   b People also have their faces lifted in order to look younger.   c In a recent poll, many people admitted that they had had / admitted having their noses altered.   d Several people had also had their eyes reshaped.   e One woman had also had her lips thickened.   f Psychologists are worried that so many young people want to have their appearance changed.   g So if you're thinking of having an operation performed, think again.   h People can also have their lives ruined by plastic surgery.

Ex 4

a Did you get your project finished in the end? b Did David get sent to the head teacher's office? c Did you get all your homework done?   d Did Susan get chosen as class representative?   e When are you getting the school sports programme sorted out?   f Did you get your revision organized? / Have you got your revision organized?   g Did Tony get injured playing basketball?   h Did you get invited to Maria's party?

Ex 5

a was offered a job in Dubai   b was promised a good position   c was sent a letter explaining all   d would be given   e was lent some money   f was given some CDs

Ex 6

a is believed to be seriously ill.   b is thought to be in hospital.   c is supposed to be flying to Washington tomorrow.   d is understood to be remaining in London.   e is not said to be dangerously ill.   f is expected to leave hospital in a few days.   g are believed to be at her bedside day and night.   h is known to be a kind of flu. i is understood to be taking antibiotics.   j is reported to be in good spirits.

Unit 22

Ex 1

a can't reach   b can hear   c can't open   d haven't been able to take   e can't come   f to be able to use g can't swim   h haven't been able to sleep

Ex 2

a mustn't   b must   c mustn't   d mustn't   e must f mustn't   g mustn't   h must

Ex 3

a mustn't   b don't have to   c don't have to d mustn't   e don't have to   f mustn't

Ex 4

a can cause   b has to provide   c have to produce d have to have   e can't grow   f have to control g have to take   h have to ask   i have to be j have to ask

Ex 5

a should   b should   c should   d should e shouldn't   f should   g shouldn't   h shouldn't

Ex 6

a We'd better take an umbrella.   b You'd better call a taxi.   c You'd better not play in the match. d We'd better take some sandwiches.   e You'd better wear a hat.   f We'd better leave now.   g We'd better not wake him up.   h You'd better check it in the dictionary.

Ex 7

a You need to think about all the information given.
b You needn't worry about spelling, but you should try to be as accurate as you can.   c You need to identify all the necessary steps to solve a problem.   d You need to understand technical words eg equation.   e You need to be able to use methods of multiplication and division.
f You need to know when to use an example.

Ex 8

a D   b D   c B   d B   e D   f C   g A   h C

Unit 23

Ex 1

a couldn't   b could   c couldn't   d could   e could, couldn't   f couldn't   g could   h couldn't   i could
j could

Ex 2

a I needn't have worked so hard!   b I didn't need to work at the weekend.   c I didn't need to borrow any books.   d But I needn't have given up so much of my spare time.   e I needn't have spent a lot of time reading and writing every evening.   f But I managed to do it on my own, and I didn't need to ask for any help.   g And I didn't need to give up playing tennis.   h I needn't have used the Internet so much.   i But it was quite easy in the end, and I didn't need to think too hard!   j In the end, I needn't have worried about it so much!

Ex 3

a didn't have to go   b couldn't pay   c had to find
d had to work   e had to sign   f had to climb   g had to be   h had to use   i had to pay   j couldn't employ
k could work   l could put   m had to limit

Ex 4

Suggested answers: a He should have conducted an experiment.   b He should have worn warm clothes.
c He shouldn't have tested it on his students. / He should have tested it on himself.   d He shouldn't have carried radioactive substances in his trouser pockets.
e He should have told people about his sister.
f The French revolutionary authorities shouldn't have executed him.

Ex 5

a should have been   b couldn't find   c had to look for   d had to avoid   e could kill   f shouldn't have told
g needn't have worried   h had to work   i couldn't stop
j should have shown   k couldn't tell   l had to admit

Unit 24

Ex 1

a may   b may not   c may   d may   e may not   f may
g may not   h may   i may   j may

Ex 2

a might   b can, may not   c may   d can   e might   f will   g will, might   h could

Ex 3

a You must know the difference between a solid and a gas!   b If a substance does not contain hydrogen, then it can't be an acid.   c If we put some litmus paper in a solution and it turns red, then the solution must be an acid.   d If we add a substance to a red cabbage solution and it stays red, then the substance can't be an alkali.
e If we add a substance to a red cabbage solution and it turns green, then the substance must be an alkali.
f If we put some litmus paper in a solution and it turns red, then the solution can't be an alkali.   g If it's not an acid, or an alkali, then it must be neutral.   h If we use a universal indicator to check a substance, and it turns purple, then the substance can't be an acid.

Ex 4

a If the world becomes warmer as some scientists predict, Europe could change dramatically over the next century.   b There might be no snow-covered mountains in Europe by then.   c And areas in the south of Europe could become deserts.   d Heavy rain might become normal in northern Europe.   e While southern Europe could be always short of water.   f There might be some benefits for some people.   g Summers could become longer, and hotter, and winters could become warmer.
h On the other hand, some species of plants and animals might become extinct.

Ex 5

a A, B   b A, B   c B, C   d C   e B, C   f B   g A, C   h A, B, C   i A, C   j A   k A, B, C   l A, C   m A   n A   o C

Unit 25

Ex 1

a You could have damaged the computer!   b You might have been more careful!   c You might have asked for help!   d You could have broken the printer.   e The computer could have got a virus.   f You might have checked the name of the sender!   g You could have lost all your work.   h That could have been a very serious problem.   i You might have told me you hadn't used a computer before!   j You might have turned the computer off when you finished!

Ex 2

a If you go near the edge, you could fall.
b If you hadn't rescued me, I might have drowned.
c If somebody had seen Tom come in late, he could have got into trouble.   d If you run a bit faster, you might win the race.   e If Maria's explanation had been detailed, we might have believed her.   f If you lift such heavy weights, you could hurt yourself.
g If you don't put your wallet in your pocket, somebody could steal it.   h If you had dropped the plates, you could have broken them.   i If you phone him, he might still be at home.   j If United had scored an early goal, they might have won.

Ex 3

a The Ancient Egyptians might have crossed the Atlantic.   b The Egyptians could have had traded with America more than 3,000 years ago.   c Traces of tobacco have been found in Egyptian mummies and this may have come from Central America.
d The discovery of silk in mummies also suggests that the Egyptians could have traded with China.
e And because there are pyramids in Central America, the Mayas might have got the idea for building pyramids from Egypt.   f On the other hand, as Egyptian pyramids and Mayan pyramids are so different, the two civilizations may have had similar ideas.   g There has even been a claim that aliens from another planet might have built the Mayan pyramids.   h According to this theory, the aliens could have used the pyramids as landing places for their flying saucers.

Ex 4

a The local people must have been shocked when they saw the Spanish armies.   b They can't have known where the Spanish came from.   c They must have soon realized that they were enemies.   d They can't have been aware of the invaders' intentions.
e They must have wondered whether they were gods.   f The Spanish can't have expected to beat the local people so easily.
g They must have thought they would be killed.
h They can't have realized what the Incas were like
i The local people must have given up when faced by horses and guns.   j The Spanish can't have expected to find so much gold.

Ex 5

a If the Trojans hadn't taken the wooden horse into Troy, they might / could have won the war.
b If Alexander the Great hadn't died at an early age, he might / could have conquered the whole world.
c If the Romans hadn't spent a lot of time fighting among themselves, their empire might / could have lasted longer.   d If the medieval Europeans had known that America existed, they might / could

have gone there sooner.   e If the Aztecs hadn't thought the Spanish used magic powers, they might / could have beaten them.   f If the Spanish had succeeded in invading Britain in 1588, they might /could have then conquered all of Europe.

Ex 6

Suggested answers: a The Mayan ruling class might have died out because rulers did not work.
b Farmers might have been unable to grow enough food to support large populations in cities.   c A natural disaster, such as an earthquake, might have occurred.   d Another Mexican people might have conquered the Mayas.   e There might have been a revolution.   f An epidemic of some kind might have caused the disappearance of the Mayas.
g The Mayan cities might have suffered from an environmental disaster.   h The people might have abandoned their cities because their priests told them to do it.

Unit 26
Ex 1

a May I   b Could you   c Would you mind taking
d Shall I   e I wouldn't leave   f I don't think you should spend   g Do you think you could explain
h Why don't you ask   i Would you like   j Can you

Ex 2

a B   b C   c C   d A   e B   f C   g A   h A   i B   j C

Ex 3

a Shall   b could   c were   d mind   e about   f Can / Could / May   g if   h wouldn't   i let's   j should

Ex 4

a 9   b 5   c 7   d 10   e 1   f 4   g 8   h 6   i 3   j 2

Ex 5

a Is it all right if I keep my coat on?   b Shall I give out the books?   c I think you should buy a dictionary.   d Do / Would you mind sharing with Mary?   e How about playing volleyball for a change?   f I won't forget my homework.   g Do you think you could explain / Do you mind explaining what this means?   h If I were you, I'd read it again.
i May I leave the room?   j I don't think you should touch that.

Ex 6

a Would you like to go to lunch now?   b Do you think you could collect in the homework, please?
c Why don't we have another look at the table on page 218?   d If I were you, I'd revise all of Unit 6.
e Shall I explain it again?   f Can you stay behind

for a moment?   g Is it all right if I sit near the front?   h How about looking for the information on the Internet?

Ex 7

Suggested answers: a Could you tell me?   b Why don't you make / How about making notes so you don't forget?   c Can / Could you speak more slowly?   d Shall I speak more slowly?   e Can you tell me what happens next?   f Shall I tell you who wins?   g Can you stop / Do you mind stopping, please?   h You should read the play. / If I were you, I'd read the play.   i Shall we go to the library?   j Let's go now. / We could go now.

Unit 27

Ex 1

a sheep   b thanks   c person   d knives   e stairs
f clothes   g belongings   h mouse   i aircraft
j goods

Ex 2

a salt   b travel   c wood   d hair   e advice   f iron
g salts   h wines   i knowledge   j information

Ex 3

a The students' accommodation was of a very high standard.   b The weather has been very bad this year.   c The furniture is arriving tomorrow.
d There is a lot of / lots of rubbish at the edge of the sports field.   e The new equipment cost a lot of money, so look after it.   f The work in the factory was very difficult.   g The scenery in this country is very beautiful.   h Most of the clothing was destroyed in the fire.

Ex 4

a B   b A   c A   d A   e A   f B   g A   h A

Ex 5

a is   b are   c is   d are   e are   f is   g are   h is

Ex 6

a B   b A   c A C   d The temperature / temperatures, electricity   e Air, gases   f lights

Extension Activity

2 her hair, some accommodation, some advice

Unit 28

Ex 1A

a It opens bottles.   b It sharpens pencils.   c It makes coffee.   d It mows lawns.   e It washes dishes.

Ex 1B

f a watch strap   g a keyhole   h a tennis racket
i a street light   j a library book

Ex 2

a mountain range   b desert areas   c sea levels d export income   e wool exporter   f beef farming   g irrigation systems   h mineral resources   i export earnings
j business district

Ex 3

a temperature of the air   b the formation of rain and snow   c the temperature of the clouds   d droplets of water   e size of the droplets   f currents of air
g drops of rain   h crystals of ice   i flakes of snow

Ex 4

a room temperature   b exhaust fumes   c mineral salts
d food chemicals   e future generations   f heart disease
g salt solution   h air pollution   i climate change
j electricity bill

Ex 5

a shop window   b bus ticket   c front door key
d bicycle chain   e telephone directory   f glasses case
g computer engineer   h bookshelf   i alarm bell
j school bus

Ex 6

David Copperfield, the novel by Charles Dickens, is a story of one boy's struggle after losing his parents. David's father dies when he is young, and his mother remarries. His stepfather, Mr Murdstone, treats David unkindly, and he can only find happiness with the Peggoty family, his nurse's relatives. At school, at first he is unhappy but then wins his friends' respect. However, when his mother dies, his stepfather sends him to work in a factory in London, where the other boys make fun of him. David runs away and walks to his aunt's house in Dover. Here he grows up happily, goes to school and becomes a clerk in a lawyer's office in London. He falls in love with Dora, his employer's daughter, and when his aunt's money is lost in a bad investment, he works writing reports of parliament for the newspapers. Many parts of the story follow the events of Dickens' / Dickens's own life.

Extension Activity

1   a desk lamp, a door handle, a water jug, an exercise book, the front door, a computer room

Unit 29

Note: As article use depends a lot on context, there may be alternative answers for some items in this section. The answers given are the most likely ones.

Ex 1

a The   b the   c a   d A   e a   f an   g the   h the   i A , a   j The

Ex 2

a B   b C   c A   d C   e A   f C   g C   h B   i C   j B

Ex 3

a The   b a   c a   d a   e the   f the   g an / the   h the   i the   j the   k the   l the   m the   n the   o The   p a   q The   r the   s the   t The   u the   v the   w the   x the   y the   z the   1 the   2 The   3 the   4 the

Ex 4

a -   b -   c a   d the   e a   f The   g the   h a   i the   j -   k the   l a   m a   n -   o -

Ex 5

a the   b the   c -   d the   e -   f a   g -   h the   i -   j -   k -   l -   m -   n -   o -   p -   q the   r the   s -   t -   u the   v The   w -   x The   y -

Ex 6

a a   b the   c the   d a   e the   f the   g the   h the

Unit 30

Ex 1

a The, the, -   b the, the, the, the   c -, -, the   d -, -   e The, -   f -, -   g the   h the, the, -

Ex 2

a -, a, a   b The, -   c -, a   d -   e a, a   f -, a, -   g a   h -, -   i -   j -, the, -

Ex 3

a -   b -   c the   d a   e a   f -   g -   h the   i the   j a   k -   l the   m -   n -   o -   p a   q -   r the   s the   t the

Ex 4

a ✓   b a (warm)   c ✓   d ✓   e the (less)   f the (real)   g the (tropical depressions)   h a (maximum)   i ✓   j the (meteorologists)   k ✓   l the (low)   m ✓   n a (heavy)   o ✓   p ✓   q the (June 1st) .

Ex 5

a -   b -   c -   d -   e A   f -   g -   h the   i the   j the   k a   l the   m -   n -   o -   p the   q the   r the   s the   t a

Ex 6

a the   b the   c the   d the   e the   f -   g -   h a   i a   j a   k -   l -   m a   n the   o the   p The   q -   r -   s -   t the   u the

Unit 31

Ex 1

a Is there any oxygen on Mars?   b Is there any cheese on the Moon?   c Are there any mammals with beaks and webbed feet?   d Is there any weather on other planets?   e Are there any fish that can walk on land?   f Are there any birds that can't fly?   g Is there any water on the Moon?   h Are there any apes that can be taught to speak?   i Is there any oil or coal on the Moon?   j Are there any living dinosaurs left on Earth?

Ex 2

a There aren't any cars that use water as fuel.   b There aren't any mammals that lay eggs.   c There aren't any polar bears (that live) in the Antarctic.   d There aren't any alien beings in our galaxy.   e There aren't any volcanoes in Britain.   f There isn't any rain in the Sahara desert.

Ex 3

a an   b some, some   c any   d some, any   e some   f a   g a   h some   i a   j some

Ex 4

a a   b any   c Some   d any   e an   f any   g any   h an   i some, any   j some

Ex 5

a crowd   b can   c packet   d tube   e cloud   f bar   g slice   h piece   i sheet   j carton

Ex 6

a Some mountain ranges are only 15 million years old, while others are 400 million years old.   b Some pine trees depend on birds to spread their seeds while others depend on forest fires to release the seeds from the cone.   c Some frogs 'fly' from tree to tree using webbed feet as parachutes, while others jump using their powerful back legs.   d Some rivers in desert areas evaporate in the desert and disappear, while others flow into rivers, lakes or into the sea.
e In some places the difference in sea level between high tide and low tide can be almost nothing, while in others it can be as great as 10 to 15 metres.

Unit 32

Ex 1

a How many   b How much   c How many
d How much   e How many   f How many   g How
much   h How much

Ex 2

a isn't much   b aren't many   c isn't much
d aren't many   e aren't many   f isn't much
g isn't much   h aren't many

Ex 3

a Only a few   b few ways   c No divers   d A few people
e only a few hours.   f There are a lot of
g there is none.   h There are few

Ex 4

a Few   b little   c few   d little   e few   f little
g few   h little

Ex 5

a Many   b many   c lots   d much   e few   f many
g lots   h little   i Many   j lots   k little   l much
m many   n few   o many   p few   q lots   r lots
s lots   t none

Ex 6

a much   b little   c Much   d plenty / lots   e lot
f much   g enough   h lots   i much   j few

Ex 7

a little   b lot   c Many   d not enough   e Lots
f many   g little   h few   i lots   j Many   k many
l little   m lots of   n many   o little   p few

Unit 33

Ex 1

a All   b Most   c No   d All   e Most   f No   g Most
h All   i no   j Most / All

Ex 2

a the whole family   b the whole country   c the whole
series   d a whole generation   e the whole area   f her
whole life

Ex 3

a all of   b Most of   c none of   d all of   e most of
f most of   g all of   h none of

Ex 4

a all   b each   c every   d each / every   e each   f all
g every   h all   i every   j All

Ex 5

a Both Alexander and Napoleon   b Neither A nor N
c Neither A nor N   d Neither A nor N   e Both A and N
f Both A and N   g Both A and N   h Both A and N
i Neither A nor N   j Both A and N

Ex 6

a B   b A   c B   d C   e A   f C   g B   h B   i A   j C

Unit 34

Ex 1

a He, his   b him   c He, his   d his, him   e he   f their
g he   h their   i they   j his

Ex 2

a mine   b his   c hers   d us   e yours   f ours   g them
h me   i theirs   j you

Ex 3

a Harry is a friend of mine.   b That was their idea.
c This one is ours.   d This is my pencil, but where's
yours?   e Sue is talking to a friend of hers.   f This bike
belongs to him.   g Is that house theirs?   h That is your
cup.

Ex 4

a yourself   b yourself   c ourselves   d themselves
e myself   f yourself   g himself   h themselves
i ourselves

Ex 5

a Everyone / everybody has   b No-one / Nobody
knows   c everyone / everybody   d someone /
somebody   e there is nothing   f anyone / anybody
g Everyone / Everybody supposes   h No-one / Nobody
visits   i No-one / Nobody knows   j is something
interesting.

Ex 6

a something else   b somebody / someone else
c Something else   d Everyone / Everybody else
e nothing else   f anyone / anybody else   g anyone /
anybody else   h anything else   i someone / somebody
else   j Someone / Somebody else.

Ex 7

a nowhere   b anywhere   c somewhere   d everywhere
e anywhere   f somewhere   g somewhere   h anywhere
i everywhere   j Nowhere

Ex 8

a his   b anyone   c everyone / everybody   d No-one /
Nobody   e something   f No-one / Nobody   g him
h himself   i themselves   j them / anything

Unit 35

Ex 1

a The boy in the painting seems to be asleep.
b The girls in this painting look alike.   c I think the person in this painting is dead.   d He is awake, but looks as if he is in a dream.   e Are you afraid of this painting?   f It's a painting of a battle and very few soldiers are alive.

Ex 2

a big, red *London*   b wonderful, old *Venice*   c vast, stone *Cairo*   d graceful, iron *Paris*   e well-known, medieval *Moscow*   f busy, commercial *Tokyo*
g tall, modern *Istanbul*

Ex 3

a really, absolutely   b -   c very   d absolutely
e very   f extremely, very   g very, really

Ex 4

a depressed   b confusing   c exhausting
d embarrassed   e worried   f interesting
g surprised   h annoying   i excited   j satisfied

Unit 36

Ex 1

a adjective   b adjective   c adjective   d adjective
e adverb   f adverb   g adverb   h adjective
i adverb   j adjective

Ex 2

a slowly   b happily   c beautifully   d badly
e really   f truly   g incredibly   h unbelievably

Ex 3

a I often finish sentences for other people.   b Other people usually seem to be comfortable when they talk to me.   c When people talk to me, I sometimes look at the floor.   d If I don't like a person's voice, I never pay attention to them.   e I usually try to be sympathetic when people talk about their problems.
f I always try to give people my complete attention when they speak to me.   g I rarely interrupt people before they have finished what they are saying.
h I sometimes laugh at what people say to me, and upset them. *Poor listener*: a, c, d, h

Ex 4

a properly   b Unfortunately   c easily   d wrongly
e usually   f thoroughly   g dreadfully   h definitely
i carefully   j entirely

Ex 5

a Do you usually take the lead in discussions?
b Do you sometimes feel unable to say anything interesting?   c Do you often change your opinion after you hear what others say?   d Do you always listen carefully to what all the others are saying?
e Do you sometimes feel that nobody is interested in what you say?   f Do you usually find ways of keeping other people's attention?   g Do you often avoid saying what you really think?   h Do you always encourage other members of the group to speak?

Ex 6

a very   b very   c too   d very   e very   f very
g too   h very

Ex 7

a adjective   b adverb   c adverb   d adjective
e adverb   f adjective   g adverb   h adverb

Ex 8

a ill   b hardly   c hard   d badly   e well   f hard
g bad   h hardly

Unit 37

Ex 1

a The River Mackenzie is longer than the River Niger.   b Lake Victoria is larger than Lake Michigan.
c The Marianas Trench is deeper than the Japan Trench.   d Mount Elbrus is higher than Mont Blanc.
e Arica, Chile is drier than the Libyan Sahara Desert.
f The oldest rocks in Canada are older than the oldest rocks in Scotland.   g The lowest recorded temperature in Finland is lower than the lowest recorded temperature in Sweden.   h Monaco is smaller than Nauru.

Ex 2

a more difficult than the first one   b are tastier than yours   c is more expensive than staying at home   d is more modern than the Royal Hotel
e is more comfortable than this chair   f more refreshing than milk (is)   g romantic films more interesting than war films   h wasn't as heavy as Jack's suitcase

Ex 3

a worse   b cleverer   c larger / bigger   d younger
e funnier   f further / farther   g longer   h warmer / hotter   i happier   j better

Ex 4

a This book is less interesting than that one.
b A scooter is more expensive than a bike.   c I'm

not as tall as you (are).   d The first explanation is just as unlikely as the second.   e The accident was more serious than Carol thought (it was).   f My arm is less painful than it was.

Ex 5

a essential   b easier and easier   c cheaper and cheaper
d important   e more up-to-date, the faster
f difficult   g cleverer and cleverer   h important

Ex 6

a A   b C   c B   d A   e B   f A   g C   h B   i A   j C

Unit 38

Ex 1

a heaviest   b longest   c oldest   d fastest   e deepest
f speediest   g most ferocious   h most poisonous
i largest   j smallest

Ex 2

a This is the most comfortable classroom I've ever sat in.
b This is the tastiest school lunch I've ever eaten.
c This is the worst book I've ever read.
d This is the most useful English lesson we've ever had.
e This is the easiest problem I've ever solved.
f This is the longest test I've ever taken.   g This is the most difficult test I've ever written.   h This is the most entertaining school play I've ever seen.   i This is the most interesting textbook we've ever used.   j You are the best friend I've ever had.

Ex 3

a harder   b faster   c more often   d more slowly
e more easily   f longer   g better   h more heavily

Ex 4

a more easily   b more quickly   c more quietly
d faster   e more carefully   f more loudly   g more heavily   h more clearly   i earlier   j more slowly

Ex 5

a A   b C   c B   d C   e D   f A   g B   h C   i D   j A

Ex 6

a the largest   b lower   c the most popular   d most famous   e wider   f the dirtiest   g cleaner   h the best
i the most exciting   j the least expensive

Unit 39

Ex 1

a to   b under   c over   d to   e outside   f on   g of
h above   i in   j in

Ex 2

a Can you tell me whether Jim is in?   b Mary has gone to live abroad.   c Shall we go indoors now?   d This snake is red on the top but green underneath.   e Wait / Stay outside, please.   f David has gone away / is away (on a trip).   g Alan lives opposite.   h Sorry, but Sue is out at the moment.

Ex 3

a in   b in   c on   d On   e at   f On   g at   h in   i at
j in   k At   l in   m on   n in

Ex 4

a to   b at   c to   d to, on   e to   f on   g on, on
h to   i in   j in

Ex 5

a at   b in   c at   d in   e At   f on   g at / by   h at

Ex 6

a B   b D   c A   d C   e C   f A   g A   h D   i C   j D
k B   l B   m A   n C   o C

Unit 40

Ex 1

a in, on, at   b in, on, in   c in, at, on   d in, at, in, on
e in, on   f in, on, at   g in, on, at, in   h on, in, in
i in, on, in   j in, at, on

Ex 2

a next   b in   c last   d on   e at   f last   g on   h next
i at   j In

Ex 3

a last   b ago   c Since   d for   e next   f last   g next
h ago   i Since   j for

Ex 4

a from, to / until   b until   c during   d By   e During
f until   g Until   h During   i during   j from, to

Ex 5

a Paula didn't arrive at school until 12.30.   b My library card runs out on the last day of July.   c By the time we arrived at the cinema, the film had finished.   d What were you doing at the time of the accident?   e I've been waiting for an hour.   f During the night there was an earthquake.   g I waited until 4.30 and then I left.
h I'll have finished within a week.   i It's ages since I saw George.   j I'll see you in a week. / in a week's time.

Ex 6

a for   b ago   c After   d from   e to / until   f later
g during / in   h until   i Since   j during / in   k at

Unit 41

Ex 1

a B   b D   c D   d D   e C   f C   g A   h A

Ex 2

a by now   b in time   c after   d now on   e until
f then   g once   h At   i then   j As soon as

Ex 3

a B   b A   c B   d C   e A   f B   g A   h A   i C   j B

Ex 4

a They'll be back in the afternoon.   b Can you do it at once, please?   c At the end of the lesson, Helen asked the teacher a question.   d My head is still aching.   e Jan was in time for his music lesson.
f I've been waiting since six o'clock.   g The film began, and soon after all the lights came on.
h Lunch isn't ready yet, so until then we'll sit in the garden.   i I haven't finished my homework yet.
j I'll finish watching TV and start my work afterwards.

Ex 5

a Until   b ago   c Until / Before   d from   e until
f already   g by   h in   i at   j At   k during
l in   m later   n In   o afterwards   p in   q Since
r still

Unit 42

Ex 1

a from   b to   c about   d on   e with   f from
g on   h at   i with   j on

Ex 2

a Sometimes I'm really annoyed with you.   b We were all shocked by the things we saw on the news.
c I'm sorry for losing your magazine.   d Who was responsible for the accident?   e I'm not keen on horror films.   f Football is different from rugby.
g Is Madonna married to Guy Ritchie?   h Are you interested in playing computer games?   i I'm bored by doing the same things every day.   j Some people are afraid / frightened of going to the top of high buildings.

Ex 3

a theory   b purpose   c impression   d practice
e all   f trouble   g control   h fact   i average   j end

Ex 4

a In the end I succeeded in finding the answer.
b Martin's teacher accused him of cheating.   c Our school provides us with a free lunch.   d I insist on

having my money back!   e They blamed the fire on Anna. / Anna was blamed for the fire.   f You remind me of my sister.   g I'm not used to getting up early in the morning.   h Don't worry, you can depend on Chris.   i What were you two talking about?   j I prefer jazz to rap.

Ex 5

a On   b on   c under   d for   e with   f on   g in
h in   i In   j from   k of   l in   m in   n after

Ex 6

a Is your bike for sale?   b I'm out of practice.   c In the end we stopped and turned back.   d Are you on holiday here?   e I thought it was Andy, but in fact it was David.   f I think you broke the window on purpose.   g They told him that he was in danger of losing his life.   h The train was out of control.   i I was under the impression it was a holiday today.
j We turned left instead of right by mistake.

Unit 43

Ex 1

a looked into   b took after   c heading for
d looked after   e joined in   f came across
g running through   h getting over   i getting at
j running into

Ex 2

a look   b get   c run   d take   e stand   f run
g look   h come   i join   j head

Ex 3

a Don't forget to give in your homework at the end of the lesson.   b The maths teacher has put the test off until Friday.   c I'll come round and pick the letter up tomorrow.   d Make sure you look up every new word.   e Remember to turn the TV off when you go to bed.   f Don't worry, we'll sort out the travel arrangements next week.   g Please fill the form in as carefully as you can.   h The bus drops passengers off right outside the hotel.   i You have let the whole class down, and I'm very disappointed.
j An elderly couple brought up the children after their parents died.

Ex 4

a carry out   b sort out   c getting over   d put off
e came across   f work out   g look into   h join in
i ran into   j let down

Ex 5

a The trip to the National Gallery has been put off until next Friday.   b Make sure you look up these words / look these words up in a dictionary.
c You can miss out Exercise 9 / miss Exercise 9 out.

d A special team is looking into the cause of the accident.   e I will not stand for such bad language in the classroom!   f Turn off the computer / turn the computer off on when you leave.   g A taxi will pick you up at 7.30.   h I wish I could give up chocolates / give chocolates up.   i Please fill in the application form / fill the application form in.   j Tina hasn't got over her illness yet.

Ex 6

a Have you ever come across this word before?
b I'm looking after the children until their mother comes home.   c Dina takes after her mother's side of the family.   d The basketball match has been put off to next Wednesday.   e Make sure you turn the lights off.
f The police are looking into a fight outside the cinema.
g Let me run through the details of the plan just once more.   h Jane found it hard to get over the death of her pet dog.   i Mr Sims had to give up driving when he reached the age of 85.   j Peter promised to come and sing in the concert, but he let us down.

Unit 44

Ex 1

a A   b D   c B   d D   e C   f A   g D   h A

Ex 2

a I'm finding it difficult to get round to my geography project.   b I'm afraid we've come up against a rather serious problem.   c Tim thought he got away with cheating in the exam.   d Have you come up with any good ideas yet?   e The school did away with end-of-year tests.   f Unfortunately Helen went down with flu on the first day of her holiday.   g I kept up with the rest of the class.   h I'm sorry, but I really can't put up with this terrible noise.   i Tom ran out of money three days before the end of the holiday.   j Kate seems to get on / along with her new teacher.

Ex 3

a up   b off   c on   d up   e off   f down   g up
h out   i up   j down

Ex 4

a leave out   b get over   c are looking into   d Fill in
e come up with   f work out   g dropped him off
h has been put off   i give up   j got away with

Ex 5

a Most students searching for information look up the details on the Internet.   b Doctors say that the unpleasant effects of the new malaria pill soon wear off.
c The battery runs out / runs out of power completely after about three months.   d The three astronauts said they were looking forward to coming back down to Earth.   e Keep up with the latest science news with *Science Magazine*.   f There is a great deal of confusion and the authorities are still trying to sort out the situation.   g The launch of the next Mars mission has been put off until next April.

Ex 6

a come up against   b speak out   c getting along / on with   d come up with   e going on   f turns up   g get round to   h build up   i breaks down   j catch up with

Unit 45
Ex 1

a According to experts, school science textbooks are not good at teaching science.   b According to their reports, most books cover too many topics.   c According to these experts, the classroom activities in the books don't help students learn basic scientific ideas.   d According to one scientist, the books are 'full of unconnected facts'.   e According to some educational experts, students learn science more effectively when they try to answer an everyday question.   f According to these experts, a question such as 'Why is the sky blue?' is the kind of science question students like answering.
g According to this theory, students learn better if they carry out project work based on this kind of question.
h However, according to many science teachers, the school syllabus does not allow enough time for this kind of exploration.

Ex 2

a You don't have to use butter, you can use olive oil instead.   b Cooking spoils the flavour of carrots, so eat them raw instead.   c This is usually made with apples, but you could try pears instead.   d Fresh fish is best for this recipe, but you can use frozen fish instead.   e Try leaving out salt, and use other spices instead.   f Sweets are fattening, so eat fresh fruit instead.   g You don't have to use cream, you can use yoghurt instead.   h In some versions of this dish, lamb is used instead of beef.

Ex 3

a You need a schedule , so work out how long you've got to prepare and then divide the time into short manageable sections.   b Don't set unrealistic goals, as you risk losing motivation if you fail to reach them
c Make sure your goals follow the SMART system, since these are the best types of goals.   d Try to be very precise about what you want to achieve, because this will give you a definite target, eg I will read three pages of history before 6.00.   e Ask someone to test you on what you have studied, so you can measure what you have achieved.   f You have to be honest with yourself about what you can achieve, because if you set yourself too much, you won't be able to do it.   g Give yourself a reward when you achieve your target, as this will make

you feel good! **h** Give yourself a deadline, since you need to feel some pressure if you want to work well.

Ex 4

a However **b** while **c** while / even though
d While / Even though **e** although **f** However
g While **h** Even though

Ex 5

a Every living organism needs energy to maintain its body and also grow. **b** Omnivores are animals that eat plants and other animals too. **c** Decomposers are organisms that eat dead animals and dead plants, and enable other plants to feed off the dead material as well. **d** Producers are plants that use photosynthesis to convert the energy of the sun into food, and they are also the lowest layer of the food web. **e** Primary consumers are the animals that eat the producer layer, and are also called herbivores.
f Secondary consumers eat the primary consumers and are carnivores, though some of them eat plants as well.

Ex 6

a Although **b** because / as **c** for example **d** However **e** so **f** although **g** also **h** such as
i As / Since **j** instead **k** Although / While **l** While / Although **m** also **n** for example **o** Although

Unit 46

Ex 1

a No **b** ✓ **c** No **d** ✓ **e** ✓ **f** No **g** ✓ **h** No
i ✓ **j** ✓

Ex 2

a 4 Linnaeus was a botanist who worked out a method of naming plants and animals. **b** 2 Marie Curie was a physicist and the first woman who received a Nobel Prize. **c** 7 Aristotle was a philosopher who taught Alexander the Great.
d 3 Mary Shelley was a writer who wrote the novel *Frankenstein*. **e** 1 André-Marie Ampère was a physicist who made an instrument for measuring current and voltage. **f** 5 Sonja Henie was an ice-skater who took part in the Olympic Games at the age of 11. **g** 8 Maria Montessori was a doctor who invented a new method of teaching young children.
h 6 Marco Polo was a merchant who visited China in the 13th century.

Ex 3

a J S Bach had two sons whose music was better-known than his for many years. **b** John F Kennedy had a brother, Robert, whose death was also a political assassination. **c** Lord Byron the poet had a daughter, Ada Lovelace, whose work in mathematics led to the development of the first computer.
d Pablo Picasso had a daughter, Paloma, whose fashion designs have become famous worldwide.
e John Lennon had a son, Julian, whose music career has not been as successful as his father's. **f** The astronomer William Herschel had a sister, Caroline, whose research contributed to his discoveries.
g Paul McCartney has a daughter, Stella, whose career in fashion design has been very successful.

Ex 4

a The word cell comes from the Latin *cella* which means a *small room*. **b** All cells have a membrane or skin which covers the cell. **c** Inside the cell is a substance called the cytoplasm which contains a number of chemicals. **d** All cells contain DNA which holds genetic information. **e** They also contain RNA which includes the information the cells need to build proteins. **f** All cells contain a nucleus which controls the actions of the cell.
g Bacteria consist of only one cell which can divide and make other new bacteria. **h** One of the most complex structures is the human body which contains over 100,000 billion cells.

Ex 5

a Einstein is a scientist who I admire.
b Shakespeare is a writer I don't understand.
c Marie Curie is a scientist whom we are studying.
d Newton is a physicist we often discuss.
e Homer is an ancient Greek writer who we study in translation. **f** Leonardo is an artist that everybody knows. **g** Jane Austen is an author most people enjoy. **h** Beethoven is a composer that I like.

Ex 6

a This is the lamp I made in a craft lesson. **b** This is the ball we lost in the park last week. **c** This is the poem I wrote in my first year. **d** This is the portrait she painted as part of her project. **e** This is the computer we used to get the results. **f** This is the dog we found in the playground. **g** This is the book I borrowed from the library. **h** This is the photo Mr Smith took of the basketball team.

Ex 7

a which / that   b which / that   c which / that
d which / that   e who / that   f which / that   g -
h which / that   i of which   j which / that   k which /
that   l who / that   m whose   n which / that   o -

Unit 47

Ex 1

a The polar bear, which is also known as the white bear,
is a large bear that lives in the Arctic.   b The polar
bear, which has a population of about 20,000, is found
all across the Arctic.   c About 60% of the bears, which
hunt well on land and in water, are found in Canada.
d The polar bear, which is threatened by global
warming, may become extinct by the end of the century.
e The sea ice in the Arctic, which bears use as a platform
when they hunt seals, is beginning to melt.   f The polar
bear, which is twice the weight of a lion or tiger, is the
largest land predator.   g The males, which are twice the
size of the females, weigh between 400kg and 600kg.
h The bear cubs, which are born helpless and blind,
remain with their mothers for ten months.   i Adult
bears, which do not hibernate, live for as long as 30
years.   j Polar bears, which are excellent swimmers, can
often be seen in open water kilometres from land.

Ex 2

a Alan Graham is the teacher I've learnt most from.   b
He is someone I have the greatest respect for.   c We
all admire people we owe a lot to.   d Especially if it is
a person we enjoy working with.   e There are some
people you can easily form a relationship with.   f But
you don't always work with people you feel admiration
for.   g And now here is the person we have all been
waiting for.   h He is the man I am pleased to present
the Teacher of the Year Award to.

Ex 3

a   There are a number of trees and plants from which
    rubber is taken.
b   The Para rubber tree is the major commercial source
    from which rubber is extracted.
c   Brazil is the country from which rubber originates.
d   Ancient Central American cultures collected rubber,
    from which they made balls.
e   The Mayas made temporary shoes by using a rubber
    mixture, into which they dipped their feet.
f   The people in Brazil used a mixture of rubber, from
    which they made waterproof clothes.
g   In England people noticed it was a substance with
    which you could rub out marks.
h   This was the origin of the name by which English
    people called it.

Ex 4

a which is   b which   c which   d which   e -   f which
g -   h which   i which   j which   k which   l which
m which was   n which   o with which

Ex 5

a why   b when   c where   d when   e when
f why   g when   h why   i when   j when

Ex 6

a who   b where   c which   d which   e -   f which
g who   h which   i which   j whom   k where   l which
m which   n when   o who

Unit 48

Ex 1

a Roman slaves worked hard so that rich Romans could
have a comfortable life.   b When enemies shot arrows
at Roman soldiers, they put their shields over their
heads to protect themselves.   c The Romans built a
road system all over Europe so that their armies could
move quickly from one place to another.   d When the
Romans wanted to catch mice, they used other animals
to catch them.   e The Romans used a pointed metal
stylus to write on pieces of wood covered in wax.
f The Romans buried their dead beside the road outside
their town so that the ghosts couldn't return to their
old homes.

Ex 2

a A barometer is used for measuring air pressure.
b A microscope is used for looking at things that are
too small to see.   c A microphone is used for making
someone's voice louder.   d A calculator is used for doing
maths problems.   e A pipette is used for measuring and
moving liquid.   f A hygrometer is used for measuring
humidity.   g A Bunsen burner is used for heating things
in a lab.   h A thermometer is used for measuring
temperature.

Ex 3

a Some parts of the universe are too distant to visit.
b The atmosphere of Mars is too thin to breathe.
c Venus is too hot to land on.   d For most people, a
journey into space is too expensive to take.   e Trips
to most other planets are too dangerous to consider.
f The universe is too large to explore completely.
g Perhaps its meaning is too difficult to grasp.

Ex 4

a If all the blood vessels in the body formed one line, it
would be long enough to reach more than twice round
the Earth.   b Some metals, eg sodium, are light enough
to float.
c A week after it is born, a baby gazelle is strong enough
to run with adults.   d The planet Pluto is not large

enough to have a proper atmosphere.   e The dinosaurs were not adaptable enough to survive climate change.   f If a spider's web had threads as thick as a pencil, it would be strong enough to catch a Boeing 707 jet!

Ex 5

a Tropical rain is sometimes so heavy that it can damage the leaves of trees.
b The bee hummingbird is so small (6.2 cm long) that people often think it is an insect.
c Jupiter's moon Europa is so cold that the ice on the surface is probably as hard as rock.
d A camel spider is such a greedy eater that it will eat until it cannot move.
e The Sun is so hot that the chemical elements found on Earth exist on the Sun as gases.
f The African Elephant is so heavy that it's only able to move at the speed of a fast walk.

Ex 6

Suggested answers:
a Because of its caves, more than half a million people visit Han-sur-Leses every year.   b As a result of falling rocks, most of the caves are too dangerous for visitors to enter.   c Because of the river's disappearance beneath a hill, ancient people threw objects into the water.   d Because of the beauty of its unexplored cave system, it was a challenge to cavers for many years.   e As a result of its disappearance under the rocks, the course of the river through the cave was unknown.   f As a result of the ice-cold water, many explorers of the cave system lost their lives.   g However, because of the importance of the caves, they are open to scientific researchers.   h And as a result of recent explorations, the course of the river has now been traced.

Ex 7

a so   b that   c for   d Because   e so   f such   g so
h so   i that   j so   k to   l such

Review Answer Key

Unit 2
a am sitting   b don't know   c are travelling   d is dripping   e apologize   f are running out   g rains
h call   i suppose   j isn't raining   k am having
l am finding out   m grow   n makes   o travel
p are taking   q want   r smells   s seem   t is crawling

Unit 3
a was / were   b went   c had   d ate   e waited
f bought   g studied   h paid   i brought   j cooked
k made   l won   m wrote   n drank   o swam
p told   q read   r picked   s sang   t ran

Unit 5
a been   b gone   c had   d eaten   e waited
f bought   g studied   h paid   i brought   j cooked
k made   l won   m written   n drunk   o swum
p told   q read   r picked   s sung   t run

Unit 6
a B   b B   c A   d B   e A   f A   g B   h A

Unit 7
a were   b had copied   c saw   d had succeeded
e used   f had heard   g was   h had written

Unit 8
a has become   b reached   c has recorded   d made
e was performing   f found   g tried / had tried
h started   i made / had made   j felt   k thought
l was doing / had done   m believe   n had been changing   o had done   p needed   q has been
r is thinking   s has been performing   t has appeared

Unit 10
a are, going to   b is going to   c are going to, Shall
d will   e is going to, Shall   f will

Unit 13
a didn't he   b were they   c did they   d didn't it
e didn't they   f didn't it   g didn't he   h didn't it
i didn't it   j didn't he

Unit 15
Suggested answers: a eating   b having   c shopping
d cooking   e washing up   f to lose   g to exercise
h eating   i cooking   j finding   k cooking   l going
m to eat   n preparing   o to do   p cooking

Unit 18

1 a If weather patterns change, droughts and floods will be more frequent.   b If water becomes warmer in the gulf of Mexico, the strength of hurricanes will increase.   c If rain falls at the wrong time, farmers will be unable to grow their crops.   d If rainfall increases, there will be more soil erosion, and deserts will spread.   e If glaciers vanish, local areas will become short of water.   f If permafrost melts in polar regions, the landscape will change.   g If polar ice melts, sea levels will rise.   h If ecosystems change, some plants and animals will change their habitat.   i If the Gulf Stream grows weak, northern Europe will become colder   j If temperatures rise, forest fires will become more frequent.

2 a If you melted a medium-sized iceberg, you would have enough water to supply a big city for several weeks.   b If Amazonia was / were a country, it would be the ninth largest in the world.   c If you put all the cells from your brain in a straight line, they would reach for 1,000 km.   d If you were a sloth, you would spend 18 hours a day sleeping.   e If you had a piece of the Sun 2.5 cm square, it would shine brighter than 1000 60 watt light bulbs.   f If you had a piece of the Sun, it would burn you to nothing!   g If you flew a plane to Neptune, it would take nearly 290 years to get there.   h If all the matter in a baby became energy, it would run a power station for a year.

Unit 20

a are produced   b are made   c are directed   d is spent   e are watched   f are made   g are loved   h are shown   i was directed   j was based   k was threatened   l was released   m has been enjoyed

Unit 23

a Ancient sailors couldn't travel far because they usually followed the coastline.   b Early ships were very small, but they had to carry a lot of fresh food and water.   c Small sailing ships were unable to survive heavy storms and very bad weather.   d There was no radio, so they could only send messages home if they met other ships.   e They didn't have accurate maps, so they had to guess their exact position.   f They didn't have radar, so they needed to keep a close look-out for dangerous rocks.   g They had to be able to see the Sun or the stars in order to navigate   h There were no rescue organizations, so if they got into trouble, they had to look after themselves.

Unit 24

a A lot of terrible things might happen to the Earth.   b An object from space might hit it.   c Or a huge volcanic eruption might change the climate.   d Hurricanes and tornadoes might spread across the world.   e Or climate change might lead to a sudden Ice Age.   f Before that, a nuclear accident might destroy life on Earth.   g A new disease might kill nearly everyone.

h Aliens might invade the Earth and might do the same thing.   i On the other hand, things might continue as they are!   j So it might be better not to worry so much.

Unit 27

a C   b C   c UC   d UC   e C   f C   g C   h UC   i C   j C   k C   l UC   m UC   n UC   o UC

Unit 30

a the   b -   c a   d the   e -   f -   g the   h the   i the   j A   k a   l the   m -   n –

Unit 35

1 a beautiful small white   b large round medieval   c interesting new German   d famous French renaissance   e tiny green plastic   f small Italian glass   g large old Spanish   h shiny circular metal   i large transparent plastic j wealthy young American

2 a bored   b surprising   c worrying   d confusing   e relaxed   f worried   g interested   h entertaining   i surprised   j distracted

Unit 36

1 a very   b too   c too   d very   e enough   f too   g very   h enough   i very   j too

Unit 43

a C   b A   c D   d C   e D   f C   g A   h B   i C   j D

Unit 45

a Human activities can upset the balance of nature. (1) For example, when humans burn wood, coal or petrol, sulphur and nitrogen compounds are added to the air, and these fall in rain and cause changes to the water of lakes and rivers so that fish die.

b These games help younger children understand basic number concepts. Adding, subtracting, and getting to know numbers are explained in cartoons of everyday activities, (5) such as playing football, getting on a bus, or going to the beach.

c Some energy sources are called 'non-renewable' because in the end they will run out. (3) For example, we cannot make oil, which was formed millions of years ago from the remains of ancient sea plants and animals.

d A risk factor is anything that increases a person's chance of getting a disease. (2) For example, sunbathing too much is a risk factor for skin cancer and smoking is a risk factor for lung cancer.

e The Wild Information page tells you what you want to know about wild animals. It includes information about dangerous predators, (6) such as tigers, cheetahs and great white sharks.

f *Science Now* is a great magazine which explores the science behind the news,(4) such as why planes crash, and why athletes shouldn't use drugs.

Unit 46

a who b - c which d who e which f -
g which h - i which j -

Unit 47

a In the 14th century, Ibn Battuta, the Moroccan explorer, travelled more than 120,000 km on his journeys, which would be difficult even for a modern traveller. b In the early years of the 15th century, European sailors usually refused to sail further south than the Canary Islands, which was understandable, as they believed that it was too dangerous to go further.   c In 1487, Bartolemeu Dias and his ships reached the Indian Ocean, which was a great achievement for the time.   d In 150 AD, the Greek geographer Ptolemy made a map of the world showing two lakes in Africa as the sources of the Nile, which was remarkable, considering that modern European explorers did not discover these lakes until the 1860s.   e Nobody thought that Marco Polo's book about China was true, which was not surprising because some parts of his story were so unbelievable.   f Archaeologists have found the remains of a Viking settlement in North America, which proves that the Vikings were the first Europeans to reach America.

Unit 48

a   You need a ball, two teams and goal posts for playing football. To play football, you need a ball, two teams and goal posts. You need a ball, two teams and goal posts so that you can play football.

b   You need bats, a hard ball and two teams for playing baseball. To play baseball, you need a hard ball, two teams and bats. You need a hard ball, two teams and bats so that you can play baseball.

c   You need a ball, a table and small bats for playing ping pong. To play ping pong, you need a ball, a table and small bats. You need a ball, a table and small bats so that you can play ping pong.

d   You need a puck, an ice rink and ice skates for playing ice hockey. To play ice hockey, you need a puck, an ice rink and ice skates. You need a puck, an ice rink and ice skates so that you can play ice hockey.

e   You need a ball, horses and mallets for playing polo. To play polo, you need a ball, horses and mallets. You need a ball, horses and mallets so that you can play polo.